Acc 5227

. J88
. HOL

Managing behavioural treatment

Managing Behavioural Treatment is aimed at all professional groups concerned with the care of delinquent adolescents.

While there is a great deal of behaviourally oriented treatment taking place, practitioners invariably focus on the mechanics of treatment programmes, only to meet obstacles at a system or policy level. *Managing Behavioural Treatment* therefore concentrates on the neglected issues of organizing and managing the delivery of the behavioural programmes to produce the maximum effect. The authors discuss organizational structure, policy-making, clarity in institutional and professional needs, staff training and evaluative research.

There is a vast network of provision for delinquent adolescents, both in the community and in residential and secure institutions. *Managing Behavioural Treatment* will be an indispensable resource for all those psychologists, psychiatrists, teachers, social workers, probation officers, nurses, and prison staff who come into contact with this client group.

Clive R. Hollin is Senior Lecturer in Psychology at the University of Birmingham and is Director of Rehabilitation in the Youth Treatment Service. His earlier books include *Psychology and Crime* and *Cognitive-Behavioral Interventions with Young Offenders*. **Kevin J. Epps** is Principal Psychologist and **David J. Kendrick** is Senior Groupworker in the Youth Treatment Service, Glenthorne Centre, Birmingham.

International Library of Psychology

Editorial adviser,
Clinical psychology:

Kevin Howells
University of Birmingham

H5

Managing behavioural treatment

Policy and practice with delinquent adolescents

Clive R. Hollin, Kevin J. Epps, and David J. Kendrick

UNIVERSITY OF OXFORD
CENTRE FOR CRIMINOLOGICAL RESEARCH
12 Bevington Road, Oxford OX2 6LH
Telephone: (0865) 274448   Fax: (0865) 274445

95 /5227

London and New York

First published 1995
by Routledge
11 New Fetter Lane, London EC4P 4EE

Simultaneously published in the USA and Canada
by Routledge
29 West 35th Street, New York, NY 10001

Typeset in Times by LaserScript, Mitcham, Surrey
Printed and bound in Great Britain by
Biddles Ltd, Guildford and King's Lynn

British Library Cataloguing in Publication Data
A catalogue record for this book is available from the British Library.

Library of Congress Cataloging in Publication Data
Hollin, Clive R.
    Managing behavioural treatment: policy and practice with
    delinquent adolescents/Clive Hollin, Kevin Epps, and
    David Kendrick.
    p. cm. – (International library of psychology)
    Includes bibliographical references and index.
    1. Problem youth – Behavior modification. 2. Juvenile delinquents –
    Mental health services. 3. Behavior therapy for teenagers.
    I. Epps, Kevin. II. Kendrick, David. III. Title. IV. Series.
    RJ506.J88H65   1994
    364.3′6 – dc20   94-16008
                                                                CIP

ISBN 0–415–05005–7 (hbk)
ISBN 0–415–05006–5 (pbk)

Contents

List of illustrations   vii
Preface   ix

1 Treatment and delinquency: a behavioural approach   1

2 A model for behavioural management and structure   25

3 Managing behavioural assessment   72

4 Designing and managing the treatment regime   102

5 Staff training and development   136

6 Legality and integrity   162

Epilogue   181
References   182
Name index   196
Subject index   200

Illustrations

FIGURES

2.1	Organizational structure in the Youth Treatment Service	40
2.2	Factors influencing policy formation	55
2.3	Long-term goals in the management and treatment of delinquents	57
2.4	Outline of violent incident report	65
3.1	A-B-A single case design	75
3.2	Multiple baseline (across behaviours) case design	77

TABLES

2.1	Policy areas in child care	56
2.2	Child-care policy and practice areas	56
3.1	Major reasons for pre-intervention assessment	74
3.2	Important principles in behavioural assessment	79
3.3	Main sources of information for assessment	79
3.4	Brief profile format for the organization of archival and other information	81
3.5	Simple A:B:C analysis of functionally similar inappropriate behaviour which may be displayed by a child to gain parental attention	97
3.6	A:B:C analysis of temper loss by young person illustrating antecedent and consequential variables	98
3.7	A:B:C analysis of adult work avoidance behaviours	99
3.8	Key issues in assessment	100
4.1	Developmental processes during adolescence	104
4.2	Factors that enhance treatment relevance	109
4.3	Behavioural management problems	111
4.4	Example of a management rule	113
4.5	Glenthorne level system	117
4.6	Extent of orientation of behavioural management systems	119
4.7	Example of programme expectations	120

4.8   Examples of good and bad programme goals   122
4.9   Main elements of sequential functional analysis   124
4.10   Advantages and disadvantages of various treatment modalities   127
4.11   The 'Highway Code' team-building exercise   133

5.1   Examples from a 44-item inventory of behavioural knowledge   137
5.2   The format of the 'Behaviour Observation Instrument'   144
5.3   Typical items from the 70-item 'Knowledge of behavioural
       principles as applied to children' inventory   145
5.4   Stages in the professional career of a behavioural practitioner   152
5.5   Outline of areas to consider in developing a curriculum for induction
       training   153
5.6   Core topics from an advanced course in behavioural theory
       and practice   157

6.1   Principles of the Children Act 1989   163
6.2   Main changes introduced by the Children Act 1989   163
6.3   The welfare checklist   167
6.4   Implications of the Children Act 1989 for residential settings   168
6.5   Early release system under the Criminal Justice Act 1991   169
6.6   Translating psychological into managerial jargon   174

Preface

To be honest, which is always the best policy, this was an extremely difficult book to write. The first difficulty we faced was in finding a title that would accurately describe the type of book we wanted to write. The eventual title that we settled on encompasses several compromises. To begin, we have used the word 'managing' in a broad sense: while much of the material is concerned with management, we are aware that some topics we discuss might equally well be described as supervision. However, as it is more difficult to subsume management under the general heading of supervision than to do vice versa, we settled on 'management'.

The next word in the title is 'behavioural', a term that does not pose any problems for us, but will not be greeted with universal acclaim (see Chapter 1). We might have fudged it with, say, 'cognitive-behavioural' but, for the reasons given in Chapter 1, we have gone for terminological purity. Well, almost. In truth we should have used the term 'applied behaviour analysis', but perhaps the exactness of that term is just too far removed from everyday usage.

The next word in the title, 'treatment', was perhaps the most difficult of all: even now we can hear reviewers sharpening their pencils, and sniffs of disapproval from certain professional and academic quarters. It is therefore important that we say what we mean by the word 'treatment'.

The main criticism of the term 'treatment' when applied in the context of delinquency is that it implies via medical associations that antisocial behaviour is an illness to be cured by putting the individual right. The theoretical ramifications of this view, it follows, are that delinquency can be accounted for in terms of individual psychopathology, thereby negating the putative role of social and economic factors. Those who proffer 'treatment' therefore collude with this theoretical position, a collusion that is damaging on two fronts. First, it provides respectable cover for those within society who have a vested political and economic interest in blaming the individual for crime. Second, an extreme focus on the individual is simply poor theory and not academically sustainable.

We will take each of these points in turn.

We recognize immediately the shifting sands that underpin the association between the words 'treatment' and 'delinquent'. There are alternatives – for example, 'intervention with delinquents' and 'working with delinquents' – but we felt these were not quite right for this book with its given focus. Having made that choice, it is important to state that we are not adherents to psychopathological views of delinquency. (Indeed, this would be an extremely strange behavioural analysis.) We prefer to view antisocial behaviour as the outcome of a highly complex interaction between the individual and his or her environment. The individual brings an array of biological, psychological, and developmental factors to the interaction. The environment brings a vast assortment of social, physical, economic, political, and legal forces that both affect the individual and, to a greater or lesser extent, can be modified by the individual's actions. Thus, the individual is simultaneously a product and a creator of his or her environment – which is a very behavioural statement!

In constructing the argument for treatment of antisocial behaviour an analogy can be drawn with poverty and famine. There are few who would dispute that poverty and famine have their roots in social and economic imbalance and injustice. This does not mean, however, that efforts should be abandoned to relieve the suffering of the victims of poverty. The delivery of food and medicine to those in need will maintain life, although this in itself does little or nothing to change the forces that produce the impoverished circumstances.

In a less dramatic way, a similar argument can be sustained for treatment of offenders. There are without question environmental factors that contribute massively towards the commission of antisocial acts by young people. To work individually with the young people is not going to change those environmental factors. However, the delivery of appropriate help (i.e. treatment as we call it here) to the individual might well help to maintain that young person within society, and lower the probability that other people will be victimized by that young person. Thus the position is a utilitarian one: the system, whatever that may be, produces young offenders, and until the system is changed the needs of those young offenders cannot be ignored. It is not right to talk of curing crime, but there is a case to be made for treating some young people who commit crimes.

The theoretical argument is slightly different. If the effective ingredients of successful treatment programmes can be identified, as the meta-analyses suggest (Chapter 1), then this might begin to shape our thinking about the theoretical role and importance of certain factors. This is not to say that these are the only factors to consider, or even that they are the most important, but that perhaps a small theoretical step might be taken based on the empirical advance made by the meta-analyses.

By this stage it is not too difficult to see the difficulties with our title: 'Managing Behavioural Treatment' might equally well have been 'Managing and/or Supervising Applied Behaviour Analysis Programmes for Behaviour Change (with Some Theory but without Claiming Theoretical Dominance and Not Colluding with the System)'. Admittedly it has a certain ring, but not one that publishers like to hear!

Another difficulty we faced was in striking a balance between defining areas for policy and practice and actually giving the fine details. For example, we felt it was right to say that organizations offering treatment should have a policy on equal opportunities, and should design programmes that in practice are sensitive to the needs of the individual young person. While, of course, we have views on how such policy and practice might look, we drew away from being prescriptive. There are several reasons for this decision: first, we cannot claim any special knowledge in this area and it would be misleading for us to do so; second, such policies should be dynamic and changing, not static in a text; third, there is merit in each organization being moved towards policy and practice through thought, discussion, and guidance, rather than by something written in a book. Thus we have highlighted and stressed as appropriate, but have not offered answers and solutions.

We faced a similar dilemma concerning presentation of the details of behavioural theory and practice, an area where we might hope to claim some special knowledge. The great temptation was to write a 'how to do it cook book', going through the fine details of assessment, practice, and so on. There are several such books available but we wanted to try to do something a little different: that is, to talk about the management, organization, and supervision of behavioural programmes. Thus we found ourselves in the impossible position of having to assume the level of knowledge, for both management issues and for theory and practice, of the reader. As there will be more than one reader, so levels of knowledge will vary. We have attempted to compromise by discussing actual theory and practice where we felt it was essential, and by giving references to other sources as often as possible. At the same time, we have attempted as much as possible to keep the focus as clearly as possible on management issues. Any compromise is bound to be unsatisfactory in parts, but we hope that readers will bear with us when material is covered of which they are already knowledgeable.

Finally, we would like to thank the supporting players. Eugene Ostapiuk did much to mould the shape of this book: had it not been for the time-consuming administrative demands of policy and practice he would have been an author. Tracey Swaffer did sterling work on the referencing of the manuscript; Mark Jackson and Vince Johnson offered helpful comments on the legal matters in the first part of Chapter 6; and Rita Granner typed the references with her customary speed and accuracy. The publishers were more than patient in waiting for a manuscript that was somewhat overdue by the time it was delivered. While it would be nice to share the blame, any errors are our own responsibility. Last but not least, thanks to our partners and families who, even without a policy, some-how manage us!

Clive Hollin
Kevin Epps
Dave Kendrick
January 1995

Chapter 1

Treatment and delinquency
A behavioural approach

UNDERSTANDING BEHAVIOUR

Since its very beginning *homo sapiens* has struggled to reach some form of self-understanding; indeed our history is littered with attempts to explain why we are what we are. Perhaps the earliest belief of all was that our actions are governed by mystical forces, by gods and demons who could inhabit our earthly bodies and mould our thoughts, words, and deeds. A different belief found, for example, in the writings of the ancient Greek teacher Hippocrates, is that it is biological forces that determine our personality and behaviour. While differing in emphasis, these time-honoured beliefs in the forces of the spiritual and biological worlds have one important similarity: they locate the cause of behaviour *inside* the person. The emphasis on an inner world – be it a biological, a mental, or a spiritual world – in seeking to explain our behaviour is to be found in more recent philosophical and psychological theories. Certainly this is true of the theories of Sigmund Freud, undoubtedly the most widely known and influential of contemporary psychological theorists.

The essence of Freud's position is that our outward, observable behaviour is a result of a constant tension and conflict between inner forces. These inner forces, thought by Freud to be psychological in nature but biological in origin, were portrayed as part of an intricate psychodynamic system, operating at both conscious and unconscious levels. Freud's ideas proved a rich source of inspiration for following generations and there are several post-Freudian schools offering variations on Freud's original theories (Brown, 1961; Kline, 1984).

If Freud followed a spiritualistic, or at least mentalistic, path, then others have taken a biological road. Again at around the turn of the century, the thesis was developed by several eminent scientists, including Sir Francis Galton, that genetic forces govern the level of mental abilities such as intelligence and therefore our behaviour. This form of biological determinism, popularly called a 'medical model', although better termed a 'physiological model', has been extended to include many other biological factors such as neurotransmitters and hormones. It is important at this point to make the distinction between correlation and cause: for example, most experts agree that schizophrenia *involves* (i.e.

correlates with) various changes in physiological functioning; however this is not to say (as some might, perhaps rightly) that it is these physiological changes that *determine* (i.e. cause) schizophrenia.

Thus the search for an understanding of the causes of behaviour has a long history steeped in the tradition of looking inside the person to explain his or her outward behaviour. The beginning of a different way of explaining behaviour took place around the turn of this century, in the laboratories of the Russian physiologist and Nobel prize winner, Ivan Pavlov. Pavlov's research was concerned with the digestive system in canines and it was while engaged in this work that he made what was to prove a significant observation. He noticed that dogs accustomed to the laboratory salivated not only at the sight or smell of food, as expected, but also salivated to cues related to the presence of food such as the sound of the food pails. Hungry dogs salivate naturally to the sight or smell of food but why should these dogs salivate to the noise of clanking pails? The answer, as of course Pavlov discovered, is to be found in the process of learning by association: certain stimuli such as sights or sounds become associated over time with a naturally occurring reflex response, such as salivation, so that these stimuli gain the power to elicit artificially the reflex response. Thus the laboratory dogs had learned an association between a certain sound and the arrival of food, so that the sound itself could elicit the salivation even if no food was forthcoming. This process of learning by association is called *classical conditioning*.

Pavlov's work heralded the notion that behaviour could be explained through interaction between the person (or animal) and the outside world. Thus, rather than seeing behaviour as the product of some biological or psychological force *inside* the person, an alternative understanding of the world was beginning in which the emphasis was on events *external* to the person. This idea was to revolutionize the discipline of psychology, in terms of both theory and method, as researchers turned to the study of behaviour as a phenomenon worthy of attention in its own right, rather than treating it simply as a by-product of some mysterious inner system. The founding father of this behavioural approach was the American psychologist John B. Watson, whose 1913 paper 'Psychology as the behaviourist views it', caught the mood of the times in an American university system unhappy with the unscientific European mentalistic tradition.

Simply, Watson argued that humans, like other animals, are born with various innate stimulus-response reflexes: the grasp reflex, the eyeblink reflex, the suckle reflex, and so on. Through classical conditioning, Watson argued, we learn more and more complex chains of behaviour. The task of psychology was therefore scientifically to develop an understanding of learning and thereby to discover the laws by which behaviour could be predicted and nurtured. With the benefit now of almost eighty years of research and debate we know that the acquisition and development of behaviour is too complex to be reduced to chains of association stemming from innate reflexes. In a sense, however, that restriction in explanatory power hardly matters; it is the line of thought invoked by Watson and the ensuing years of research and debate that is important. (This is not to say that classical conditioning has been dismissed – far from it as Rescorla (1988) shows – rather that other explanations are also needed to account for the richness of learning.) Pavlov and Watson, like Freud, had set into motion a new way of thinking about the world, and in the same way that Freud's ideas were developed by the post-Freudians, so Watson's ideas were developed by the neo-behaviourists.

The individual destined to be the most influential of the neobehaviourists was a young researcher at Harvard University who between 1930 and 1935 developed the basic concepts for a new way of analysing and understanding behaviour. This new approach was called *behaviour analysis* and its main proponent was the American psychologist B. F. Skinner.

Behaviour analysis

As Kazdin (1979) notes, one error made in many textbooks is to dismiss the principles of behaviour analysis as simplistic and mechanistic. While the founda-tions of behaviour analysis may be understandable, the philosophical and theore-tical issues are complex and taxing. It is not our aim here to discuss these theoretical issues in depth; readers who wish to grapple with the complexities of behaviourism should refer to the recent books by Catania and Harnad (1988), Lee (1988), Modgil and Modgil (1987), Nye (1992), and Zuriff (1985).

The basis for Skinner's contribution can be traced to a line of research – perhaps most often associated with Edward Thorndike, an American psycho-logist working in the early 1900s – concerned with the relationship between the outcome of a behaviour and the probability of that same behaviour recurring in the future. Skinner's quest was to understand the nature of this relationship between behaviour and its consequences. As was the fashion in the 1920s and 1930s, Skinner's early studies were carried out with animals such as rats, pigeons, and squirrels. In a typical study the animal would be placed in a closed box – now known as a Skinner Box – and its behaviour closely observed and recorded. The use of a closed environment such as a box allows the researcher to control external events and so see precisely their effect on behaviour.

When placed in a Skinner Box the animal, say a rat, will explore its new environment. One feature of a Skinner Box is a bar. The researcher has arranged that when the rat first approaches the bar food will be delivered into a tray inside the box. After eating, the rat will return to the bar and explore further, eventually placing its front paws on the bar; with a click, the bar drops down and food is automatically delivered into the tray. Very quickly the rat learns that its behaviour, the bar press, can operate on the environment to produce a certain consequence; it is food in this example, although other consequences are possible such as drink and access to other rats. This type of behaviour, which operates on the environment to produce certain consequences, Skinner called *operant* behaviour and hence this type of learning, *operant learning*. The relationship between behaviour and its consequences is called a *contingency*, and Skinner formulated the principles of two important types of contingency that he termed 'reinforcement' and 'punishment'.

Reinforcement

A reinforcement contingency is by definition a situation in which the consequences of a behaviour *increase* the likelihood of that behaviour occurring in the future. There are two types of reinforcement contingency: positive reinforcement and negative reinforcement. *Positive* reinforcement takes place when behaviour is either maintained or increased by producing consequences that the person (or animal) finds rewarding. *Negative* reinforcement, on the other hand, occurs when the behaviour produces the consequence of avoiding or escaping from an aversive situation. These principles can be used to change behaviour. Suppose a teacher wishes to increase the amount of classwork handed in by a certain pupil; the wish to increase behaviour immediately signifies that a reinforcement programme is required. The teacher has to make a choice between using rewards and aversive control. Increased classwork might be made contingent on a pleasant outcome, such as praise or more time at preferred activities; alternatively, a failure to increase classwork might be made contingent on some aversive outcome such as detention or loss of some privilege. Both approaches may well increase behaviour, assuming accurate identification of a reinforcer; however, the first uses positive reinforcement, the second negative reinforcement. Although the two strategies have the same effect they will be very different in practice; we will return to this issue when we discuss the management of programme design in Chapter 4.

The point above regarding the accurate identification of reinforcers is important: it is sometimes assumed that the same things, such as money or praise, are rewarding for everyone. This is not true: for example, some people, perhaps particularly adolescents, find praise far from rewarding (Brophy, 1981). Alternatively, events that are seen by most people as unrewarding or even aversive, such as verbal or physical abuse, can in some situations be rewarding and so reinforce behaviour.

Punishment

The term 'punishment' as used in behaviour analysis has a different meaning from that found in everyday usage. A punishment contingency is one in which the consequences of a behaviour lead to a *decrease* in the frequency of that behaviour. As with reinforcement there are two types of punishment, sometimes termed positive and negative punishment, which can be used to change behaviour. Suppose a schoolteacher is faced with a child who shouts in class, a behaviour that the teacher wishes to stop or, in operant terms, punish. The teacher has a choice of two strategies: the shouting can be followed by the delivery of some aversive outcome, such as extra schoolwork or detention; or the shouting can be followed by the loss of a reward such as a place on a sports team or another privilege. In the former instance an unpleasant outcome is made contingent on the behaviour, which is positive punishment; in the latter case the loss of a reward is negative punishment. As with reinforcement, the strategy is only punishing if it leads to a change in behaviour.

It is important to emphasize that in the sense used by behaviour analysts punishment refers to a particular relationship between behaviour and its consequences. Punishment emphatically *does not* mean physical pain or highly distressing events.

Three-term contingency

Having considered behaviour and its consequences there is one more factor to discuss to complete this brief introduction to behaviour analysis. Behaviour, in the main, does not happen at random; environmental events signal that if a given behaviour is carried out then it is likely to be reinforced or punished. The errant child shouting in the classroom is unlikely to do so when the classroom is empty. It is more likely that several cues – the presence of certain other children, a particular teacher, a type of lesson – will prompt the shouting. The child has learned that shouting in the presence of these cues produces either rewarding outcomes such as peer approval (positive reinforcement), or avoids other outcomes such as having to do a disliked lesson (negative reinforcement). The relationship between setting or antecedent events, the behaviour, and the consequences is called a *three-term contingency*. This gives rise to the much used A:B:C analysis: Antecedent : Behaviour : Consequence.

The goal in conducting a behavioural analysis is to come to an understanding of a behaviour through the formulation of an A:B:C sequence for a given behaviour. In essence, the goal is to understand the *function*, in terms of reinforcement and punishment, of a behaviour for the individual concerned, hence A:B:C analysis is properly called a *functional analysis*. A useful distinction can be made here between assessment and analysis: the former is the gathering of data and information; the latter is the process of making sense of this information and so simplifying the process of setting goals for change. The management of assessment, analysis, and goal-setting is discussed in detail in Chapter 3.

While it is historically true that the principles of behaviour analysis were formulated in studies with animals, often called the *experimental* analysis of behaviour, the task of *applied* behaviour analysis is to use these principles to understand human behaviour. The movement away from the laboratory and the controlled environment of the Skinner Box into the real world makes this an immensely difficult task. The difficulties are twofold: the complexity of most people's lives makes it impossible to discover every event in their learning history and to appreciate every influence on their behaviour; further, people differ from animals in some important ways – principally in their cognitive abilities, in their highly evolved use of verbal language, and in the nature of their social environment – which requires some adjustments in the principles derived from animal studies. Several points follow from these two difficulties. The first is that the completeness of an assessment and the analysis that flows from it will always be limited. The second is that applied behaviour analysis depends on the skill and ability of the analyst: it cannot be reduced to rigid, mechanical formulae. Third, our understanding of the place of 'human' factors in behaviour analysis is constantly changing as research progresses (e.g. Lowe, 1983). These considerations clearly point to the need for training for those who wish to practice applied behaviour analysis (see Chapter 5).

The 'problem' of private events

In seeking to establish a scientific basis for the emerging discipline of psychology, Watson proposed that because the private world inside the skin is impossible to study scientifically it should not be of concern to the psychologist. An unfortunate legacy of Watson's behaviourism is the mistaken belief that behaviourism denies the existence of, or at best ignores, 'private' events such as thoughts and feelings. Such a criticism is entirely misplaced if directed at contemporary behaviourism: indeed, as Skinner (1974) states, 'A science of behaviour must consider the place of private stimuli ... The question, then is this: What is inside the skin and how do we know about it? The answer is, I believe, the heart of radical behaviourism' (pp. 211–12). In part answer to his own question, Skinner (1986a) has suggested the place of private events in a sequence as follows: 'In a given episode the environment acts upon the organism, something happens inside, the organism then acts upon the environment, and certain consequences follow' (p. 716).

The key issue that arises, which is the heart of the 'problem', is whether what happens inside the skin can be considered as behaviour, and therefore be part of behaviour analysis; or whether internal events should be accorded a separate, perhaps mentalistic or spiritualistic, status and so fall outside the realms of behaviour analysis. The radical behaviourist position is that private events are behaviours and so can be understood within the terms of behaviour analysis: that is, private events are seen as established by a particular environment, and they are maintained and modified by environmental consequences.

Do private events cause behaviour? Again Skinner is clear: 'Private events ... may be called causes, but not initiating causes' (see Catania and Harnad, 1988, p. 486). The initiation of behaviour, including private behaviour, is to be found in the environment – most often our social world. However, once initiated, one behaviour can lead to another and so on: thus private behaviour can act as the stimulation for overt, observable behaviour. For example, if someone steps on your toes and hurts you, then you might become angry and shout (or worse!); in an applied behavioural analysis you shouted not because you were hurt and angry, although the pain and emotion were undoubtedly involved, but because initially the environment acted on you to set in train a sequence of reactions that culminated in your verbal behaviour. The consequences of your behaviour – remembering that behaviour includes the private events – will produce environmental consequences that, the next time your toes are stepped on, will either reinforce or punish the chain of behaviours that culminated in your shouting on this occasion.

The practical or technical difficulty lies in the assessment of private events. By definition, private events are not observable and so we must rely on self-report to find out about them; the problems here are concerned with the accuracy and reliability of self-reported information. Self-report can be unreliable for several reasons: the person may want to withhold the truth; or the very act of self-observation can change the nature and functioning of the private event; or private events may in part occur outside awareness, such as when dreaming, and so are not amenable to self-observation. It may be that as technology progresses these problems will be overcome; for the present we must work within these limitations.

Cognitive theories

Of course, not all theorists agree with radical behaviourism – the world would be a duller place if they did – and there are several other important contemporary psychological theories. *Social learning theory* is in part an extension of operant principles, but with changes in the role and status of cognition (Bandura, 1977, 1986). In operant theory behaviour is initiated and reinforced by the environment; however Bandura prefers the use of the term 'motivation' to reinforcement. Motivation can take three forms: *external reinforcement*, as in operant learning; *vicarious reinforcement*, which comes from observing other people; and *self-reinforcement*, as in a sense of personal pride or achievement. The introduction of motivation as a cause of behaviour, alongside the concept of internal as well as external reinforcement, marks a clear divergence from radical behaviourism. While social learning theory retains some overlap with behaviour analysis, the recent moves towards the separation of cognition and behaviour as exemplified in cognitive theories such as information-processing (Anderson, 1980) is clearly at odds with behaviourism. The theoretical research and debate continue apace and, as the theories advance, so do treatment styles and methods (Fishman *et al.*, 1988). In little more than two decades behaviour modification has been supplemented by cognitive-behaviour modification, followed by the rise of cognitive therapy, quite different in form and emphasis from its predecessors (Brewin, 1988).

At this stage we should perhaps declare our hand for what is to follow. Without being dogmatic or disparaging, we can say that we are not cognitive theorists or therapists, and this book is not concerned with this approach. We are all applied behaviour analysts, although perhaps admitting to healthy differences of opinion regarding the status of cognition, and it is therefore applied behaviour analysis that provides the foundation for this book.

Of course applied behaviour analysis can be used to develop an understanding of all social behaviours, from the 'micro' level of the individual to 'macro' level of a culture (Lamal, 1991; Skinner, 1986b). Given this scope, it is not surprising that applied behaviour analysis, with associated learning theories, has informed attempts to account for delinquency (e.g. Morris and Braukmann, 1987).

DELINQUENCY

The topic of delinquency has generated a vast amount of research and there are several texts that offer summaries of current knowledge (Henggeler, 1989; Quay, 1987a; Rutter and Giller, 1983; West, 1982). However, before looking at some of the research, it is important to clarify exactly what we mean by the term 'delinquent'.

The term delinquent is typically used in two ways in relation to child or adolescent behaviour: the first is in connection with behaviours, such as lying or defiance, of which an adult disapproves; the second is to describe behaviour that is illegal and can be dealt with by criminal law. For present purposes we will use the term in keeping with the second sense: the former is perhaps better thought of as 'antisocial behaviour' or 'conduct disorder' rather than criminal behaviour. Thus a delinquent can be defined as a young person who commits an act forbidden by criminal law who can be dealt with by criminal proceedings. There are several reasons why, after committing a criminal act, young people may not be dealt with under criminal law. Most obviously, they may not be caught: substantial numbers of offences go unreported or unsolved and it is reasonable to assume that some of these offences are committed by adolescents. Alternatively, young people may not have reached the age at which they are held fully responsible for their behaviour and so they cannot be prosecuted for a criminal offence. The age of criminal responsibility varies from country to country and legal system to legal system. For example, in Scotland the minimum age of criminal responsibility is 8 years of age, in England and Wales it is 10 years of age, in France it is 13 years of age, and in Sweden it is 15 years of age. At the other end of the scale, there is a cut-off point between juvenile and adult offenders; this tends, as for example in England and Wales, to be approximately 17 to 18 years of age. Finally, the presence of mental disorder, again as defined by different legal systems, may mean that a young person is not dealt with under criminal law.

These points allow us to arrive at a more exact definition of the meaning of the term delinquent as we intend it to be understood here. A delinquent is a young person, over the legally defined age of criminal responsibility but not an adult, not suffering from a mental disorder, who commits an act capable of being followed by criminal proceedings. Thus we are not concerned here with children below the age of criminal responsibility, or with disturbed young people in medical, psychiatric, or other facilities (although some of what we have to say may be applicable to these other groups). Our concern here is with the population of 'normal' young people who commit criminal offences.

Juvenile crime

What types of offences do young people commit? How many young people commit criminal offences? With regard to type of offence, the distinction can be made between *status* offences and *index* (or *notifiable*) offences. Status offences are those acts that are peculiar to young people and so do not apply to adults – truancy, drinking alcohol, driving a motor vehicle under age, and so on. Index offences, on the other hand, are serious offences – such as murder, rape and sexual assault, burglary, arson, robbery – which are criminal acts whatever the age of the perpetrator. It is true that young people commit both status and index offences but, to turn to the second question, how many young people commit offences?

If we consider both status and index offences, the research strongly suggests very high rates of offending among adolescent populations: estimates of over 80 per cent of adolescents having committed a criminal offence are not uncommon. Indeed, Farrington (1987) suggests that if unrecorded offences could be included with official figures then this would 'undoubtedly push these figures close to 100 percent' (p. 34). What percentage of these offences are minor status offences as opposed to serious index offences? Farrington notes that in both England and the United States about 30 per cent of criminals apprehended for serious crimes are juveniles. As this figure is based on official records it can, of course, only include those offences known to the authorities. It is possible therefore that more adolescents are committing serious offences than this figure suggests. How much greater is a matter for conjecture, but it is highly unlikely that the number of serious offences even begins to approach the high levels of status offences.

While statistics of this type tell us something about delinquency rates, they do not tell the whole story. There are two sides to the coin: *prevalence* rates are the numbers of young people committing offences; and *incidence* rates are the numbers of offences committed per offender. The importance of this distinction is seen, for example, when we consider the relationship between age and offending. It is well established that for the adolescent population delinquency rates increase from the lowest age of criminal responsibility, reach a peak at 16–17 years of age, then rapidly decline in the late teens and early twenties (Farrington, 1986). Is this picture of rising crime among young people due to increasing prevalence, i.e. more young people committing crimes? Or is it due to a rise in incidence, i.e. the young people who commit crimes committing more as they grow older? For many reasons it is difficult for researchers to disentangle absolutely prevalence and incidence rates, but nonetheless there is general agreement that the rise in delinquency rates with age reflects a rise in prevalence not incidence. For example, from their longitudinal study carried out in the United States, Wolfgang *et al.* (1987) argued that the peak in rates of offending at 16–17 years of age is due 'almost entirely to an increase in the number of active offenders and not to an increase in their annual "productivity"' (p. 44).

While acknowledging that various demographic variables – such as sex, race, socio-economic class – have some influence on both prevalence and incidence, can we conclude that the general message from research on age and offending is that if young people are left alone they will 'grow out' of delinquency? It is tempting to think that no action is needed at all, but this is highly unlikely to be true for all offenders. Although most of the offences that contribute to the increase in offending are relatively trivial, research has suggested several factors that are associated with chronic long-term offending. For example, West (1982) reported several individual, family, social, and economic factors that characterized serious young offenders. These predictive factors included being labelled as 'troublesome' at primary school, coming from a large family with a low income, a parent with a criminal record, and poor parenting. In addition, it is also known that children who commit their first serious offence at an early age, and those adolescents who accumulate more than six criminal convictions, are at greatest risk of progressing to an adult criminal career (Farrington, 1983). While these findings are important in describing the types of condition associated with the aetiology of delinquency, they also demand an explanation of *how* they cause delinquent behaviour. In other words, we need a theory to explain the process by which the interaction between the young person and the events outlined above combine to cause the delinquent behaviour. It is to this end that behavioural theories have been applied to attempt to explain delinquent acts.

Behavioural theories of delinquency

The study of crime is a highly specialized topic, drawing on knowledge and theories from a range of disciplines including sociology, biology, economics, and psychology. The multidisciplinary flavour associated with criminology has given rise to a plethora of theories of crime: Siegal's (1986) criminology text, for example, reviews classical and neoclassical theories, biological theories, psychological theories, social structure theories, social process theories, and social conflict theories. It should be clear that there are many ways to understand crime and delinquency, some directly opposed, some with a degree of overlap. Within psychological theories of criminal behaviour, the application of theories of learning to delinquent behaviour has a relatively long history (Blackburn, 1993; Hollin, 1989, 1992).

Differential association theory

The foundations for differential association theory were laid by Sutherland (1939), and there have been several subsequent modifications (e.g. Sutherland and Cressey, 1974). This theory is concerned with both the environmental conditions that produce criminal behaviour, and with the learning processes by which an individual becomes criminal. Sutherland begins from the standpoint that crime is socially defined: in other words, there are some people within society, the law-makers, who hold the power to dictate what behaviour is acceptable and what cannot be tolerated. Within such a social structure some people are law-abiding, while others commit acts judged as unlawful. Why do some people remain within the law while others do not?

The answer, Sutherland proposed, is to be found in learning – learning no different from any other behaviour. In keeping with the predominant theoretical views of the time, i.e. the mid-1920s, Sutherland suggested that the learning takes place through *association* with other people. It should be noted that Sutherland does not suggest that the association is with criminals, rather that the association is with other people favourably disposed towards breaking the law who fail to deliver sanctions for offending. Following this line of argument, Sutherland also argues that the content of learning includes not only the specific skills for committing certain types of crime but also the attitudes and motivations conducive to offending.

It is remarkable how Sutherland anticipated later developments in both learning theory and criminology. He suggested that important, formative learning takes place in close social groups and intimate personal relationships; this is now to be seen in social learning theory (Bandura, 1977), and in social process and social structure theories in criminology (Shoemaker, 1990). Further, the idea that the content of learning includes both skill and cognition is exactly in line with contemporary learning theory (Hayes, 1989), and stands comparison with contemporary criminological research on crime specialization (e.g. Klein, 1984) and cognitive processes in offenders (e.g. Cornish and Clarke, 1986). Finally, the view that criminal behaviour is *acquired* behaviour, and therefore no different from any other behaviour, argues against the position, popular at the time Sutherland was writing (e.g. Aichhorn, [1925] 1955), that criminal behaviour is evidence of underlying psychopathology. A nonpathological view of criminal behaviour is very much in keeping with the opinions of many contemporary criminologists and psychologists.

When Sutherland was developing his theories, he did not have an empirical base or a well-developed theory of learning from which he could hypothesize about how differential association might work. However, the work of figures such as Skinner and Bandura made possible an increase in theoretical sophistication leading both to an expansion and modification of Sutherland's original theory.

Reinforcement theory

Jeffery (1965) suggested that advances in operant learning could be used to refine differential association theory. In essence, Jeffery proposed that criminal behaviour is an operant behaviour: in other words, criminal behaviour is acquired and maintained by the reinforcing environmental consequences it produces for the individual. Thus, to understand why a person commits a crime, it is necessary to understand that individual's learning history and so the rewarding consequences for the criminal act. In most cases of acquisitive crime – theft, burglary, embezzlement – the consequences are financial and material gain. These gains can be positively reinforcing in themselves, or alternatively they may be negatively reinforcing in that they allow the offender to avoid the unpleasant position of having no money. As well as material rewards, criminal behaviour can produce social rewards. For example, within delinquent cultures repeated criminal acts are often rewarded with peer approval and positions of leadership within groups.

Jeffery also suggested that criminal behaviour can produce aversive consequences – such as being caught, loss of liberty, disruption of family relationships – which might have a punishing (in an operant sense) effect on the behaviour. Thus, it is the balance of reinforcement and punishment in the criminal's learning history that determines, given the right antecedent conditions, the occurrence of criminal behaviour. In keeping with operant learning theory, it follows that each individual will have a unique learning history, thereby demanding analysis in its own right. This is a crucial point when it comes to the organization of assessment, functional analysis, and intervention programmes (Chapters 3 and 4).

Social learning theory

The ideas and concepts heralded by the emergence of social learning theory have also been applied to the analysis of delinquency. Akers (1977) is perhaps most closely identified with attempts within mainstream criminology to develop a theory of crime based on elements from differential association theory, reinforcement theory, and social learning theory (see Krohn *et al.*, 1987). Thus the acquisition of criminal behaviour, in terms of both attitudes and skills as proposed by differential association theory, is explained either through direct reinforcement, as in operant terms, or via modelling as understood by social learning theory. While learning can and does occur in non-social situations, Akers maintains that most learning takes place in social contexts when other people make reinforcers and punishers available for certain behaviours. Thus it is argued that criminal behaviour is similarly maintained by the tangible, social, and vicarious rewards it produces.

In keeping with Sutherland's original theory, Akers also turns to the definitions or meanings of the criminal behaviour for the offender. These definitions may be positive, so that criminal behaviour is seen as desirable or permissible; for example, car thieves may argue that it is desirable to steal cars to experience the joy of driving. Alternatively, definitions may be neutralizing, so that they negate the impact of what are considered intolerable behaviours; for example, tax dodgers may agree that it is wrong to steal, but neutralize their wrongdoing by arguing that the sum involved is very small, or that as there is no 'real' victim then no harm is done. These definitions, which clearly involve sophisticated cognitive processes, set the meaning of the criminal behaviour for the individual and so form a highly personalized aspect of the individual's criminality.

More recent research following a social learning approach has focused on two aspects of delinquent functioning, social cognition and social skills. A brief overview of these areas is given below; more comprehensive discussions are given by Hollin (1990a) and Ross and Fabiano (1985).

Social cognition can be thought of as that part of cognition concerned with other people, their behaviour, and our own behaviour in relation to other people. Several types and styles of social cognition have been associated with delinquency. The ability to see things from the other person's point of view – i.e. to display *empathy* – is an important part of social cognition. Most studies, although not all, have suggested that delinquents do not score highly on measures of empathy: the lack of unanimity in the research may be due to differences in empathy associated with the delinquent's age, sex, and offence type.

The term *locus of control* is used with reference to the degree to which individuals see their behaviour to be under their own *internal control*, or under the control of *external* forces such as luck or people in positions of authority. Some studies have shown that delinquents tended to see themselves as externally controlled; that is, they see their behaviour as caused and maintained by forces outside their own control. Again the findings are not unanimous, which may be due to variations such as type of offence: for example, violent young offenders have been shown to display a greater belief in external control than non-violent young offenders.

A lack of *self-control* is often linked to impulsive behaviour, often described as a failure to stop and think between impulse and action. Some studies have shown that delinquents are characterized by high levels of impulsivity although, again probably for the reasons already discussed, not all studies have found this link between low self-control and delinquency.

Moral reasoning is another facet of social cognition that has been associated with delinquency. Specifically, it is suggested that delinquency is associated with a delay in the development of moral reasoning so that given the opportunity the delinquent does not have the cognitive ability to control and resist temptation (see Blasi, 1980). While there is evidence in support of this position, it is likely that the strength of the relationship varies in accord with other factors. For example, a study reported by Thornton and Reid (1982) found that young offenders who had committed offences without financial gain (assault, murder, sex offences) showed more mature moral judgement than another group of young offenders who had committed crimes of acquisition (burglary, robbery, theft, fraud).

Finally, *social problem-solving* refers to the ability, needed in most social situations, to weigh up the situation, generate possible courses of action, consider the various outcomes that might follow, and plan how to achieve desired outcomes. Several studies have shown that compared to non-delinquents, young offenders use a more restricted range of alternatives to solve interpersonal problems, and rely more on verbal and physical aggression. This appears to hold true for both male and female young offenders.

Social problem-solving, as well as an important component of social cognition generally, is also an integral part of the second aspect of delinquent functioning that has attracted a great deal of recent attention: *social skills*. The concept of social skills refers to the individual's ability to perceive and understand social cues and signals, generate feasible courses of action (i.e. social problem-solving), and act in a socially appropriate manner (see Argyle, 1983). Some studies have shown that, compared to non-delinquents, delinquents show on average lower levels of social skills in the three areas of social perception, social problem-solving, and social performance (see Hollin, 1990b).

The recent research into social cognition and social skills in delinquents raises several important issues. The first is that much of the evidence is gathered using group designs. Typically the performance of a group of delinquents on, say, a test of moral reasoning ability is compared to the performance of a group of non-delinquents on the same test. Comparison of the average performance of both groups shows that the delinquents score significantly lower than the non-delinquents. While this might be interesting, it says nothing about variations *within* the sample of delinquents: while the average performance of the delin-quents may be lower, this is an average. Some delinquents will therefore perform above average levels compared to other delinquents and may well perform better than those non-delinquents who scored below average. Apart from the theoretical dilemmas set by such a pattern of scores, this point has an important practical side. While these research findings may usefully point to potential targets for intervention, it cannot be assumed that all delinquents experience social skills difficulties. In other words, the research may suggest targets for assessment but it does not obviate the need for careful detailed assessment at an individual level. The second major point to be made is that while the research may show patterns of average ability in delinquents on measures of social ability, it is altogether less clear how, if at all, any shortcomings in social behaviour are related to offending. This is a point made repeatedly in the past both for young offenders (Henderson and Hollin, 1986; Hollin, 1990b) and adult offenders (Howells, 1986), and to which we will return in Chapters 3 and 4.

In total, therefore, we have at our disposal a wealth of research concerning the aetiology and epidemiology of delinquency, and we have sophisticated behavioural theories of delinquency. How has this knowledge been used in formulating policies to respond to delinquency?

RESPONDING TO CRIME

Within any society most people would probably agree that delinquency, certainly serious delinquency, should be prevented. The problem is how to achieve this goal; by what means should delinquency be prevented? Morris (1987) describes three prevention strategies that can be applied to all criminal behaviour, including that committed by young offenders. *Primary prevention* has the aim of pre-venting the whole of the population from breaking the law; *secondary prevention* aims to prevent offending among 'at risk' individuals and groups; and finally *tertiary prevention* has the goal of preventing further offending by those indivi-duals who have already committed an offence. The notion of prevention and the development of prevention programmes is attracting increasing attention generally (e.g. Edelstein and Michelson, 1986), as well as for crime and delinquency specifically (Burchard and Burchard, 1987).

Primary and secondary prevention

There are two, diametrically opposed, ways in which both primary and secondary prevention of criminal behaviour might be achieved. The first way is by implementing policies, made known to 'honest citizens' and 'at risk' groups alike, that if they commit a crime then severe unpleasant consequences will follow. This type of thinking, embodied in the principle of deterrence, is at the basis of many western legal systems. It has its roots in conservative, classical criminology that espouses the view that in committing a criminal act the individual, aware of the consequences of his or her actions, is exercising free will in making a perfectly rational decision to break the law (Roshier, 1989). It follows from this line of thought – increasingly popular at present as testified by the rise of the, so-called, neoclassical theories – that to prevent crime the public has to be made aware that offending will attract stiff penalties. Of course, this also demands that the legislation is in place to ensure that stiff penalties can be handed out by the courts.

An alternative approach to deterrence, usually associated with a liberal, *positivist* criminology, is based on the notion that criminal behaviour is a result of forces, either psychological or social, over which the individual has little or no control. In order therefore to prevent crime, according to this way of thinking, it is necessary to change the conditions that set the scene for criminal behaviour. To achieve this goal, we need precise knowledge of the individual and social factors associated with criminal behaviour. As discussed previously, researchers such as Donald West and David Farrington have uncovered several predictors of later criminal careers, and suggestions have been advanced of how such research can be put into practice. In a statement remarkable for its frankness, Nietzel and Himelein (1986) note that, 'We believe there is enough knowledge about etiologic factors in crime to justify aiming our interventions at some prevention targets' (p. 197). Nietzel and Himelien give five such areas:

1 diversion of youth away from the adverse labelling effects of the criminal justice system;
2 tackling family violence as the source of antisocial behaviour by those abused as children;
3 parent training for better child management;
4 development of young people's cognitive, behavioural, academic, and occupational skills and competencies;
5 situational measures to reduce opportunities for criminal behaviour.

As Nietzel and Himelein note, the first option is secondary prevention, the others, depending on whether they are targeted at the whole population or 'at risk' groups, have the potential to be used as either primary or secondary prevention.

At the level of primary prevention, a moment's thought shows that to achieve even one of the latter four points requires a huge investment, an investment not just in terms of time and money, but also a political investment in changing many long-established social and cultural traditions, values, and 'freedoms'. At the level of secondary prevention, the strategy of intervening with 'at risk' – or 'predelinquent', as they are sometimes termed – groups to divert young people away from a life of crime has a certain appeal. However, a note of caution must be sounded when we look at the results from previous attempts at early intervention. The most widely cited study of this type is the American Cambridge–Somerville Youth Study (Powers and Witmar, 1951). In this study young males, living in high crime areas and therefore judged to be at risk of offending, were recommended to the programme by welfare agencies, police, and members of the local church. When the referral to the programme was accepted, the young person was randomly allocated to either an intervention or a no-intervention group. For the intervention group, counsellors were assigned to the young person's family, visiting on average about twice a month. In addition, the families themselves could call for help when they felt it was needed. Along with the counselling, the intervention programme also included improved access to medical and psychiatric facilities, academic teaching, and other community programmes. The length of intervention varied from family to family, lasting for anything between two and eight years. The no-intervention control group were simply contacted at regular intervals and asked for information about themselves.

As the study began in 1939, it has been possible to collect long-term follow-up data. A follow-up study by McCord (1978) traced the records of over 500 men who had participated in the original study. The follow-up information revealed that those adults who had taken part in the programme expressed fond memories of the project, particularly recalling their counsellors with affection. However, the rate of offending, as both juveniles and adults, did not vary to any significant degree between the intervention and no-intervention groups. Further, McCord notes several *adverse* effects associated with the intervention: these adversities included more mental illness and alcoholism in the intervention group, and even a tendency to die at a younger age. In seeking to explain these findings, McCord suggests that the intervention may have acted to create a dependency on outside agencies that then caused problems when later removed. Alternatively, the values of the counsellors were so far removed from the families with whom they associated that this raised internal conflicts for the young person, thereby precipitating the later disorders. McCord concludes with the warning that 'Intervention programmes risk damaging the individuals they are designed to assist' (p. 289).

A more recent study by Palamara et al. (1986) arrived at a similar conclusion: both police and treatment-orientated interventions with young people had the effect of increasing juvenile deviance. In yet another American study, Davidson et al. (1987) looked at the long-term effects of diversionary treatment for over 200 juvenile offenders. They reported that while the diversionary programmes had some effect as measured using official measures of criminal behaviour (e.g.

police arrests), self-reported delinquency remained steadfastly unchanged. While results such as these should rightly give occasion for thought, it should also be remembered that, in total, the evidence is very limited. Experience in planning and designing programmes continues to grow, and it may be that more effective secondary prevention programmes can be developed in the future by building on existing knowledge.

Despite the debate concerning the relative merits of primary and secondary prevention, it is a reality that many practitioners have their first contact with young people when the 'at risk' has become a reality – *after* an offence has been committed. Indeed, in many, but not all, instances this first contact is not only after the offence, but after the court has passed sentence. Such practitioners are, by definition, concerned with tertiary prevention; that is, their aim is to prevent further offending by those young people who have already broken the law. While we hope that much of what we have to say will be of interest to all those concerned with all levels of prevention, particularly those working in the field of Intermediate Treatment, it is with practitioners working with convicted offenders at the forefront of our thoughts that we have written this book.

For a practitioner to make a commitment to tertiary prevention based on changing the offender's behaviour through positive rather than punitive means demands a specific philosophical and moral stance. It demands a belief that it is right to follow liberal rather than conservative thinking on the causes of criminal behaviour. It demands a belief that it is better to try to modify behaviour through positive, caring methods, rather than by punitive, aversive means. In total, it demands a belief that rehabilitation is preferable to retribution and harsh punishment. It is important to state that in adopting a treatment approach, one is not seeking to excuse the offender, offer easy options, or neglect victims. Treatment programmes should aim to make the young person more responsible for his or her actions and try to make the young person work at challenging and changing his or her behaviour. The process of change is, as all concerned will testify, much harder than sitting idly in a prison cell, while few would argue against the view that victims deserve all the help that can be offered. Indeed, on the latter point, many people talk as if offender programmes and victim support schemes are somehow exclusive: there is no reason why both cannot exist. Indeed, the force of some recent research is to show that many offenders are also victims (e.g. Widom, 1989).

To adopt a treatment philosophy in working with young offenders therefore demands a moral and social judgement by each practitioner. Of course there is a range of issues associated with such a stance; however perhaps the most fundamental is the politics of appearing to focus on the offender.

INTERVENTION AND DELINQUENCY

If, as many theories including behavioural theories maintain, delinquent behaviour is a product of an interaction between a host of economic, social, political, and individual forces, can it be right to focus attention on the individual offender? Do advocates of an intervention approach that is based on changing the offender's behaviour also divert attention away from the injustices and in-equalities of society, and therefore away from the need for social change, by putting the blame squarely on the offender's shoulders? Yet further, do advocates of this approach really 'medicalize' antisocial behaviour, creating a market for their treatment skills that are needed to 'cure' the offender?

West (1980) has discussed these issues in detail. He suggests that paying heed to the offender as an individual, and seeking to understand his or her behaviour in the context of family relationships, interactions with authority, and other social factors, actually has the effect of highlighting the importance of environmental influences. Indeed, if we look to the research discussed previously, we can do little else but take account of environmental factors in seeking to understand criminal behaviour. This awareness of environmental influences on behaviour must therefore influence our planning of assessment (Chapter 3), programme design (Chapter 4), and return to the community after institutional care (Chapter 4). In broader terms, Burchard (1987) makes the distinction between therapeutic contingencies and social/political contingencies. Those concerned with thera-peutic contingencies and those concerned with social/political contingencies come from very different worlds. The therapist is concerned with the individual offender and perhaps his or her close social contacts such as family and peers. Administrators and politicians, on the other hand, are concerned with laws, with budgets, with personnel, and with the disposal of offenders on a grand scale. There is a vast power differential between therapists and administrators; at the most basic level the policy-makers control the funding necessary for therapeutic contingencies to function – put simply, they have the power to hire and fire. It follows, as Burchard states, 'If the issue is the prevention of delinquency, or even a reduction in the incidence of delinquent behaviour, behaviour analysts must broaden their focus. Social/political contingencies should be brought into the realm of behaviour analysis and behaviour therapy' (p. 88). This issue, of 'managing up' as well as 'managing down', is addressed in Chapter 6.

However, to return to the central point, if delinquency is to be explained principally in terms of environmental or societal factors – which is making the same error as in seeking an explanation solely in individual terms – then this would mean that attempts to change offending through working with the offender are doomed to failure. In other words, when it comes to rehabilitation, it would be predicted that nothing works.

The 'nothing works' debate

In 1974 Robert Martinson published an article titled 'What works? Questions and answers about prison reform'. This article has become one of the most widely cited pieces in support of the doctrine that, when it comes to rehabilitation of offenders, nothing works. However, as Cullen and Gendreau (1989) note in their discussion of the effectiveness of rehabilitation programmes with offenders, the view that 'nothing works' owes more to rhetoric than to scientific evidence. Given the centrality of this issue to this book it is worthwhile looking in some detail at this topic.

Martinson's 1974 paper, based on a much larger research report (Lipton *et al.*, 1975), was concerned with the evaluation of 231 outcome studies of treatment programmes with offenders conducted between 1945 and 1967. Martinson concluded that most of these programmes appeared to have had little or no effect on recidivism, and he was less than optimistic that the ideal of rehabilitation could be achieved. However, he also noted the possibility of a variety of procedural shortcomings in both the implementation of the rehabilitation programmes and the evaluative research that would account for the lack of success. In other words, there may be explanations for the null findings other than 'nothing works'. With this in mind, a recent re-examination by Thornton (1987) of the 231 studies used by Martinson is of interest. Thornton rigorously examined the 231 studies according to three criteria: (1) the use of recidivism as an outcome variable; (2) a research design involving either random allocation of offenders to treatment or control conditions, or matched treatment and control groups; and (3) a level of methodological sophistication acceptable by criteria defined by Lipton *et al.* in their study. When subjected to this level of scrutiny, Thornton found that only 38 of the 231 studies satisfied all three stringent criteria demanded of strong clinical evaluation studies. Of these 38 studies, 34 involved a comparison between a group of offenders treated using a psychological therapy, such as psychotherapy or counselling, and an untreated control group. The first point to be made is that the small number of highly robust studies immediately limits the size of the data base from which any conclusions can be drawn. Second, the limited range of psychological therapies in these studies leaves open to speculation the effects of other interventions based on, say, education, skills training, or behavioural principles. In examining the results of these 34 studies, Thornton found that 16 studies showed a significant advantage after treatment; 17 showed no difference in outcome between treatment and control groups; and one study reported a worse outcome for the treatment group. Thornton concludes,

> Either the catalogue of studies on which Martinson based his assertions may properly be read as indicating that psychological therapy can have positive effects on recidivism, or it can be read as indicating that no conclusion can safely be drawn. The one interpretation that is not acceptable is that it has been shown that 'Nothing Works'.
>
> (p. 188)

Thus Thornton's conclusions, made decades later, bear out the reservations expressed by Martinson in 1974 about the outright rejection of rehabilitation programmes for offenders. Yet further, a second paper by Martinson, published in 1979, explicitly stated that some treatment programmes can and do have a beneficial effect on recidivism rates.

A major difficulty when attempting to establish the overall effectiveness of a body of research work lies in comparing across studies that have used different designs, different statistical tests, and even different definitions of 'success'. Yet further, different studies examine different variables such as style of intervention, types of measures, type of setting, and so on. As there are literally hundreds of outcome studies, it is impossible to draw meaningful conclusions about what works, for whom, and under what conditions simply by pooling the results. Until quite recently this inability to draw a meaningful conclusion from the literature was a problem in any area of research (in many disciplines) for which there was a large and diverse body of experimental evidence. However, the development of the statistical technique of *meta-analysis* has gone some way towards solving this problem.

As Izzo and Ross (1990) explain, meta-analysis is

A technique that enables a reviewer to objectively and statistically analyse the findings of many individual studies by regarding the findings of each study as data points . . . The procedure of meta-analysis involves collecting relevant studies, using the summary statistics from each study as units of analysis, and then analysing the aggregated data in a quantitative manner using statistical tests.

(p. 135)

When applied to treatment outcome studies, meta-analysis provides a means by which to produce a detailed picture of what works. There have been several meta-analyses in the field of offender rehabilitation (see Andrews *et al.*, 1990; Izzo and Ross, 1990). For example, in a typical meta-analytic study, Garrett (1985) included 111 studies reported between 1960 and 1983, involving a total of 13,055 young offenders (mainly male) of average age 15.8 years. The first step in the meta-analysis is to calculate the *effect size*; that is, the extent to which the treatment groups differ from the control groups after the treatment. A positive effect size shows an advantage to the treatment group; a negative effect size shows a disadvantage after treatment. Garrett reported an effect size of +0.37 across *all* the studies on *all* measures, which is relatively modest, but nonetheless evidence for a positive advantage resulting from treatment. However, the effect size for different therapeutic approaches is of greater interest. Garrett subdivided the treatment studies into several groups, which included: psychodynamic; behavioural, including contingency management and cognitive-behaviour modification; and life skills, including academic and vocational training. The effect sizes for these groups were +0.63 for the behavioural treatments, +0.31 for the life skills training, and +0.17 for the psychodynamic treatments. Garrett also calculated the effect sizes for the different types of intervention specifically with regard to recidivism. In this respect, she found that the contingency management programmes had an effect size of +0.25 and the cognitive-behavioural pro-grammes an effect size of +0.24. In other words, both styles of behavioural approach had modest but positive effects on later offending. Garrett concludes, 'Perhaps the most interesting finding with respect to specific treatments was that a cognitive-behavioural approach, a relatively recent development, seems to be more successful than any other' (p. 304).

In considering the findings of the meta-analysis studies it is important to make the distinction between *clinical* and *criminogenic* outcome; it is, for example, quite possible for rehabilitation programmes to produce good outcomes in terms of, say, improved psychological adjustment or improved social skills, but to have little or no effect on recidivism and further acts of delinquency (Hollin and Henderson, 1984). As a generalization, programmes with a specific aim tend to produce specific outcomes. Thus the crucial question that follows is: what can be said about the interventions that have the most *criminogenic* success? Several firm statements, based on the two most recent meta-analysis studies reported by Andrews *et al.* (1990) and by Lipsey (1992a), can be made:

1 Indiscriminate targeting of treatment programmes is counterproductive in reducing recidivism: important predictors of success are that medium to high risk offenders should be selected, and programmes should focus on criminogenic areas.
2 The type of treatment programme is important in that structured treatments, such as behavioural and skill-orientated programmes, are more effective than less structured and focused approaches such as counselling.
3 The most successful studies, while behavioural in orientation, include a cognitive component to focus on the attitudes, values, and beliefs that support and maintain delinquent behaviour.
4 With respect to the type and style of service, some therapeutic approaches are not suitable for general use with offenders. Specifically, Andrews *et al.* argue that 'Traditional psychodynamic and nondirective client-centred therapies are to be avoided within general samples of offenders' (p. 376).
5 Treatment programmes conducted in the community have stronger effects on delinquency than residential programmes. While residential programmes can be effective, they should be structurally linked with community-based interventions.
6 The most effective programmes have high 'treatment integrity' in that they are conducted by trained staff and the treatment initiators are involved in all the operational phases of the treatment programme. In other words, there is effective management of the process of treatment.
7 Further, as indicated in a separate meta-analysis reported by Roberts and Camasso (1991), effective programmes also include an element of family work.

Given the above, Lipsey (1992b) states that treatment programmes can produce 'reductions of 20% or more in the recidivism of treated juveniles compared to control juveniles' (p. 142).

We believe that it is simply untrue that 'nothing works' when it comes to treatment with offenders: intervention, particularly behavioural intervention, can have an impact on a range of target behaviours, including criminal behaviours. The 'failures' of the type discussed previously can be accounted for in terms of the above conclusions; thus low impact studies are characterized by the use of non-directive therapeutic approaches that are not focused specifically on offending behaviour, and treatment programmes with low-risk offender populations. However, to return to the meta-analysis conclusions, the real issue, to our way of thinking, is what are the barriers that prevent behavioural treatment from enjoying an even greater success than the figure noted above?

BARRIERS TO SUCCESS

A treatment programme, of whatever type, can only stand a chance of being successful if it is properly implemented: if there is, in other words, a high degree of *treatment integrity*. Solid and effective treatment programmes do not magically appear overnight. They require planning for both content and resources; trained personnel to conduct assessments and deliver treatment; and the flexibility to cope with the varying demands and problems presented by different individuals. These goals all require clear management to achieve treatment integrity, to ensure that what happens in practice is in accordance with both theory and planning. However, there are various obstacles to success that are a function of the running of an organization; we have therefore called these obstacles *organizational* barriers.

Organizational barriers

Organizational barriers are to be found in any system – be it within a residential setting or in the community – and they impede the progress that might be made with a properly implemented treatment programme. In the history of behavioural work with offender populations there have been several graphic accounts of organizational barriers. Laws (1974) describes the barriers he faced in attempting to carry out a behavioural programme: there were clashes between behaviourally orientated practitioners, who judged an offender's progress in terms of behaviourally defined gains, and psychodynamically orientated administrators who wanted a different type of evidence of change. Laws also describes how a lack of control over rates of admission to the programme stretched resources and hence the ability to devise flexible, individually tailored programmes. In addition, a lack of control over selection of staff to work on the programme made it impossible to ensure a consistent approach by properly trained personnel. Laws eventually concluded that, given these constraints, treatment integrity was impossible and he abandoned the work.

Clashes between staff have been documented elsewhere: Quay (1987b) describes a programme in which the staff responsible for treatment delivery were antipathetic to a behavioural approach, believing that it would not influence later offending, and were poorly trained in behavioural work. Quay notes that the treatment programme was not well conducted, was not successful, and was written off as a 'failure' of behavioural practice. Cullen and Seddon (1981) similarly note how their programme was sabotaged by psychiatrists who refused to comply with agreements made to ensure treatment integrity. Milan (1987) lists a catalogue of further difficulties including confusion over what is meant by behaviour modification, a lack of resources, and a lack of control over key administration policies such as decisions concerning admission and release.

Overcoming barriers

Reppucci (1973) has defined six principles that need to be implemented to overcome these organizational barriers to treatment integrity:

1 A clear guiding philosophy that is understood by *all* those involved in a treatment programme.
2 An organizational structure that facilitates communication and accountability.
3 Involving all staff in decision-making.
4 Using everyone's skills to the maximum effect, whatever the constraints of credentials and job descriptions.
5 Maintaining both a community orientation and community involvement.
6 Setting reasonable time constraints in developing and 'tuning' programmes, thereby resisting the pressure to try to achieve too much in too short a time.

Each of these six points specifies a target to be achieved by establishing and maintaining a system of management to facilitate treatment integrity. Thus, Reppucci's first point suggests a need for staff training and clear organizational literature; the second, third, and fourth are concerned with the structure within which treatment takes place; while the fifth and sixth deal with the monitoring of the functioning of that structure.

Finally, we arrive at perhaps the most important barrier to treatment: the acceptability of behavioural programmes in legal, ethical, and professional terms. It is unfortunate that anything that bears the label 'behavioural' is likely to be greeted with suspicion and hostility by large numbers of people. This suspicion is often based on serious misconceptions about behavioural theory and practice. In our experience, most people do not understand behavioural theory; it is wrongly said to be 'mechanical', thought to be based solely on research with animals, and said to deny the existence of thoughts and feelings. Following from this, any intervention based on behavioural principles is viewed as manipulative, controlling, denying clients their rights, and sure to inflict pain and suffering. It would be nice to be able to say that abuse never took place, but this would be quite wrong. There are documented instances of behavioural programmes going badly wrong, and real suffering and infringement of human, civil, and legal rights taking place; see, for example, Milan's (1987) discussion of the ill-fated START programme in the United States. However, the fundamental mistake made by many critics is to place the blame for the abuse of theoretical principles and associated practice at the door of the theory. If we consider the issue from the standpoint of applied behaviour analysis, we see that the theory is neutral; it is the individual practitioner who delivers unacceptable programmes. Yet, as applied behaviour analysis further suggests, we must consider not only the individual practitioner but also that person's environment – the management system responsible for professional practice and programme delivery. Behavioural techniques, as countless studies have shown, are very powerful – if they were not then it seems unlikely that there would be such concern about their use – but they must be used sensitively, clearly, openly, and above all ethically. In other words, there is an overwhelming need for the proper and informed management of behavioural treatment.

That is what this book is about.

Chapter 2

A model for behavioural management and structure

There are many different types of service provision for young people: some are based in the community, others in various gradations of security; some are supported locally, others nationally; some work with low-tariff young offenders, others with young people who have committed grave offences. While there are obvious differences between services, what we have to say about the management of behavioural treatment is applicable to all these settings and groups. However, behavioural programmes cannot operate in a vacuum, independent of the rest of the organization; indeed, when they do this it is a recipe for conflict (Cullen and Seddon, 1981; Laws, 1974). It is important initially therefore to step back from the details of managing specific treatment programmes, to consider the broader picture of organizational structures and procedures. Simply, the way any service is organized, resourced, and managed will determine its effectiveness in managing and treating this group of young people. This chapter outlines some important organizational factors that need to be considered when setting up services for difficult, disturbed, and delinquent young people. This, in turn, will set the scene for the treatment orientated chapters that follow, which deal specifically with assessment (Chapter 3), management and treatment (Chapter 4), and staff training (Chapter 5).

AIMS OF THE SERVICE

Consideration first needs to be given to the aims of the service. Specifically, who will be the clients? What geographical area will be served? What is the service aiming to achieve?

Client characteristics

The client group for whom the service is intended will inevitably influence the functioning of the service and the way in which it develops. It is important to have a firm idea of the needs of the client group, and how the service is going to fit into the wider network of services provided for the management and treatment of delinquent and disturbed young people. These issues can best be addressed by carefully defining the characteristics of the young people at whom the service is aimed.

Age

In England and Wales the term 'juvenile delinquent' applies to young people aged from 10 to 17 who have been convicted of an indictable offence. Young people at the lower end of this age range (i.e. early adolescence) have different needs from those at the upper end (i.e. middle adolescence). It is also important to provide a service for those past the age of 17 (i.e. late adolescence), who often fall between the adolescent and adult services, and for whom it is often unclear who, if anyone, has statutory and legal responsibility. Programmes for delinquents often fall short of providing an effective service because they are not funded to cater for youngsters aged 18 to 20. Many of these young people return to the community with little help or support, thus increasing the chances of failure and, perhaps, a return to crime.

Returning to the issue of developmental needs, any service must ensure that it can realistically meet those needs. Youngsters aged between 10 and 16 years have a statutory right to education, while older adolescents, many of whom may have failed in mainstream education, will require work skills and help with finding employment in an increasingly competitive job market. Young adolescents may respond more to a care and management system in which the adults are perceived as care-givers and, with a degree of authority, take on a parent-teacher role. Older adolescents, on the other hand, may well respond negatively to such a system, and expect more autonomy and independence. Thus an environment in which young people perceive staff as advocates and equals may be more appropriate for older adolescents.

The provision of recreational facilities is also dependent to some extent on the age of the young people. Young adolescents are just emerging from their childhood, where games and activities play an important role. Many young delinquents have often missed normal childhood experiences and appear older in their interests, making it easy for care staff to lose sight of their need for play and games. It is not unusual, for example, to find a 'hardened' delinquent with an extensive criminal history who becomes excited and animated when playing a board game, or who takes a cuddly toy to bed.

To summarize, the age group at which a service is aimed has a variety of implications for service delivery, including provision of after-care and support, education, leisure and recreational facilities, work experience, as well as staff skills and staff training. Careful thought and planning needs to be given to mixing youngsters from across a wide age range. While mixing age groups can have benefits, there are disadvantages if this involves exposing relatively inexperienced delinquent young people to older, more experienced recidivists, who often gain status from boasting to young children about their criminal exploits (Short, 1968).

Legal status

The legal status of the young people at whom a service is directed will be dependent upon age. Age plays a part in deciding how a young person is dealt with by the courts, and the kinds of legal restrictions that may be imposed on their liberty. A 12-year-old arrested for child molestation is likely to be managed within the child-care system, while a 16-year-old convicted of the same offence is likely to receive a custodial sentence. These legal orders have different consequences for the organization or service charged with looking after the young person. For example, a young person held under a Secure Accommodation order will need social work involvement and frequent returns to court. Thus, there must be access to a qualified social worker; while court appearances will have resource implications, especially if the young person's home address is some distance away. Older adolescents on probation orders, or those sentenced under Section 53 of the 1933 Children and Young Persons Act (reserved for grave crimes such as murder, manslaughter, rape, arson, and robbery), will impose different organizational demands. For these young people there may be strict restrictions on their freedom and movement, and the need for appropriate levels of security to prevent escape. Overall, the legal status of the young people, particularly issues surrounding restrictions of liberty, will have implications for the way a service operates on a daily basis. It is essential that staff are well informed about legislation pertaining both to child care and to the criminal justice system (Chapter 6).

Gender

As noted in Chapter 1, most convicted juvenile delinquents are male, and it is probably true to say that most services for delinquents are geared towards adolescent boys. The question of what to do with the minority of difficult and delinquent young women has always been an administrative problem. Those young women who do end up in services for delinquent young people often present difficulties that are less frequently encountered in boys. Services for adolescent males often have to deal with aggressive and violent behaviour; however adolescent young women are, on the whole, more likely to inflict damage upon themselves, typically through cutting and overdosing (Green, 1978; Hawton and Goldacre, 1982; Hawton *et al.*, 1982). These different problems have implications for staff training and resource management.

Services that provide for both sexes also need to consider carefully the ratio of male to female staff, and the mix of male and female clients. It is likely that mixed groups of young people will need closer supervision. This is especially important if young women are to be placed on the same residential unit or community programme as young men with a history of sexually aggressive behaviour and where there is therefore an increased risk of sexual harassment.

Referral problems

The distinction was made in Chapter 1 between those delinquents convicted of serious offences, such as murder, rape, arson, and robbery, and those convicted of less serious offences, such as car-theft, shoplifting, and burglary. It is usually the latter group that are referred to in much of the research literature on delinquency (see West, 1967), while it is the former group who often end up in programmes for delinquents (Bullock *et al.*, 1990). Adolescents convicted of serious offences are more likely to be perceived as disturbed and to have damaged personalities (Miller *et al.*, 1986). Generally speaking, such adolescents need to be managed and treated within a forensic setting, where issues of dangerousness and risk can be addressed. Young people convicted of less serious offences, on the other hand, tend to benefit more from an approach that emphasizes integration with the local community, one that attempts to divert them from custody and long-term residential care (Davidson *et al.*, 1990).

Service-providers for young people also need to consider the extent to which they can manage and tolerate particular behavioural problems – such as absconding, substance abuse, violence, persistent self-injurious behaviour, and sexual misbehaviour – all of which are frequently found among groups of delinquents. These kinds of behavioural problems often present a serious challenge to the staff working with this client group. Effective management of these problems requires specific policies and practices based on behavioural principles (see section on policy and practice), with additional implications for staff training (see Chapter 5) and resource management. It is in relation to the management and treatment of these kinds of problems that close contact with other services is beneficial. Advice and consultation can then be sought from other services with more experience or expertise in dealing with specific kinds of problems. It is important, for example, that a good relationship exists between services for delinquent young people and the adolescent psychiatric services, which tend to have more expertise in dealing with mental health and emotional problems. In today's climate such arrangements will probably have to be on a contractual basis, specifying costs, responsibilities, and so on.

Catchment area

Services for difficult and delinquent young people can be differentiated according to whether they provide a local, regional, or a national service. The size of the catchment area has implications in terms of cost and resources, as well as the nature of the relationship with the community in which the service is based. If the service overlaps with other similar services, issues of responsibility across the services concerned will need clarification.

Local services, serving a town or a rural community, have the opportunity to become well integrated into the local community. Such integration can be of great benefit in helping to achieve aims such as diversion from custody, normalization, and deinstitutionalization. Intermediate Treatment, in which the young person may remain living at home and attend the treatment centre on a daily basis, is an example of this approach (Preston, 1982; Tutt, 1982). The emphasis with this type of local service is on keeping the young offender at the lower end of the tariff system, and minimizing the negative effects of labelling and stigmatization. This kind of approach is also consistent with the concepts of secondary and tertiary prevention referred to in Chapter 1.

Local services tend to be most effective when they are part of a regional strategy to respond to juvenile delinquency. This broader strategy helps in the coordination and integration of the various agencies responsible for delinquents, including the police, social workers, probation officers, and the courts. At a regional level there is often the need for some kind of residential service, which provides for the most difficult and dangerous young offenders, who cannot otherwise be managed and contained safely in the community. Many such centres provide secure accommodation as well as open facilities. Some, but not all, also try to provide various forms of treatment to reduce the risk of further reoffending, and to ease the young person's adjustment to the community. Another advantage inherent in a regional strategy is the opportunity to maintain close links with the young person's family, school, and local community. This enables problems to be realistically tackled in their natural environment, and reduces the risk of institutionalization.

There is, however, a case to be made for residential resources that operate at a wider, national level, to cope with the most difficult and demanding young people, and to compensate for the absence of regional initiatives in some areas. There are many problems inherent in a national catchment area, not least of which is the difficulty of maintaining contact with families and local services over a wide geographical area. This geographical scatter can have enormous resource implications, most obviously in terms of the cost and time spent travelling. It also poses problems for reintegrating young people into their home area, while older adolescents may decide not to return home, thus placing an extra demand on local services. National resources also depend heavily on good communication and contacts with regional provisions and other sources of referral. It is essential therefore that a system of 'gate-keeping' is set up, by which only young people for whom there is no suitable alternative are admitted to such a national resource.

In summary, the geographical size of the area and the population within that area are important considerations when setting up a programme. While there are some disadvantages with large catchment areas it seems unrealistic to expect local and regional service to provide for the small numbers of extremely difficult and dangerous young people.

Outcome expectations

Any service dealing with difficult and delinquent young people should have some idea of the outcomes they hope to achieve for the young people for whom they work. Many factors already referred to above, such as age, sex, and presenting problems, will influence the type of outcome that is realistically feasible with any one individual. Setting clear targets and goals enables a service to be organized in such a way as to maximize the chances of meeting those goals; and of structuring the task so that progress towards achieving those goals can be monitored and evaluated. (Further discussion of this point is given in the section on service monitoring and evaluation.) The specification of outcome expectations also helps when planning and organizing resettlement in the community. The provision of after-care and support is frequently lacking in many programmes for delinquents. The amount of time available for planning a return to the community can determine whether a young person ultimately succeeds or fails. It is therefore desirable that planning begins at the point of admission. Particular considerations in care planning include: the availability of education or work experience; social service and probation support; psychiatric services; and links with family, relatives, and friends.

SERVICE LOCATION

The question of where to locate a service is obviously dependent on some of the issues raised above, such as the population for whom the service is designed. There are, however, several other factors that need to be considered.

Geography

The relationship of the service to other facilities is an important consideration. The proximity of local amenities – such as sporting facilities, centres of further education, hospitals, fire and emergency services, and even shops – have an important bearing on the quality of life for young people. Links with such amenities increases the chance of successfully generalizing any behavioural change achieved within a programme to real life community settings. Research evidence consistently shows that while residential and community programmes can produce significant and positive changes in behaviour, these effects are often short-lived (Blakely and Davidson, 1984; Braukmann and Wolf, 1987; Dunlop, 1974; Hollin and Henderson, 1984). Attention to the problem of generalization, which will be discussed in more detail later in this chapter, is particularly important for young people who have deficits in social abilities that are functionally related to their offending behaviour. An opportunity to test out new-found skills in the natural environment must be an integral part of any intervention programme. While there are some advantages in locating residential services away from populated areas, particularly in reducing the risk of absconding, this must be balanced against the need for generalization of behavioural change.

Another important geographical consideration is access to road and rail services. Quick and efficient access to transport, such as proximity to motorways and mainline rail services, minimizes travelling time for families, relatives, and other professionals involved in the care and treatment of young people. Considerable problems can also be encountered when transporting difficult and potentially violent young people on long journeys to and from court.

Community relations

Another important consideration is the relationship with the local community. The significance of fostering good relationships with local people, particularly those in positions of authority and influence, should never be underestimated. This is perhaps especially true if a service intends to deal with young people with a history of serious and grave crimes, such as murder and rape. Poor community relations and adverse publicity can effectively destroy a service.

The development of constructive relationships with the local community should begin in the early stages of service planning and development. Local people and significant figures of authority, such as councillors, politicians, school governors, and police inspectors, should be invited to planning meetings to discuss developments and service aims and objectives. The worries and concerns of those involved can then be dealt with from an early stage, and mutual trust and cooperation can be established. People from the local community may have a variety of realistic concerns, and be ill-informed about the nature of the client group. A certain amount of resistance is inevitable: it is not uncommon for one or two individuals to set up a local pressure group. It may be necessary to hold open meetings, to which all local residents are invited and given the opportunity to voice their concerns.

One strategy to improve wider community relations is to offer the public limited use of facilities, such as meeting rooms, gymnasiums, or even swimming pools. This type of 'open' relationship not only helps to overcome hostility and resistance, but may also provide established links with the 'real world' for the young people, who may be isolated from their own family and friends.

The cementing of constructive community relationships takes on extra significance during times of crisis, such as when a young person reoffends in the local community, or a dangerous offender absconds. It is at such times that underlying hostility and resentment can become destructive. A history of cooperation and openness can help resolve such a crisis, and reactions from local residents may prove helpful in improving practice.

Police relations

Services dealing with disruptive and delinquent youngsters also need to have a good working relationship with local and regional police forces. It follows that representatives from the police should be involved at an early stage in service development. Effective lines of communication are important in times of emergency, such as when a dangerous offender absconds, or if there is a hostage situation or a riot. Liaison with local police forces helps to negotiate effective contingency plans to deal with such crises, where timing and rapid decision-making are important. Procedures for contacting and involving the police should form part of the policy and practice manual of the service.

Constructive police relations are also important on a day-to-day basis. Most behaviourally based programmes for delinquents have a community orientation and aim to generalize behaviour change back into the real world. It is inevitable that certain risks are associated with this process, such as an increased risk of absconding or offending while in the community. Keeping police informed of the activities and rationale of the service can help towards a constructive working relationship. The young offenders themselves may also benefit from police involvement: informal police contact can help young people to see the police in a different light. It is a fact of life that for many delinquent young people their experience with the police will usually have been related to their offending behaviour. Invariably these encounters with the police will be acrimonious, typically making matters worse for the young person. In this light, some social skills programmes for delinquents have successfully enhanced adolescents' skills in managing encounters with the police (Kifer *et al.*, 1974). Similarly, police cadets can be invited to undertake placements as part of their training, and activities can be organized that involve the police, such as demonstrations of police dog handling, which can also involve the local community.

Service networks

The concept of networking was hinted at earlier when referring to the importance of making links with other services that are geographically close. These services may include: *health services*, for general health problems, dental checks, immunizations, accidents, and emergencies; *psychiatric services*, both for psychiatric oversight and for handling emergencies; and *counselling services*, such as pregnancy advisory services and HIV counselling. In addition, a range of services is provided by ethnic minority and religious organizations, who offer a consultancy to the service on issues of care and management, and who may make a direct input to the young people themselves in the role of either advocates or befrienders.

PHILOSOPHY AND OPERATIONAL FRAMEWORK

Any service or organization has to decide how it is going to achieve the aims or goals that it sets itself. The organization also needs to understand the constraints that act upon it, and which help to shape the framework within which the work must be carried out. Work with young people, for example, must be carried out with reference to legal and ethical guidelines. Appendix 1, taken from our own organization, provides an illustration of guidelines that shape our work. Further discussion of legal issues is given in Chapter 6.

The nature and structure of the framework should be specified as early as possible in service development. It will affect all that is to follow, including building design and structure, service organization, referral and admission policies and procedures, operational policy and practice, and staff training. One strength of the behavioural model is that it can contribute to developments in all these areas, providing a frame of reference for discussing a range of different issues arising from work with difficult and delinquent young people. Further, the adoption of a cogent theoretical framework has several important advantages. The concept of 'organizational barriers' has already been referred to in Chapter 1: the six principles advanced by Repucci (1973) offer a way of overcoming these barriers (see p. 23). A behavioural framework facilitates the application of these principles as discussed below.

Terminology and communication

Programmes set up to help delinquent young people implicitly attempt to manage and change socially unacceptable behaviour. It is important, therefore, that those managers responsible for such programmes can communicate effectively, clearly, and precisely about the behaviour of the young people. As Barlow (1979) points out, 'If consistency is difficult to achieve with two parents, it is far more so with a dozen different adults working with the same group of children' (p. 215). The behavioural model can simplify communication by using defined concepts, each of which conveys useful information about the way in which a young person interacts with his or her social and physical environment. Terms such as *positive reinforcement, negative reinforcement, extinction*, and *contingency management* are all parts of the mutually understood vocabulary of staff trained in behavioural theory and practice.

Objectivity

The behavioural model emphasizes the importance of observable and quantifiable information. Given that most young people enter programmes because of their actions, it makes sense to use a framework that strives to identify, quantify, and understand the likely causes of behaviour. The behavioural model minimizes reference to speculative determinants of behaviour. This approach therefore avoids reliance on guesswork and unfounded assumptions about the causes of behaviour. It is not difficult to see how an overreliance on speculation and assumptions can lead to practices based on personal bias and opinion. This, in turn, is likely to result in abuse and malpractice: too many people think they can offer their own private explanations and therefore claim to know what is 'best' for troubled young people.

Emphasis on objectivity and factual information also has benefits when communicating with outside agencies, many of whom may be unfamiliar with the client group and the problems they present. In turn, clear objectivity also enables outside agencies to give constructive feedback on practice, which can prevent bad practices developing and help to keep the service up to date.

Policy and practice

The behavioural model demands that operational practices and the rationale behind them are clearly stated, so that all members of staff know what is expected of them and can respond to situations in a consistent way. A policy and practice manual should be issued to all staff as part of their induction training (see Chapter 5), and should be referred to at times of uncertainty. Explicit statements on policy and practice also clarify discrepancies between existing practices and legal and ethical requirements. Any behavioural programme must be acceptable in legal, ethical, and professional terms.

Understanding behaviour

Adults who work with difficult and delinquent adolescents, some of whom exhibit dangerous and sometimes bizarre behaviours, are constantly faced with the complex task of trying to understand what is happening. A lack of understanding can result in feelings of impotence and unpredictability, which can lead to apathy – the 'nothing works' attitude referred to in Chapter 1. An air of nihilism is particularly damaging and counterproductive when the quality and outcome of young people's lives are in the hands of those who run an organization. An operational framework based on behavioural principles and methodology will reduce the risk of institutional apathy. It provides staff with clear goals and objectives, and a framework within which to assess, understand, and work with the actions, beliefs, and attitudes of the young people with whom they work. Further, a behavioural framework creates opportunities for research and development that helps to maintain and stimulate staff interest.

BUILDING DESIGN AND STRUCTURE

Many management difficulties frequently encountered by practitioners when working with delinquent young people can be minimized, or avoided altogether, through careful attention to the architecture and design of the building. We now have the advantage of being able to learn from past mistakes to ensure that new buildings are purpose-built. For example, close liaison between practitioners, architects, and building engineers has resulted in the development of expertise in the design and building of secure units (Blumenthal, 1985). More generally, Canter and Canter's (1979) book, *Designing for Therapeutic Environments: a Review of Research*, offers a variety of suggestions for improving building design.

Consultation with architects is essential at the earliest stages of service development, preferably at the point at which blueprints are drawn up. Although architects and designers often have to work within constraints such as secure unit guidelines and budgetary limits, there is often room for negotiation and improvement to existing plans. After all, the people who live and work within such buildings are usually those who are most aware of the limitations of existing building structures.

In general, buildings either ease or hinder the task of managing and treating difficult young people. The extent to which the building structure helps to prevent the occurrence of dangerous situations, and enables staff to control and manage such situations when they do occur, is particularly important. Several factors can be identified that influence both prevention and management of emergencies.

Prevention of emergencies

Environmental control

Applied psychologists have for a long time been aware of the effects of living environments on human behaviour. Of particular significance for environments for potentially aggressive and disruptive clients are the levels of noise and temperature, and the effects of overcrowding: these factors have been associated with aggressive and violent behaviour (Health Services Advisory Committee, 1987). Environments that are hot, crowded, and noisy or disruptive invariably have an adverse effect on the people living in them. It is therefore desirable that staff should have some control over these factors.

An admission policy that controls numbers and so prevents the number of residents rising above a given level eliminates the possibility of overcrowding. Control over levels of temperature and light enables the environment to be controlled to suit the activities and mood of the young people. For example, in the evenings the lights can be dimmed in the living area to produce a more convivial and relaxing atmosphere, thus reducing the risk of arguments and aggression; other parts of the building where staff or youngsters may be vulnerable to attack can be kept well lit. Double glazing and sound proofing can also be used to reduce disruption from external noise, especially when services are situated near busy main roads.

Personal space

It is not unusual to find buildings, or parts of buildings, which restrict freedom of movement: corridors that are too narrow, or a dining area that is too small. This lack of space increases the risk of accidental physical contact that, in turn, increases the potential for confrontation and aggression (Hollin, 1993). Indeed, studies of institutional violence have found that most violence occurs around meal times (Fottrell, 1980), which suggests that special consideration should be given to the design and layout of dining areas – a point that applies to all types of building.

The size of the young people needs to be considered. Some facilities intended for young adolescents find themselves admitting older adolescents who are physically larger and simply need more space: fixed dining tables and chairs designed for 13- and 14-year-olds, for example, may be unsuitable for 17- and 18-year-olds. Research into 'body-buffer zones' suggests that habitually violent people require more personal space, and are particularly sensitive to what they perceive as intrusions into their own space (Kinzel, 1970; McGurk *et al.*, 1981).

Recreational facilities

The provision of adequate sporting and recreational facilities is usually compulsory in mainstream education, yet is often lacking in programmes for young offenders. Many secure units, for example, offer a limited choice of table-tennis and weight-training, both of which can be carried out in small areas but do not give the young people adequate opportunity to burn off excess energy and provide the freedom to run around. As a generalization, delinquent young people are notoriously bad at occupying themselves and a dearth of recreational facilities can make it very difficult for staff to find ways to occupy the young people in their care.

Staff supervision

Most staff time will be spent supervising the young people. This task can be either hindered or eased by the design and geography of the building. It is usually necessary to have different levels of supervision, depending on the circumstances. Each supervisory level should be operationally defined so that staff know what is expected of them. Young people at serious risk of harming themselves, for example, may need constant supervision. A building that makes it difficult to sustain supervision not only places young people at risk – either from themselves through self-injurious behaviour, or from each other through bullying and physical assault – but also places staff at risk. Staff who are left alone with a young person, perhaps at the end of a long corridor or in an isolated room, are vulnerable to attack, and may be unable to call for assistance.

Good building design allows staff effectively to supervise all the young people with minimal demands on time and energy. Single-storey buildings, built around a central point, like the hub of a wheel, simplify supervision, while multi-storey buildings that are long and narrow hinder supervision. In these situations there may be only two options: either part of the building is closed off, or staff are put at risk. It may be possible to offset some effects of poor building design through closed-circuit television cameras and two-way radios. However, these are rarely adequate substitutes for good design and, in any case, are often necessary in even the best designed units when dealing with particularly dangerous offenders.

Furniture and fittings

A variety of objects can be used to inflict harm on others or on oneself. Young people who are determined to injure themselves can use virtually anything to achieve this, from self-strangulation with curtains to swallowing screws removed from a light fitting. Adolescents have been known to swallow batteries, bed-springs, and parts of a light bulb. One way of reducing the likelihood of such behaviour is to minimize the use of unnecessary furnishing and fittings, and to ensure that those in use are difficult to destroy or dismantle. Spongy foam chairs can be used in place of hard plastic chairs, and curtains can be fitted using velcrose instead of plastic curtain rails and fittings. The problem with minimization is that unless carefully managed, it can result in a bare, under-stimulating, and harsh environment. These sparse living conditions can in turn contribute to high levels of disruption. Yet further, under-stimulating environments are inconsistent with behavioural practice: the technique of time-out from positive reinforcement depends on the 'time-in' environment being reinforcing and stimulating. In particular, an impoverished environment causes problems when looking after long-term residents, when it is crucial to maintain a good quality of life. In practice a compromise needs to be made between providing a safe environment and providing a good quality of life. One solution that has been put forward is to create several different environments, so that an individual progresses from a bare, under-stimulating environment, where safety is the main concern, to a more open, enriched environment. However, this kind of system can result in a variety of problems. For example, some young people may not progress through the system and so remain at lower levels. A better alternative is to create an environment that is suitable for all clients, which is pleasurable and reinforcing, but where effort has been made to reduce risk through careful attention to fixtures and fittings. Additional measures of control, such as restraint and separation, can then be carried out as and when needed.

Security

Security precautions serve two main functions: simply, to keep people in and to keep people out. Security is increasingly becoming an issue for most types of care and treatment settings, whether or not they are purpose-built secure facilities. Indeed, some young people are admitted into residential care for their own protection, for example, those involved with adult sex offenders, or those who have received threats from adult co-defendants. Staff working with such young people need to be aware who is on the premises at all times, and to know the identities of people who visit youngsters. Purpose-built secure facilities should be reserved only for the most difficult and dangerous young people. Two forms of security can be distinguished; these are *external* and *internal* security.

External security refers to the restrictions applied outside the building, such as high perimeter fences and surveillance cameras. The use of external security measures can often enhance the quality of life for residents. They may allow youngsters to have more freedom within the campus, such as access to playing fields and recreational areas with minimal staff supervision, thus enabling them to be used more frequently. *Internal security* refers to the use of closed-circuit television (CCTV) and specially designed windows and doors within the building. CCTV is important in parts of the building where young people may remain unobserved for relatively long periods of time. With regard to doors and windows, doors should open outwards and be easily removed to prevent barricading, and windows should be shatterproof. Davies (1989) makes several useful suggestions regarding building and office design that can reduce the risk of violence.

Responding to emergencies

Although attention to building design can prevent emergencies, it is inevitable that such situations will occur. A variety of factors concerned with building design can, however, influence the effectiveness with which these situations are managed and resolved. The use of proper fire procedures and alarm systems, and the use of separation rooms particularly deserves further consideration.

Fire procedures

The effectiveness of systems and procedures for detecting and responding to fire is particularly important when dealing with young offenders, some of whom may have a history of fire-setting. The situation is exacerbated in secure conditions where residents and staff are locked in. Building design should simplify evacuation, and door locks should preferably be capable of being deactivated from a central locking system. Adolescents are notorious for deliberately starting fire alarm systems, either by smashing break-glass units or throwing talcum powder into smoke detectors. Some of the more recently developed detection systems reduce the risk of these problems, and can also give information regarding the exact location and time of the incident.

Separation rooms

Separation rooms (also called seclusion or segregation rooms) are only really necessary in secure conditions. In any case, separation must be used sparingly, only when managing highly disturbed and difficult behaviour. The use of separation is one area where there is a particular need for clear policy and practice statements, with close monitoring of both frequency and duration in its use. Young people should only be placed in separation when they are in serious danger of inflicting harm to themselves or others, or when they may cause extensive damage to property. The use of separation as a short-term management response also has the advantage of containing the disturbance away from other youngsters, thus minimizing further disruption and upset.

Separation rooms need to be easily accessible and safe. It is not unusual, however, to find them located in obscure parts of the building, or even upstairs, so that young people have to be restrained and carried for several minutes through narrow corridors or up flights of stairs. This greatly increases the risk of injury, whether accidental or deliberate. Seclusion room doors should be wide enough to enable easy access, and open outwards, to prevent a barricade. The room should contain a mattress and blanket, and be without fittings, sharp corners, or protruding objects such as door handles. All parts of the room must be observable, so that the young person is unable to hide from view. Clear visibility also ensures the continuing safety of the young person, and avoids staff having to enter the room before he or she is sufficiently calm and controlled. Placing a young person in a room that is unsafe often increases the risk of injury. The young person is likely to become even more angry and uncontrolled at the point of separation, and may actively seek ways either to harm him- or herself or to draw staff into the room. Unsafe separation rooms should not be used until they satisfy rigorous safety standards.

STAFFING

The way in which an organization is staffed depends on its aims and objectives. A long-stay residential facility, for example, will have different staffing requirements from an open community-based resource. There are two issues of particular relevance: the organization of staff teams or groups and the qualities of the staff.

Staff organization

Several principles can be identified that help the delivery of behavioural management and treatment programmes.

Roles and responsibilities

If the aims and objectives of an organization are clearly specified, it is possible to identify what tasks need to be performed and by whom. This can be achieved by delineating particular roles and responsibilities for each member of staff, then formulating these into written job descriptions. At risk of stating the obvious, a list of the advantages of job descriptions can be made: it helps to ensure that individual members of staff are aware of what is expected of them; it helps to identify training needs; and it makes explicit the nature of staff relationships to the organization as a whole. Overall, a clear understanding of roles and responsibilities helps to give a sense of shared purpose across the whole of the organization. A typical example, taken from our own place of work, is shown in Figure 2.1.

Communication and decision-making

The importance of good communication between staff has already been emphasized. Delinquent young people, especially those with long histories of antisocial behaviour, constantly pose management difficulties that require fast and effective responses. It is important that information is reliably communicated to those staff

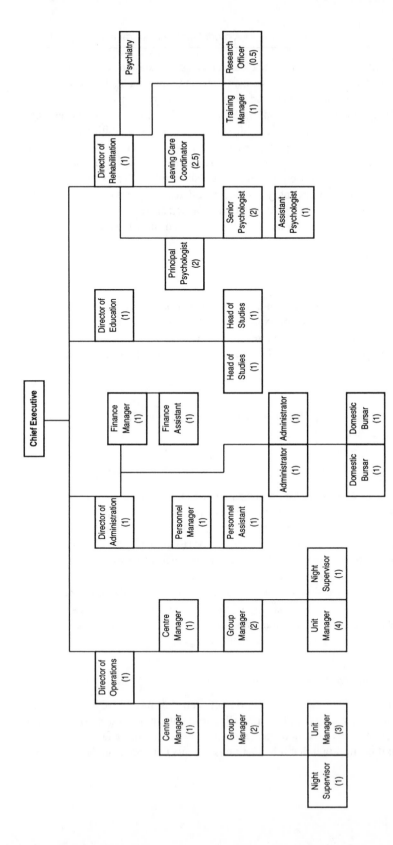

Figure 2.1 Organizational structure in the Youth Treatment Service

Note: A general practitioner and a consultant psychiatrist visit the Centre on a regular weekly basis.

responsible for making managerial, legal, and clinical decisions. The need for fast and effective communication has several implications for the ways in which staff groups are organized.

To begin with, an organizational structure is needed that allows important decisions to be made at any time during the day or night. Should a violent young person be separated? Does a young person who has cut his or her arms need to be taken to a hospital? Should the police be called to take a statement from a youngster who has disclosed an unknown offence? Each of these situations requires rapid, clear, and well-established lines of communication, often cutting across a range of different settings and professionals. A hierarchical organizational system, such as that shown in Figure 2.1, is one possible solution to this problem. Information can then be passed up and down the hierarchy, and decision-making points can be clearly specified.

However, it is also important that information spreads laterally across the system; other staff members need to be kept informed of what is happening. This lateral communication helps to create an environment that is consistent in its response to behaviour; such environmental stability and predictability is fundamental to the behavioural model. Regular multidisciplinary meetings and daily information meetings are needed to achieve a constant flow of information. Treatment meetings, on the other hand, are concerned with long-term planning and goal-setting, and can be held less frequently (see Chapter 4). Given that effective communication is so important when working with delinquent young people, it is necessary for staff to possess good verbal and written communication skills. Specific skills, such as report writing and observing and recording behaviour, should therefore form part of the staff training programme (see Chapter 5).

Staff management

An effective management structure provides a variety of functions:

1 It ensures new staff are introduced and inducted into organizational procedures and practices;
2 enables monitoring and evaluation of staff performance;
3 assists in the promotion of staff development, both personal and professional;
4 informs the process of providing staff support and helping staff deal with personal problems;
5 promotes team cohesiveness and team work;
6 clarifies the process of setting goals and objectives for staff teams (see Chapter 4);
7 ensures that working practices comply with legal, ethical, and administrative guidelines.

Essentially, managers are responsible for getting the best from staff, and keeping the staff team on task. All members of staff should have an identified manager, with whom they should meet formally on a regular basis.

Type of staff

Lack of control over staff selection to carry out a programme was one of the factors identified by Laws (1974) as responsible for past failures of attempts to adopt a behavioural approach (see Chapter 1). This issue of control applies to those staff responsible for planning and delivering management and treatment programmes, and who have most contact with the young people on a day-to-day basis. There is little doubt that one of the major downfalls of many behaviourally based programmes for delinquent young people is a managerial belief that behavioural techniques can be operationalized and carried out by untrained staff. Thus behavioural programmes are run by staff who lack a good grasp of behavioural theory, and who have little or no understanding of the rationale behind behavioural practice. This managerial miscalculation can result in inflexible, mechanistic regimes and practices, and an inability to respond to novel situations in an appropriate way.

One consequence of the use of untrained staff has been the misinterpretation and distortion of behavioural programmes, sometimes resulting in practices and procedures that have no grounding in behavioural theory or research. A recent example of this was the use of the so-called 'pin-down' regime implemented in Staffordshire children's homes between 1983 and 1989 (Levy and Kahan, 1991). The term *pin-down* was first used to describe a method of controlling the behaviour of disruptive children and adolescents, within a certain children's home, in an attempt to avoid the use of secure accommodation. Essentially, the original pin-down programme consisted of isolating youngsters in a room and preventing them from leaving by placing a member of staff outside the door, although the door was not locked. The room was kept bare so that youngsters would have to 'earn access to privileges'.

This kind of regime is usually and wrongly associated with behaviour modification. The pin-down programme was not based on behavioural theory or research, and does not appear to have been devised or managed by practitioners trained in behavioural theory and practice. Further, because pin-down was originally set up by untrained staff, its initial aims and objectives were misinterpreted and became distorted over time. Whereas pin-down was originally (and wrongly) intended only to be used as a 'last resort' to control young people's behaviour, it became integrated into the ethos and daily practice of the home. Staff came to assume that pin-down was a respectable and justifiable method of child management. The technique was also adopted by other children's homes in the same vicinity; over a six-year period, until its use was rightly banned, it is estimated that at least 132 children had been subjected to the pin-down regime.

Many lessons can be learnt from an examination of the rise and decline of corrupt management regimes such as pin-down. The importance of ensuring that staff are carefully selected and trained in both the theory and practice of behavioural methods cannot be overemphasized. However, it is also important that new staff coming into the organization have an aptitude for such work and can benefit from training. One way to safeguard standards is to employ staff with a professional qualification and who have experience of working with young people. Although this has obvious implications for running costs, it is the most effective way of ensuring high quality care and treatment. Control over staff selection also helps to ensure a balanced staff group with respect to gender, race, and cultural background.

Control over staff selection also allows staff to be chosen on the basis of their commitment and motivation for working with delinquent young people. Consideration should be given to the moral and social attitudes of staff selected to work with this population. There must be evidence of a commitment to the philosophy and practice of rehabilitating offenders, and staff should show an ability to reflect upon their own attitudes, experiences, and behaviour in terms of how these affect their own working practices.

The effectiveness of staff depends to a large extent on how well they are liked by the young people. Mutually rewarding relationships between staff and young people is a desirable and in many ways an essential component of any behavioural approach to difficult and delinquent adolescents. The *Teaching Family Handbook*, based on the work carried out at Achievement Place, Kansas, has identified five reasons why it is essential for staff to be liked by the young people (Phillips *et al.*, 1972). If a young person likes a member of staff then he or she will be:

1 more affected by staff *feedback* regarding his or her behaviour (i.e. approval or disapproval);
2 more *communicative*;
3 more likely to *imitate* the member of staff. For example, he or she will be more likely to identify with the opinions of the staff member and to use the same rationales in explaining to peers why certain rules exist. Also, he or she will be more likely to model the appropriate social behaviour of the staff member;
4 less likely to *abscond*, or if he or she does, more likely to return voluntarily;
5 more likely to *protect* the organization by defending it in front of peers or adults who criticize it.

Phillips *et al.* also identify the elements of the kind of positive relationship that can help to influence the behaviour of young people.

Affection

Statements and gestures of affection are very important to young people. Direct care staff must, however, be careful to analyse what kinds of affectionate behaviour are appropriate for each young person. For example, some young people like play-fighting; however, this can sometimes escalate and result in a loss of control over the situation. It is desirable, especially within residential contexts, to have rules regarding such play. Similarly, some young people like hugging and other forms of physical contact. This can be misinterpreted, particularly by other young people or staff observing the interaction. Again, guidelines built into an operational policy can help to minimize problems arising in this area.

Sympathy

To most young people (just like the rest of us) the most important problems in the world are their own problems, especially those in relation to peers and parents. Staff should show some ability to be sympathetic to these kinds of problems. Sincere sympathy can have a very important effect on the development of a relationship between the young person and a member of staff.

Concern

The young people should feel that the staff are genuinely interested in their future. Ideally, staff should demonstrate to the young people that they are their advocates. Staff should not engage in any behaviour that would imply that they actively dislike a young person in the programme even if, on occasion, this may be true. The concern of staff can often be addressed within counselling sessions with the young person, using a problem-solving approach. This style of counselling revolves around specific problems about which the staff can show sympathy and concern and come to agreements with the young people about alternative courses of action.

Respect

It is important that staff try to respect the opinions of the young people whenever possible. For example, when a young person gives a reason for a poor day in class as the 'teacher was unfair', the member of staff can agree that teachers can sometimes appear to be unfair.

Fun

A sense of humour and the ability to help young people to enjoy themselves and have fun is important. The ability to have fun, especially with other people, involves a range of skills that many disturbed and delinquent young people may lack. If there are some young people who get too excited and out of control, then this could be a time to engage them in more socially acceptable behaviour, and to help them discriminate between different situations. It is inevitable that staff will sometimes be at the receiving end of some young people's humour, and it is important that staff can tolerate this without being too sensitive about their appearance or personality. The ability to 'take a joke' will often be used by young people to discriminate between 'good' and 'bad' staff, and can help to foster constructive relationships.

Activities as a group

Taking part in enjoyable activities as a group is an excellent way of developing relationships. In open settings, informal trips can be ways to spend an enjoyable evening, and sometimes youngsters who are quiet and withdrawn may display a skill or flair for a particular activity and therefore gain status among their peer group. Although such activities are more difficult in conditions of high security, occasions such as birthday parties can be used to initiate enjoyable group games and activities.

Pleasantness

Just as staff expect young people to be polite and considerate to them, so the young people will benefit when staff are also polite and considerate. Irrational, angry, or harsh behaviour from staff interferes with the development of good relationships. Calm and considerate social behaviour, even in the act of disciplining, is more effective and helps to build and strengthen relationships.

Flexibility

The young people should understand that the goal of the programme is to help them to be more successful and to be happier. This means that there is nothing absolute about the systems of management. If a young person wants to question or change some part of a programme, then staff should be willing to listen and negotiate, and consider the views of the young person.

The importance of a balanced and cohesive staff team cannot be underestimated but it is often neglected when setting up behavioural programmes. Staff operating such programmes often have to respond to situations in a specific and precise way, often over long periods of time, which can be very stressful. Mutual support and cooperation are therefore essential ingredients in any effective programme. The structure of staff teams, and the use of team-building and staff support systems will be discussed in Chapter 4.

ADMINISTRATION AND FUNDING

Sources of funding

Lack of funding is a major cause of programme failure. Facilities for disturbed and delinquent young people can be funded from a variety of sources. In *statutory* programmes the cost of capital expenditure is often met directly from government or local authority funds. There are, however, a range of *voluntary* organizations for young people who obtain funding from charitable sources, often in addition to some central funding or government grants. In Britain, for example, charities such as Barnardo's, The National Children's Home, and The Children's Society, provide money for projects for difficult and delinquent young people.

The names and addresses of various voluntary bodies and charities are to be found in the *Annual Social Services Year Book*. The best way to approach potential financial backers is with a written proposal, specifying the amount of money being requested, the use for which it is required, the proposed running costs, and the possibility of long-term returns on the investment.

Some projects depend on several different sources of funding. For example, initial start-up money from the Home Office may be used to provide and furnish suitable premises, and pay the salaries of several members of staff. This may then be supplemented, for example, by grants from Barnardo's with which to provide equipment, and assistance from the Department of Social Services to pay for the food and lodgings of residents.

Administration

Once a service has been set up it is important to establish and administer appropriate management and financial accounting systems. Budgetary control systems are required, covering capital and revenue expenditure. An important function of administration is to maintain strong links with financial backers, and to keep them well informed of the structure and function of the organization. Work with delinquent young people is not always looked upon favourably, and can be influenced by local and national politics. Keeping financial backers sympathetic to the general aims and objectives of rehabilitating young offenders reduces the risk of being denied further financial help. Programmes often come to an end because of underfunding, and failure to convince potential backers of their worth and value.

Perkins (1987) used a cost-benefit analysis to argue the case for treating adult sex offenders, a group which is often seen as undeserving of treatment. By comparing the cost of staff salaries and other expenses incurred (the cost side of the equation) with savings on the cost of imprisonment, such as clothing, food, laundry, and prisoners' earnings (the benefit side of the equation), Perkins was able to show that even a conservative estimate suggests that the rehabilitative work more than pays for itself. This, of course, does not include other benefits arising from treatment, such as the reduction in risk of harm to future victims. Such arguments can prove valuable when requesting further funding.

Income

It is not always obvious who is the customer when dealing with difficult and delinquent adolescents. Statutory organizations are generally set up to deal with an identified group of young people, with money allocated specifically for this task. For voluntary services, however, it may not be clear who should foot the bill. In today's economic climate few services are offered free of charge, and most agencies are expected to operate on a repayment basis and to charge users to achieve recovery of full costs.

Residential services are usually costed according to a rate based on occupying one bed for one night. A price can then be set for the financial period, and compared to similar establishments in terms of cost effectiveness. Non-residential services, however, can be more difficult to cost. For example, outreach services that operate from residential centres, offering family and community-based work, perhaps to prevent admission and thereby to reduce the costs of treatment, can be difficult to cost.

The best way to overcome potential financial disagreements is to enter into written contractual agreements with service users. The contract, signed by representatives from both parties, should specify aims and objectives of the service being offered. This specification might include residential care and treatment or outreach work; the amount of time anticipated to complete the work; the names of the people who will carry out the work; and the total cost. This level of specification will ensure that service users do not withdraw their support once the work has begun, which would mean that the remaining work is either carried out free of charge, or is not done at all; the latter can of course be damaging to the young person and his or her family.

In addition to income generated by client-related work, there are often other possible sources of finance. For example, income can be generated through offering teaching and training to other organizations, or through consultation services. Research can also attract income through grants, especially if carried out in partnership with colleagues from higher education establishments.

Budget allocation and expenditure

Budgets need to be allocated appropriately and tightly controlled by identified budget holders. Many projects often have 40 or 50 different budgets, covering diverse items such as food and possessions, pocket money, crockery and linen, library facilities, and staff training. Many behavioural programmes for young people rely in part on tangible reinforcers, where young people earn points or tokens that can be exchanged for specific rewards, such as computer games, items of clothing, and video tapes (see Chapter 4). Money for this purpose is best controlled under a separate 'treatment budget', as the success or failure of a particular intervention often depends on the delivery of the reinforcers at the appropriate time. Like most of us, young people do not like to be told to wait another week, and feel let down when what they have earned is not forthcoming.

Financial planning

Finally, some attempt should be made to project expected income and financial and work force requirements for at least the following year. Budgets may need to be reallocated or parts of the service allowed to run down in an effort to maintain other, more important, aspects of the service. Alternatively, additional sources of funding may need to be sought, perhaps in anticipation of a shortfall in particular budgets.

ADMISSION POLICY AND REFERRALS

Admission criteria

An essential feature of any service must be the operation of clear criteria and policies for admission. This is particularly important for organizations that provide specialist services across several different regions or at a national level. Admission criteria and policies serve a variety of functions. Clear admission criteria ensures that access to the service is reserved for young people in the greatest need. Conversely, these criteria will prevent young people from entering the service who will not benefit. Whittaker (1979) made the point that no single set of practices will meet the needs of all troubled children. The behavioural model is no exception, and reference will be made later in this chapter to some of the admission criteria that may be necessary in this specific instance. However, application of the admission criteria should allow some young people to be re-referred to a service that is more able to meet their needs. Finally, admission criteria simplify monitoring of changes in service demand and the needs of young people referred to the service.

Admission criteria are particularly important for residential facilities, which are expensive to operate and should therefore be used selectively. Barker (1988) identifies a number of mistaken ideas commonly held about residential treatment.

1 *Residential treatment is more intense than other forms of treatment.* This all depends on what is provided in the way of treatment. Generally speaking, the main advantage of a residential setting is the provision of 24-hour care and management. The need for a continuous 'therapeutic milieu' or management regime should therefore be the main reason for admission. Further, it could be argued that admission should only occur if it can be shown that the management regime produces significant and desirable changes in behaviour, or at least prevents further deterioration. One advantage of the behavioural model is that it more easily lends itself to evaluation, through monitoring residents' behaviour and their social environment.

2 *Young people are usually admitted to residential facilities because they need this type of 'therapy'.* Various factors are responsible for the admission of young people to residential facilities, and their need for a particular form of 'therapy' is only one of them. Admission may be arranged because other people (family, school, children's home) are no longer willing to tolerate their behaviour, which may be more to do with changes in circumstances, such as marital breakup, or staff shortages, than the behaviour of the young person.

Alternatively, admission may serve to protect the community from those young people who have committed serious, life-threatening offences and present real dangers to the public. Similarly, admission may be to protect young people who pose a serious danger to themselves: this may be through either deliberate self-harm, or because of the potentially dangerous situations in which they place themselves. A minority of young people may be at risk through no fault of their own, such as those young people who have been threatened by adult co-defendants, or who have been terrorized after giving evidence.

3 *Residential treatment and residential care are the same.* There is sometimes confusion between the idea of providing care for young people who cannot, for whatever reason, live at home, and the provision of treatment for behavioural, psychological, or psychiatric difficulties. While good care of disturbed young people may help to promote their healthy development, it is important to distinguish between generic residential care and focused treatment programmes.

4 *It is easy to combine therapy with the family and residential treatment of the young person.* Barker (1988) suggests that this is not easy to achieve, a view that is consistent with our own experience. While separating young people from their families in times of crisis often relieves families from the burden of looking after a difficult young person, it can have the effect of reducing the motivation of the family to change. Families of delinquent young people are often reluctant to take part in formal family therapy or, if they do take part, are reluctant to examine their own behaviour and the way in which the family functions. Given the importance of work with families (e.g. Roberts and Camasso, 1991), it is crucial to recognize and work with this resistance. Many families of seriously disturbed and delinquent adolescents feel resentful and dissatisfied with previous professional help and advice and are not happy about the prospect of engaging with yet another set of therapists. There may also be practical difficulties, such as the distance from the family home. These kinds of problems do not mean that family work is impossible, but that it is necessary to be realistic about what is possible. It may be more productive to invest time and energy in creating and maintaining constructive links between the young person, the family, and the service providers.

It is important to formulate admission criteria into written guidelines, and to make these available to potential referring agencies. The referral process is simplified if a proforma is administered to referring agencies at their request, specifying the criteria for admission, and requesting specific information about the young person. This not only helps when deciding whether a referral is appropriate, but simplifies pre-admission planning. An example of admission criteria, again from our own organization, is given in Appendix 1 to this chapter.

Admission process

Control over the admission process is important in preventing an overload on the service, both in terms of the number of young people and the kinds of problems they present. There may be times when a combination of events, such as staff sickness and one or two extraordinarily demanding young people, demands a temporary halt to admissions. An admission panel which meets regularly, say on a weekly or monthly schedule, is one way to 'gatekeep' admissions. Representatives on the panel should be drawn from within the service and from outside, to maintain a degree of objectivity. The admission panel has the task of considering each referral and making a decision about how best to proceed. Three main courses of action are available to the panel:

1 *The referral is appropriate for admission.* In this case an admission date should be set and contact made with both the referring agency and the young person. This pre-admission work is best done as soon as possible, by telephone, letter, and in person. A booklet outlining information for youngsters coming into the service is useful, and can help to allay anxieties about the move.

2 *The referral is inappropriate for admission.* In this case the rationale for the decision should be explicit and, if possible, alternative courses of action recommended.

3 *The referral appears appropriate for admission but a decision cannot be made.* This may be due to either the information provided being incomplete, or unresolved legal issues.

Admission procedures

Staff need to be prepared for new young people coming into the service, and procedures for new admissions should form part of the service policy and practice manual. When admitting youngsters into residential facilities the young people will be concerned with familiarizing themselves with the daily routines and getting to know the staff and other young people. The young person and his or her possessions may also need to be searched to check for illegal items such as knives, drugs, alcohol, and pornography. When admitting to conditions of high security the search needs to be very thorough and carried out before entry to the building (for this reason it is advisable to have a designated room). Search procedures need to be clear, especially in relation to intimate body searches, which may be necessary when there is evidence or suspicion that a young person has secreted an object.

It is also important to have information about the young person's state of health. Children and adolescents sometimes carry infections, such as chicken-pox, or may even be infested with head-lice.

The first few months of a young person's stay is invariably the most difficult, although many young people are initially settled after the first two or three weeks. During this time he or she is preoccupied with the new environment and adjusting to its demands, such as changes in the daily routine. The young person will also be establishing his or her place and position in the peer group, and forming new relationships, both with the other young people and members of staff. The focus for staff during this settling in period will be upon assessment (see Chapter 3). This begins with monitoring and observing the youngster, collating previous reports and written material, and contacting and establishing working relationships with other relevant professionals. Skynner (1976) has referred to this basic assessment as establishing the 'minimum sufficient network'.

Staff may need to intervene at this stage with particular management strategies, over and above those in daily operation, to deal with social behaviour that is grossly unacceptable, such as inappropriate mealtime behaviour and eating habits, or soiling and faecal smearing. Given the special difficulties that can arise during the period following admission, there are some benefits to be gained from operating an 'admissions unit'. It should be recognized that this may not, however, be always practical. In the case of facilities that run several different units, offering both secure and open provision, an admissions unit may be worthy of serious consideration. Such a system has been operated successfully for several years in our own organization (Gentry and Ostapiuk, 1989). All young people begin in an admissions unit where they stay for between three and six months, depending on their predicted total length of stay. They then move on to either one of two long-stay secure units, or directly on to the open unit. The main tasks of the admission unit are to settle the young person into the routine and expectations of the Centre, and to carry out a thorough assessment of the young person's personal, treatment, and educational needs (see Chapters 3 and 4). This sequential system has several advantages, both for staff and young people. Residents who initially present serious management difficulties have the opportunity to start afresh on a new unit, with different staff but within a similar framework. Young people can also be transferred to their next unit according to their own particular needs, thus helping to establish the highest possible quality of life, which is important within long-stay secure settings. A computerized model is currently being developed for managing movement through the four units at Glenthorne, to maximize occupancy, and minimizing time spent on the waiting list.

COMPREHENSIVE SERVICE PROVISION

Services for young people have to meet a variety of needs, some of which are statutory, such as education. Young people with histories of difficult and disturbed behaviour have a variety of additional needs, often requiring the implementation of highly structured management regimes and complex, multi-faceted treatment techniques and strategies. The way in which these different functions or tasks are organized and delivered will ultimately decide the effectiveness of any attempt to change the behaviour of the young people.

Provision of high quality child-care

An environment that nurtures the physical, intellectual, and emotional growth of the young people provides the foundation for effective treatment. The efficacy of any intervention, no matter how well it is carried out, will be diminished if the young person is living in a harsh and deprived environment. Several factors can be identified that help to ensure that a good standard of care is maintained, which may prevent some forms of institutional abuse, such as the pin-down regime referred to earlier.

Complaints procedure

Young people should have the right to make a formal complaint about any aspect of their care and treatment. Ideally, complaints should be in confidence, and directed to independent representatives. Upon entering the service young people should receive a booklet explaining the procedure for making a formal complaint, and have the opportunity to discuss this with a member of staff. Use of the complaints procedure should be monitored, especially the speed with which complaints are handled. This ensures that any particular issues that arise can frequently be properly addressed.

Young people's views

Regular surveys should be undertaken of the young people's views of their standards of care, treatment, and education. Areas covered by such surveys should include food, clothing, toiletries, pocket money, mail, room, privacy and confidentiality, effectiveness of the complaints procedure, management, treatment, and education. Ideally, the results of such surveys should be available to anyone who wishes to see them, and may form part of the annual report of the service. Findings arising from such surveys can help to address areas of dissatisfaction and reduce the risk of disruption.

Inspection from outside agencies

Inspection from outside agencies, such as the Social Services Inspectorate (SSI) in England and Wales, helps to ensure that adequate consideration is given to the rights, personal dignity, and civil liberties of the young people. Outside agencies also have the role of monitoring the quality of care, control, education, and treatment in the light of best professional practice and in accordance with relevant legislation. Outside representatives have the advantage of being impartial and objective; in addition they are well briefed with respect to changes in child-care legislation and current mainstream practice. Outsiders can often highlight areas of practice that need immediate attention, and assess the extent to which the service is meeting the needs of young people from ethnic and other minority groups.

Management and control

Rules, both written and unwritten, are important in any social organization, but particularly so within small living environments where people go about their daily lives in close proximity. The maintenance of social order depends largely on the ability of each individual to control and manage his or her own behaviour within socially acceptable limits. Services for difficult and delinquent adolescents often experience problems in controlling and managing the young people they are looking after. Many young people will have poor self-control and will not have internalized the rules that govern everyday social behaviour. Consequently, they are more likely to behave maladaptively in response to stress, frustration, and challenges. Procedures for managing and controlling behaviour need to be clear and explicit, and easily understood by both staff and youngsters. The uses of such procedures serve several objectives: (1) to prevent harm coming to young people and staff; (2) to prevent serious damage to the building, furnishings, and fabric; (3) to regulate the behaviour of staff with respect to how they prevent and respond to unacceptable behaviour; and (4) to make explicit to the young people the boundaries of acceptable behaviour, and the consequences that follow unacceptable behaviour.

Overall, the aim must be to produce a living environment that is stable, free of violence and other unacceptable behaviour, and relatively free of chaos. Many residential and community facilities struggle to achieve adequate management and control, so that a disproportionate amount of time, energy, and resources is invested in this area. Needless to say, this expenditure is at the cost of other crucial tasks such as education and treatment.

Education and work

The third component of a comprehensive service for difficult and delinquent adolescents must be the provision of an educational curriculum and, particularly for older adolescents, vocational training. In England and Wales there is a statutory requirement to provide education to anyone aged 16 and below. The curriculum should be broad based, flexible, and based on the individual's assessed needs in academic, social, and vocational skills to maximize personal development.

The relationship between education and offending in young people is a complex one. Hollin (1990a) suggests that the relationship can be viewed in two ways. The first view emphasizes academic difficulties, including learning difficulties, which are associated with poor social adaptation, and increase the probability of offending (Loeber and Dishion, 1983). At a second level, social behaviour within school is related to later offending (Elliot and Voss, 1974). Although it is unlikely that school difficulties, either academic or social, actually cause offending (Rutter and Giller, 1983), there is good reason to believe that integration of education into programmes for young offenders will have beneficial effects. Many young people will have been excluded from school because of their offending or antisocial behaviour (see Lane and Murakami, 1987), which may mean reduced school time or removal from mainstream classrooms to special schools or residential establishments. Many delinquents, therefore, have been denied access to formal education, and may be performing well below their true academic potential.

Assessment and intervention

The final task is the establishment of effective systems, procedures, and methods for assessing the needs of the young people, and delivering individually tailored interventions to promote lasting changes in behaviour. The topics of assessment and intervention will be addressed in more detail in Chapters 3 and 4 respectively. Here it is sufficient to outline some basic principles that should be followed when dealing with difficult and delinquent adolescents.

1 Make a clear distinction between institutional and referral problems. All too often staff become preoccupied with behaviours that cause problems within the institution (i.e. management issues) at the expense of the problems that resulted in the young person first being admitted. Although the two sets of problems may be related, this is not invariably the case.
2 Young people should be assessed on an *individual* basis, using a variety of assessment methods.
3 The distinction should be made between 'clinical' and 'criminological' treatment goals. For example, helping a young person to improve his or her social skills is a clinical task, and it cannot be assumed that this will necessarily reduce the risk of reoffending (Hollin, 1990b; Hollin and Henderson, 1984).
4 Have clearly defined intervention programmes.
5 Ensure that young people give fully informed consent to enter the programme.
6 Maximize treatment effectiveness by linking the intervention to all aspects of the young person's daily life (e.g. school, home, unit).
7 Ensure that staff are properly trained and supervised.
8 Build in regular treatment reviews, open to other relevant professionals and family members.
9 Evaluate treatment outcome.

POLICY AND PRACTICE

Reference has already been made to the need for clearly defined policy statements regarding key areas of working practices. Policy statements reflect on an organization's attitude towards particular issues, which can be evaluated in terms of their legal, ethical, and theoretical acceptability. Gentry and Ostapiuk (1989) have identified three main factors that influence policy formulation: (1) the characteristics of the organization; (2) the theoretical model on which the therapeutic practices is based; and (3) external policy constraints (see Figure 2.2). These three factors will each act in different ways to influence a range of policy issues. For example, policies regarding disclosure of sexual abuse by a young person will be influenced mainly by external policy guidelines.

Table 2.1 lists some areas for which statements on policy and practice are essential. Child care is the most complex area of policy and practice. Young people have a variety of needs and a significant proportion of staff time will be spent meeting those needs. In all settings, staff have a responsibility to provide a

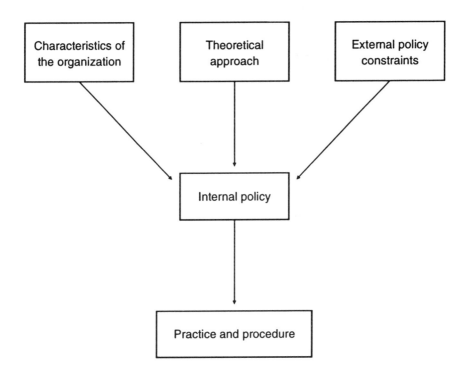

Figure 2.2 Factors influencing policy formation

caring, nurturing environment aimed at promoting the young person's personal development.

It is also essential that the care regime reflects the multi-cultured and multi-racial society in which we live. This should not be only reflected in the choices given to young people, in food, music, hairstyle, and clothing, for example, but also in the attitudes and behaviour of the staff group. Race awareness training is an essential component of any training programme for those who work with young people, and there is a need for specific policies that address acts of staff prejudice or discrimination. Staff should also have access to relevant textbooks and literature (e.g. Wing-Sue and Sue, 1990).

Specific areas of policy and practice that need to be included within the child-care category are given in Table 2.2.

From policy to practice

In many ways, formulating good policies and procedures is easy. The difficult part is actually putting them into practice. Each member of staff should be given

Table 2.1 Policy areas in child care

1   Child care
2   Anti-discriminatory practices
3   Health and safety
4   Education
5   Treatment
6   Behaviour management and control
7   Disclosure of sexual abuse by a young person
8   Disclosure of previously unknown offences by a young person
9   Allegations of assault (sexual or physical) by a member of staff on a young person
10 Assaults on a member of staff by a young person
11 Staff development and training

Table 2.2 Child-care policy and practice areas

1   Clothing
2   Food
3   Physical needs
4   Social needs
5   Developmental/emotional needs
6   Cultural needs
7   Family contact and relationships
8   Privacy and confidentiality
9   Access to files and medical records
10 Communications (visitors, letters, and telephone calls)
11 Complaints procedure
12 Spiritual and religious needs
13 Acceptable sexual behaviour
14 Availability of pornography (magazines, books, and videos)

a copy of the policy and practice manual; indeed, this should be built into the induction programme (see Chapter 5). Staff should be aware of specific practices arising from policy statements. There is a sense in which the policy reflects the attitude of the organization, while the practice guidelines aim to determine the behaviour of its staff. By way of example, Appendix 2 shows the policy and procedure from our own organization for dealing with assaults on staff.

The use of policy and practice manuals helps decision-making, especially at times of crisis when important decisions have to be made quickly. Regular reviews of policy and practice also enable changes to be made in the light of new legislation or other developments. Through this process a service can continually improve its performance in dealing with the range of complex and difficult issues that can arise when working with young people.

DISCHARGE AND FOLLOW-UP

An important consideration in any programme designed to intervene in the lives of difficult and delinquent young people are the amounts of time and effort devoted to helping the young person survive in mainstream society without the support of the programme. This issue is particularly important with respect to residential services where, in contrast to the 'real world', there is usually a high degree of structure and clear expectations. The shift from institutional control to the demands of the real world is illustrated in Figure 2.3.

In Figure 2.3 the vertical axis has the residential establishment at one pole and the real world at the other. For reasons that include legal requirements, protection of the public, and safety of staff and residents, the institutional pole of this axis is

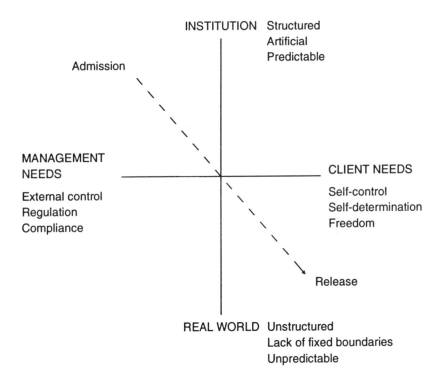

Figure 2.3 Long-term goals in the management and treatment of delinquents

Source: *Clinical Approaches to Violence*, edited by K. Howells and C. R. Hollin, 1989, Chichester: Wiley. Reprinted by permission of John Wiley & Sons.

characterized by security and predictability of routines. In total, these factors produce a highly artificial environment. The opposite end of the axis, the real world, is exactly the opposite: it lacks structure, fails to define boundaries, and is unpredictable in many ways. The horizontal axis separates management needs and client needs. Management needs, reflected in the characteristics of institutions, must have effective means of control to ensure compliance, containment, and adherence to institutional routines. The needs of young people as clients, given the ultimate goal of a return to the real world, are characterized by a need for self-control and independence.

Ostapiuk and Westwood (1986) suggest that intervention programmes must strive to be relevant to both the institution and the client. However, under the pressure of residential life it is easy for the focus to become fixed in the upper left quadrant – institutional and management needs – to the neglect of the lower right quadrant – real world and client needs. Ostapiuk and Westwood suggest that the aim should be to facilitate the client's movement, along the dashed line, from formal routines and external control to self-control in a sometimes unpredictable real world.

Obviously this progression is not going to happen without planning. To enable realistic transition from programme to real world while maintaining positive changes developed during the programme, termed *generalization*, contact between the two worlds must be maintained at all times (Burchard and Harrington, 1986).

The problem of generalization

Preventing young people's behaviour from returning to pre-intervention patterns soon after the programme is one of the most pressing problems associated with behavioural programmes (Gelfand and Hartmann, 1975). One solution is to blur the boundaries between the programme and the real world, that is, to promote generalization by making the setting in which the work takes place as similar as possible to the young person's natural environment. The young person's behaviour in real-world settings should be assessed, and problematic areas targeted for intervention. This may mean the availability of work, education, and leisure opportunities, and it requires the real world to be drawn into treatment programmes in the form of families, friends, and a peer group. For example, staff can accompany the young people on trips into the local neighbourhood and observe their ability in a range of situations. Studies have shown that such strategies can produce improved generalization with young offender populations (Emshoff et al., 1976).

Many services for delinquents were developed with the unfortunate philosophy that the young person could be removed from society, 'treated' by an expert, and then returned to the community in a 'cured' state. The behavioural approach makes explicit some of the difficulties that arise from this philosophy, and suggests methods that promote generalization. There are two areas that merit attention in facilitating the successful return of delinquent adolescents to the real world: these are preparation for discharge or release, and collection of follow-up information.

Planning discharge

The return of young people to the real world should be carefully planned, and should be incorporated into the general aims and objectives of the treatment programme. A placement should be identified as early as possible, so that there is sufficient time to prepare the young person. It is also helpful for young people to know what lies ahead of them, and to be aware of the demands that will be made upon them in the real world. Many services do not have funding or resources to provide long-term follow-up and after-care in the community (Bullock *et al.*, 1990). This places an onus on care staff to find the most suitable placement for the young person so that the risk of breakdown and a return to offending is minimized. A range of placement types is usually available, including a return home to family, hostels, independent living, and professional fostering. Each of these types of placement makes specific demands of young people. The factors that should be considered in planning the young person's discharge are discussed below.

Family structure and functioning

A return to the family may mean a return to the same setting that contributed to the young person's original difficulties. The relationship of the young person to his or her family should be carefully assessed. In particular, it is important to know the extent to which the structure and functioning of the family contributed to the young person's behavioural difficulties, and how the family has previously responded to these. Some young people choose to return home although they are aware that this is probably not the most suitable option, perhaps out of a sense of loyalty to their family. Contact with the family should begin early in the treatment programme, even before admission, and family work is central to most social-behavioural interventions with young people (Frude, 1991).

In addition to developing a constructive working relationship, it may be possible, if the family is willing, to undertake a family-based intervention. Two styles of family work are most closely associated with a behavioural approach: these are functional family therapy (FFT) and parent management training (PMT). FFT aims to improve family communication and negotiation (Alexander and Parsons, 1992), while PMT aims to change, through training, the way in which parents interact with their children (Bank *et al.*, 1987).

Professional fostering

Professional fostering schemes have developed in response to the demands of young people who wish to live in a family setting other than their own. In our own organization, such a scheme has been developed with Barnardo's (Dixon, 1984). Through this scheme it has been possible to place with families young people with long histories of disturbed and difficult behaviour, many of whom have committed serious offences, and are aged 18 or 19 years at the time of placement. The scheme has many advantages: prospective foster parents can be carefully selected and given training, advice, and support; and it is also possible to match young people with appropriate families, and arrange for pre-placement visits to ensure that both the young person and their family are satisfied with the arrangements. Young people on this scheme sometimes form long-term attachments to the family and use it as a source of support after they have left.

One issue that can cause difficulties is confidentiality of information, particularly the extent to which foster parents have access to existing records about young people. For example, a family that agrees to foster an adolescent with a history of arson may find it difficult to insure their home. On the other hand, failure to disclose background information to insurance companies could invalidate existing insurance policies should the young person set a fire.

Probation, social, and health services

The involvement of other agencies after discharge is nearly always necessary and therefore links should be made with after-care services as early as possible. It is particularly important to clarify the role of such agencies in relationship to the young person. While probation has become popular in recent years, often as an alternative to custody, many young people are unsure about the role of their probation officer. Nonetheless, it is true that probation is often recommended; Carney (1977) suggests five reasons for this: (1) the community is more normalizing than institutions; (2) probation minimizes psychological and physical degradation; (3) probation humanizes rehabilitation; (4) probation is more effective than incarceration; (5) probation costs less.

However, Stumphauzer (1986) is critical of the work probation officers undertake with young offenders in the United States. He suggests that probation services have developed methods of understanding and handling casework that simply do not work: either they fail to change offending behaviour, or are so inconsistent in their procedures that they cannot be evaluated. Nevertheless, several authors have noted the potential of probation work for enabling delinquent young people to change through the application of behavioural principles (Stumphauzer, 1986; Tharp and Wetzel, 1969). A review by Remington and Remington (1987) points out that many problems faced by offenders, such as anxiety, depression, and drug abuse, are precisely those in which behavioural intervention has proved efficacious. Further, several training programmes in behavioural skills for probation staff have been described (Novaco, 1980; Polakow and Doctor, 1974). In Britain, Hudson (1986) notes that behavioural casework is being reported with increasing frequency by probation officers, with social skills training proving particularly popular.

Some youngsters, especially those with a psychiatric history, or a history of bizarre and unusual offending behaviour, may benefit from psychiatric supervision within the community after their discharge. In such cases it is important to ask for an opinion from a consultant psychiatrist within the region to which the young person is returning. If longer-term psychiatric supervision is thought appropriate, and the young person is willing to attend, regular appointments can be arranged at the nearest psychiatric clinic. The purpose of this kind of work, particularly in relation to forensic problems, is not so much one of treatment but of monitoring the individual's mental state and social functioning with the aim of preventing deterioration and reoffending.

Neighbourhood and community

The neighbourhood and local community is known to influence the development and maintenance of delinquent behaviour (Simcha-Fagan and Schwartz, 1986; Stumphauzer, 1979, 1986). The SHAPE program described by Reid et al. (1980) paid particular attention to the relationship of the young person with the local community. SHAPE was a three-phase programme in which young offenders aged 16 to 23 years were placed (Phase I) in a group home with a relatively high level of control, reinforcement, and shaping of social skills. In Phase II the young person moved into two-person housing with continued shaping of social and employment skills, but with increased self-management. Finally, in Phase III, independent living and employment were encouraged and supported.

Aiken et al. (1977) made an interesting proposal with regard to learning from the community. They suggested that delinquent adolescents could learn and adapt the strategies used by non-delinquent young people living in the same community. In theory, the adoption of this approach should lead to strategies that help to prevent at-risk young people from engaging in delinquent behaviour.

Employment

The job market in most western countries is becoming increasingly competitive, and the demands of many jobs are complex and technical. Young people with a history of delinquency and behavioural difficulties are usually disadvantaged by a variety of problems when competing for employment. These disadvantages include a criminal history, poor social skills, verbal and communicative skill deficits, low self-esteem, and poor educational attainment. Yet it is this group of young people who desperately need the social and emotional benefits associated with employment (Morash, 1983; Winefield et al., 1993). Programmes for delinquent adolescents should therefore include provision for work preparation and experience. Vocational training can usually be integrated with external schemes operated in the local area, such as government Youth Training Schemes. Links can also be made with local career services. Young people can be encouraged to take part in pre-vocational courses, such as the Certificate in Pre-vocational

Education, which addresses the basic skills inherent in most jobs, such as health and safety at work, interview skills, and weights and measures.

Follow-up

Few services for adolescents have the time or money to provide formal long-term support and after-care. However, informal support can be offered, young people can be encouraged to telephone or drop in occasionally, especially at times when they feel in need of support, or when they feel at risk of reoffending. This kind of informal contact can be useful, especially for young people for whom the programme provided stability and the chance to form meaningful relationships.

Ideally, of course, services should be resourced to provide follow-up. Frequently young people who have made considerable progress in treatment settings find themselves struggling within a few months after discharge. It is not unusual to find new problems emerging after discharge, such as substance abuse, homelessness, and social isolation (Bullock *et al.*, 1990). Services for individuals who have persistent and chronic problems are increasingly recognizing the limitations of a 'treatment' philosophy and prefer to use the term 'rehabilitation', where the aims are more to do with preventing further deterioration and maintaining the best possible level of functioning.

The use of relapse-prevention strategies with delinquents has been one attempt to take a long-term perspective. The relapse-prevention model was developed by Marlatt and Gordon (1985), and aims to help the offender control his or her offending behaviour by paying attention to risk situations and to their thoughts, feelings, and behaviour within these situations. Although the model was developed for working with substance abusers, it has recently been extended to other groups, including sex offenders (Pithers, 1990; Pithers *et al.*, 1983). The effectiveness of this strategy, however, relies on keeping contact with the offender, in order to maintain his or her motivation, identify potentially difficult situations, and review and reinforce the offender's use of specific cognitive-behavioural techniques.

SERVICE MONITORING AND EVALUATION

The demands placed upon services dealing with delinquent and behaviourally disturbed adolescents change over time. It is therefore important to monitor the main factors that influence a service, and to develop a structure for evaluating the performance of the service in its attempts to meet those demands.

Service monitoring

Four areas can be targeted for monitoring: these are client characteristics; staffing; quality of care; and management of behaviour. The first two of these factors help to determine the ability of the service to meets its aims and objectives, while the latter two reflect the performance of the service. Given the large quantity of information that will need to be collected and analysed, the use of computerized database systems is advisable.

Client characteristics

A complex network of services exists for dealing with difficult young people. Changes in one part of the system, or a change in legislation concerning children or young offenders, can have ripple effects throughout the system. Sometimes these changes may take several years to produce noticeable effects, making it difficult for services to plan. Monitoring the client group coming into an organization helps to anticipate trends in the system, and to ensure that adequate resources are available to meet their needs. Information should be collected regularly, once or twice a year at least, on several different variables, including: (1) admission statistics (i.e. age, sex, ethnicity, previous placements, legal status); (2) length of stay; (3) presenting problems (i.e. reason for referral and admission); and (4) discharge statistics (i.e. age at discharge, type of after-care placement).

Staff characteristics

The ability of the service to meet the demands of the client group and to fulfil other aims and objectives, such as training and research, depends on being able to recruit adequate numbers of motivated staff with suitable training and experience. Monitoring of the staffing situation is essential for a variety of reasons, not least of which are the dangers that can arise through understaffing, especially when working with young people convicted of serious offences. A minimum staffing level must be maintained at all times, and consideration must be given to the composition of the staff group with respect to gender and ethnicity. Monitoring also helps to anticipate shortfalls in staffing and gives an indication of the functioning of the service as a whole. For example, high levels of staff sickness and a high staff turnover should be cause for concern. Several kinds of information about staff should be collected: (1) staff vacancies (i.e. number of vacancies, areas of vacancies, and recruitment difficulties); (2) composition of staff group (i.e. age, sex, ethnicity, qualifications and training); (3) staff sickness; (4) staff training and career development (i.e. courses completed, career plans – see Chapter 5); (5) staff turnover.

Quality of care

The term 'quality of care' is rather vague and demands an operational definition. Within this definition, it is important to monitor the living standards of the young people, perhaps particularly within residential settings, where young people have often restricted choices and where they may live for several years (CCETSW, 1992; Schaefer and Swanson, 1988). Some suggestions for monitoring quality of care were made earlier in this chapter. These included: the use of complaints procedures; surveys of the client group; regular external inspections, which help to ensure that care standards meet those laid down through regulation and accepted good practice; the availability and uptake of health-care services, such as dental and eye check-ups; the provision of health education; and the availability of specialist counselling services relating to issues such as pregnancy and HIV.

Management of behaviour

Two issues are relevant here: the general level of disturbed and difficult behaviour, and the use of specific management techniques to control difficult behaviour. Information relating to three different areas should be collected routinely: (1) absconding (i.e. number per month; where from; how returned); (2) use of additional measures of control (i.e. use of physical restraint; number and length of separation incidents; use of time-out); and (3) assaults on staff and young people.

Information about these areas serves several purposes. First, it reflects the difficulties facing staff on a daily basis enabling, for example, decisions to be made regarding the need for extra staff. Second, it gives an indication of the extent to which an organization is coping (or not) with the client group. Third, it helps to safeguard the rights of the young people and ensures that information is readily available for external inspection.

It is well established that the environment exerts considerable influence over the behaviour of young people, most markedly within residential settings (for a review see Clarke, 1985). Sinclair (1971, 1975), for example, found large differences in the rates of misbehaviour and absconding between probation hostels dealing with young offenders. These differences he attributed to the style of management in the institutions. Similar results were obtained in Dunlop's (1974) study of eight approved schools catering for boys aged 13 to 15 years on admission. She found that schools that emphasized trade-training and mature and responsible behaviour had lower rates of both absconding and other forms of misbehaviour during training, as well as lower rates of reconviction following discharge. The significance of these and other findings lies in the shift of emphasis from person-related variables, such as intelligence and personality, to the influence of the environment upon behaviour.

One area that is of great concern in managing behaviour is violence within the workplace. While research suggests that serious violence is not a regular occurrence (Fottrell, 1980), it is also recognized that because of underrecording and inaccurate recording official records do not always fully represent the extent of the problem (Weiner and Crosby, 1987). Service issues, such as increasing levels of violence, can only be properly addressed if the information is accurately recorded. It is important, therefore, that systems are set up that help recording. Specific incident forms should be available with which staff are thoroughly familiar, and which produce information that is amenable to analysis. An example of an incident report designed for recording violent incidents is given in Figure 2.4, taken from Gentry and Ostapiuk (1989).

THE INCIDENT
Where and at what time did the incident occur?

What did the client say and do?

How did the client appear?
(a) Physical state:
(b) Psychological state (confused, angry, etc.):

Who else was directly involved (clients and staff)?
What did they do?

How did the incident end?

ANTECEDENTS
What was happening immediately before the incident?

What particular event(s) triggered the incident?

CONSEQUENCES
What happened to the client afterwards?

What happened to other clients directly involved afterwards?

What did the member(s) of staff directly involved do afterwards?

Figure 2.4 Outline of violent incident report
Source: *Clinical Approaches to Violence*, edited by K. Howells and C. R. Hollin, 1989, Chichester: Wiley. Reprinted by permission of John Wiley & Sons.

There are several advantages to this kind of report. First, it can be completed in only a few minutes. A common reason for underreporting is the amount of time involved in writing a complete description of the incident, such that staff cannot be bothered, especially if the incident did not result in serious harm. Second, the form is highly structured, which helps recall and cues staff to the type of behaviour that they should be recording.

Third, the three sections, Incident (Behaviour), Antecedent, and Consequences, are consistent with the behavioural model, and facilitate analysis of each incident. This enables staff to learn from the incident, and modify future practices accordingly, as well as enabling the organization as a whole to monitor changes in the pattern and frequency of incidents. In addition, with consistent reporting it is possible to evaluate the effects of specific changes in policy and practice.

Epps (1990) carried out a retrospective study into the effects of specific policies and practices for the management of violence at Glenthorne Youth Treatment Centre. Records were examined of injuries sustained by staff at work over a ten-year period, with particular reference to injuries relating from contact with a young person. Over this period there was a shift from injuries sustained as a result of deliberate physical assaults upon staff, some of which required hospital treatment (e.g. broken nose, concussion), to injuries sustained during the course of carrying out specific procedures, such as restraint and separation, most of which were fairly minor (e.g. twisted fingers, bruised limbs). These data suggested that the organization had developed effective methods of preventing and managing violent and disruptive behaviour.

Service evaluation

Few services dealing with difficult and delinquent adolescents have made determined efforts to evaluate outcome. Roberts (1987) notes, 'In view of the millions of dollars expended each year to protect society, care for, and rehabilitate juvenile offenders, it is astonishing that so few systematic research and follow-up studies have been conducted by juvenile justice agencies' (p. 44). There are many different reasons for this, including the complexity of the task and the lack of funding. However, there has also been a degree of therapeutic nihilism, especially in relation to young offenders. There are two key points to address when considering evaluation. First, what is the *outcome* of a particular intervention? Second, to what extent was the intervention *delivered* as planned? This is called 'treatment integrity', and will be discussed in more depth in Chapter 6.

Outcome

The effectiveness of any service should be considered with respect to its aims and objectives, and the measures chosen should reflect these aims. Hollin (1990a) has pointed out the confusion between *clinical* and *criminological* variables that exists in the literature on young offenders. Clinical variables include, for example, measures of social skills, institutional behaviour, and self-esteem. Criminological variables, on the other hand, are concerned with rates of reoffending, for which data can be collected in several ways, such as self-report, reconviction, and type of offence. Conceptually these two classes of variables should be kept distinct. A service whose main aim is to reduce rates of reoffending should not have clinical variables as its main outcome measure. The reason for this is that the relationship between clinical variables and reoffending rates is an empirical question that has yet to be properly addressed. For example, there is limited empirical evidence to suggest that young offenders are less socially skilled than non-offenders, but there is little evidence to support or refute the assumption that poor social skills are functionally related to criminal behaviour (Henderson and Hollin, 1986). Indeed, it is likely that the relationship between clinical and criminogenic variables will differ from individual to individual.

Given that most services for difficult and delinquent young people aim to address both sets of factors, outcome research should include data relating to both areas. Two brief examples should make clear the reasons for this assertion:

Example 1   John was admitted to a residential centre because of a violent assault on another boy. He was discharged a year later and was followed up over the subsequent year. During that time he did not reoffend. However, he had been unemployed for most of the year; and had twice attempted suicide; abused solvents and several other substances; lived in bed and breakfast accommodation, or slept rough; and had no stable relationships.

Example 2   Stephen was admitted to the same centre for a variety of offences, including robbery, criminal damage, car theft, and burglary. Over the course of the following year Stephen was convicted for burglary and car theft. However, he managed to hold down a job in a garage; moved in with his long-term girlfriend; attended a part-time college course on motor mechanics; and remained in good physical and mental health.

These two contrasting examples illustrate some of the difficulties with evaluations. Which one is the success? How does one decide which variables should be used to measure outcome? Should different variables receive different weighting according to their significance? Historically, most studies have focused on rates of reoffending (for a review see Basta and Davidson, 1988), but more recent studies have taken a broader perspective in looking at outcome (e.g. Bullock *et al.*, 1990).

Treatment integrity

While outcome studies are interested in the product of an intervention, it is also important to examine the extent to which the intervention was delivered as planned. Often there are discrepancies between the intended treatment and the treatment that actually takes place, and these will inevitably influence the outcome. It seems that the majority of published studies take treatment integrity for granted, although there is little justification for this. It is well recognized that delinquent young people are difficult to engage in specific and focused programmes of intervention (see Chapter 4) and are frequently resistant and manipulative. In addition, they often present with a multitude of different problems, which require a range of different interventions aimed at *both* clinical and criminogenic variables. In many ways, therefore, there is little room for complacency in accepting treatment integrity, and any evaluation should examine closely the *process* of treatment delivery.

However, before moving to programme delivery, it is necessary to consider assessment. What are the issues in the management of behavioural assessment?

APPENDIX 1: CRITERIA FOR ENTRY TO A RESIDENTIAL SERVICE

Eligible children

The young person must:

- be looked after by a local authority within the meaning of Section 22 of the Children Act 1989; *and*
- be subject to an order restricting liberty under Section 25 of the Children Act 1989; *or*
- be likely to be subject to an order restricting liberty by the Wardship Court, under transitional arrangements resulting from the implementation of the Children Act 1989; *or*
- be subject to detention for a fixed term of years or for life, or detained during her Majesty's Pleasure under Section 53 of the Children and Young Person's Act 1933.

For children looked after by a local authority

The young person must:

- be aged 12–16 years; *and*
- be likely to remain in care for at least another 12 months after admission to the YTC; *and*
- be likely to be subject to grounds for fresh orders for at least 12 months after admission; *and*
- require long-term specialized help over and above what may be available in the child-care system.

When children are referred by the local authority, funding for the young person's proposed placement must be approved by the local authority at the time of the application, and authorized by the Director of Social Services. In addition, the home authority social worker must be prepared to maintain close contact during the young person's residence.

'Section 53' children

In the case of a child detained under Section 53 of the Children and Young Person's Act 1933, one or more of the following criteria should additionally apply:

- the Youth Treatment Service can offer appropriate offence-related or therapeutic treatment that could not be provided elsewhere;
- the young person would suffer significant harm if placed in the penal system (e.g. because of age, vulnerability, offence type);
- a suitable alternative placement outside the Youth Treatment Service is not available.

All children, whether being looked after by a local authority, or a 'Section 53' detainee, presenting problems should include at least *one* of the following:

- serious delinquency;
- violent or very aggressive propensities;
- actual or potential danger to self/others, or both;
- extremely disruptive in other settings;
- suicidal tendencies;
- self-harm (e.g. mutilation);
- habitual absconding;
- repeated failure to respond in other settings.

Ineligible children

Young people will not be accepted if any of the following apply:

- being on remand;
- being looked after by a local authority, but with no prospect of a Secure Order;
- amenable to non-secure intervention, e.g. juvenile justice strategy such as intensely supervised activities, specialized fostering, non-residential services, intensively supervised residential care;
- can be accommodated satisfactorily in a Community Home (with Education) with secure provision, voluntary or private sector, education sector, health sector;
- being diagnosed as mentally ill.

APPENDIX 2: YTS POLICY AND PRACTICE FOR DEALING WITH ASSAULTS ON STAFF BY YOUNG PEOPLE

Policy statement (summarized version)

Violent behaviour is one of the main reasons for a youngster being placed in a Youth Treatment Centre. In the process of changing this type of behaviour and helping youngsters to achieve self-control and learn acceptable alternative behaviours, staff must expect to receive much of the angry and aggressive responses that the young person has learned elsewhere. However, there are limits to the level of abuse which staff can reasonably be expected to tolerate. There are two basic principles:

1 For everyone's safety it must be made clear to young people that physical assault is no more acceptable within the Centre than outside.
2 The response by staff to a serious incident must be immediate and un-compromising. It is therefore essential that response options are clearly understood in order to minimize the risk of injury.

Procedure following assault

1 In the event of an assault on a member of staff, the young person concerned must be restrained as quickly as possible, using the minimum amount of force necessary to do so. Senior management should be informed immediately the situation is under control. They will consider whether to call the police.

2 Staff and the young person concerned may have suffered injury as a result of the incident. Management's first duty will be to arrange for the treatment of any injuries without delay (whether by first aid, medical treatment at the Centre, or hospital). Even if members of staff have not suffered physical injury, management will always counsel staff members, offering them the opportunity to visit their own GP, and to go off duty if they so request. They should be accompanied, if necessary.

3 The senior manager on duty will arrange to discuss the incident with other unit staff at the end of their period of duty and ask for written reports from any staff who witnessed the alleged assault. Eye witness accounts volunteered by young people present at the incident will also be recorded.

4 Regardless of its severity, every incident must be recorded in the log book held by each unit, and by the on-call manager in the daily diary. In a case of undisputed physical injury, the appropriate Accident Form held by each unit should be completed.

5 Normally a member of senior management should visit the member of staff within 24 hours of the incident. It is desirable that the staff member should produce his or her own written version of the incident, and should be asked to do so, although it is appreciated that some members of staff, for reasons of their own, may prefer to decline.

6 Head Office should be informed by telephone of the circumstances of the alleged assault as soon as practicable. This should be followed by a written account of the incident accompanied by any eye-witness statements and a report from the assaulted member of staff, if available.

7 Senior management may seek to involve a Staff Welfare Officer, particularly if the member of staff lives alone, seems likely to require sick leave for some time, or has been admitted to hospital.

8 Assault is a criminal offence involving a deliberate act as opposed to one of inadvertence. If there are reasonable grounds to suspect a deliberate assault, and where injury is inflicted, senior management will refer the matter to the police unless, in very rare circumstances, special factors would make referral inappropriate (such as professional misconduct, apparent provocation by staff, or failure to comply with Centre policy and practice).

9 If management decide not to involve the police, or the police decide not to prefer charges against the young person, the remedies of civil proceedings are available to the member of staff. This is a matter for personal decision. Legal advice can be arranged if the member of staff so wishes. If senior management are consulted by a member of staff, any form of discouragement or implication that his or her position as member of YTS staff might be jeopardized by initiating proceedings would be a serious derogation of the rights of staff, as expressed in the Staff Code. The role of senior management in these circumstances will be to offer advice about the possible courses of action. Nothing in this paragraph is intended to limit the legal rights of members of staff to institute proceedings, or to seek independent legal opinion or advice from the police as they see fit.

10 Where appropriate, senior management should advise the member of staff that:

(a) Any sick leave taken as a direct result of the assault will not count against sick leave entitlement.
(b) He or she will continue to receive full pay, including any overtime, night duty or shift disturbance allowances normally received.
(c) He or she may claim full compensation for damage to personal property arising from the assault.
(d) He or she may be entitled to claim compensation under the Criminal Injuries Compensation Board Scheme.
(e) He or she should contact the local National Insurance office about entitlement to disablement benefits.

Chapter 3

Managing behavioural assessment

When examining the issues involved in the management of behavioural assessment there are two areas of prime concern. First, the practical issues that need to be considered when carrying out behavioural assessment; second, the management of the process of assessment.

With regard to practice, this should ideally involve the use of a variety of techniques of information-gathering, such as examination of archival data, assessment interviewing, direct observation of behaviour, and self-report measures. Each of these methods has its own strengths and weaknesses and has specific functions to play in the overall assessment strategy (Hollin, 1990a). It is essential therefore that all those who are involved in both the management and practice of assessment are aware of the strengths and the potential problems and pitfalls associated with the various assessment techniques. This assessment appraisal will inform decisions as to the most appropriate method(s) to use to obtain reliable and valid information. It is this information that will form the basis of the functional analysis of the young person's behaviour.

The second prime concern noted above refers to how the practice of behavioural assessment can itself be managed, expedited, and monitored. In essence, the goal of management is to 'assess the assessment' within the constraints of the working environment. Ultimately, the issue is one of balancing the priorities given to the 'system needs', such as the institution, the case load, the family and other agencies, and the 'client needs' as highlighted by the assessment.

This chapter offers a pragmatic view of behavioural assessment methods, then examines the ways that assessment can be organized and improved by managing practice.

BEHAVIOURAL THEORY AND ASSESSMENT

Behavioural theory has generated a number of diverse intervention strategies that have been applied to a growing number of personal and social problems (e.g. Bellack *et al.*, 1986). Behavioural theory has several distinguishing characteristics: it stresses the role of individual differences in the topography and maintenance of behaviour; it emphasizes the importance of the intensive study of the individual; and it looks to the application of intervention strategies specifically designed for individual clients. Of crucial importance in practice, therefore, is the need for accurate, reliable, and valid assessment techniques. Such techniques will help identify and specify target behaviours, provide information for the purpose of functional analysis, and produce data for programme evaluation. Behavioural assessment has become increasingly important in behavioural practice over the last decade, as shown by several recent texts (Barlow *et al.*, 1984; Bellack and Hersen, 1988; Ciminero *et al.*, 1986).

The process of carrying out an assessment is not just a matter of the application of theory to practice: good assessment needs to be well planned, well designed, and well managed.

PLANNING THE ASSESSMENT AND DEMONSTRATING OUTCOME

As well as informing programme planning, from the outset assessment should be seen as a way of monitoring the outcome of a programme. Almost paradoxically we therefore include in this opening section a discussion of the way that assessment informs judgements at the end of the intervention.

Pre-intervention assessment

Assessment of a young person's behaviour before embarking on *any* type of intervention programme is essential in behavioural practice. As detailed in Table 3.1, there are several reasons why pre-intervention assessment should be carried out.

Pre-intervention assessment, therefore, plays a vital role within the total behaviour change programme. Assessment cannot be either ignored or performed incorrectly if analysis and intervention are to be successful. Thus, the first step of the assessment that calls for good management is the collection of baseline information.

Baseline information

One hallmark of good behavioural practice is an orientation that favours intervention strategies that are informed by reliably collected information. A *baseline* is formed by repeated measures over time of the frequency, intensity, and duration of the naturally occurring specified behaviour. A baseline informs not only the design of the programme and its evaluation, but should also be the basis of decisions about whether to try to change behaviour.

Useful case management information is provided by continuing to monitor behaviour after intervention, so that change (for better or worse) can be carefully supervised and intervention plans adjusted as necessary. Other advantages of a baseline include gathering an accurate estimate of the actual severity, variability, and range of behaviour; looking for any systematic changes that occur before intervention as 'reactive' effects of the assessment procedure (reactivity is explained in

---

Table 3.1 Major reasons for pre-intervention assessment

- Identification of target behaviour(s)
- Identification of appropriate measuring instrument
- Identification of environmental variables affecting behaviour
- Identification of organismic variables affecting behaviour
- Selection of intervention strategy (or strategies) with high probability of successful outcome
- Evaluation of the effectiveness of intervention

---

detail later in this chapter); and familiarizing the observer(s) with the target behaviours, the assessment procedures, and the client's behavioural repertoire.

The second management step concerns the period over which to collect baseline data. Ideally, the baseline period should be continued until a stable rate of behaviour is obvious, or until it seems that the behaviour is not consistently changing in a favourable direction (without an intervention programme), but this may not be always possible. However, measures of behaviour are usually collected for at least five to seven days and, if a formal statistical analysis of the data is to be performed, the requisite minimum number of data points within each of the baseline and intervention phases should be collected (see Barlow and Hersen, 1984).

Programme evaluation

With the baseline established it is possible to design and carry out an intervention programme – assuming intervention is judged necessary – in an attempt to bring about behaviour change. A comparison of baseline levels of behaviour with levels during and after intervention can show that it is the intervention, rather than extraneous factors, which has brought about change. The issue of effectiveness is of prime importance in behavioural practice. If an intervention can be shown to be responsible for behaviour change, it can then be used again with increased confidence.

A task of management is to plan so that the specific contribution of the programme to behaviour change can be shown. There are two principal types of evaluative design that can be used to show the effect of behaviour change programmes: these are the *reversal* (or withdrawal) design, and the *multiple baseline* design. The brief discussion below gives the basics concerning these evaluative designs; for a more detailed discussion the texts by Barlow and Hersen (1984) and by Kazdin (1982) are strongly recommended.

Reversal design

This is often called an A-B-A design, although there are many permutations on this basic design. An A-B-A design shows the effect of a behavioural programme

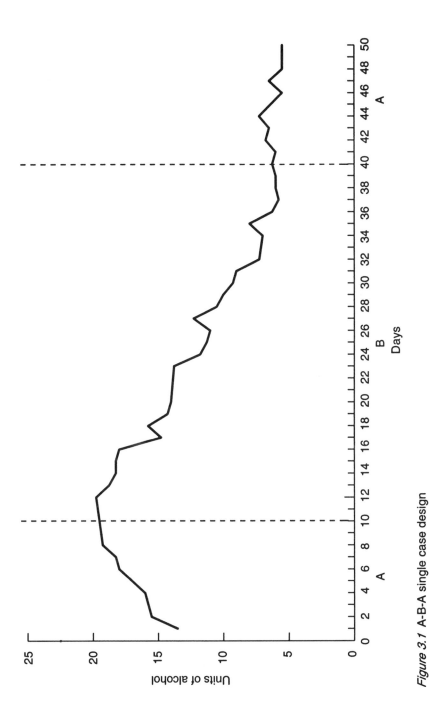

Figure 3.1 A-B-A single case design

Source: Young Offenders and Alcohol-related Crime: A Practitioner's Guidebook, by M. McMurran and C.R. Hollin, 1993, Chichester: Wiley. Reprinted by permission of John Wiley & Sons.

by alternatively presenting and withdrawing the programme over time. As illustrated in Figure 3.1, using the example of an intervention to reduce alcohol consumption, the purpose of the design is to show the relationship between changes in the target behaviour and the programme itself.

In the case example in Figure 3.1, during the baseline period, called the 'A' phase, information is gathered on the amount of alcohol drunk by the individual concerned. The second phase, called the 'B' phase, is where the intervention programme commences: in this case a controlled drinking programme over a one-month period. Typically, the 'B' phase is continued until either the behaviour reaches a stable level, or until it diverges markedly from the level seen at the baseline phase. With some reservations, changes in behaviour from A to B can be attributed to the effects of the intervention.

At the conclusion of the intervention there is a natural return to baseline conditions (the second 'A' phase); during this second 'A' phase no attempt is made to change behaviour. In the case in Figure 3.1, the control over drinking achieved during the programme has clearly lasted over a short ten-day period. It would, of course, be advantageous to continue monitoring intake of alcohol over a longer period.

The maintenance of programme gains after a return to baseline conditions is a strong indicator that the intervention was primarily responsible for the change in behaviour. A lack of maintenance of treatment gains would, on the other hand, indicate a lack of generalization, and the need to reintroduce the intervention phase, i.e. to introduce a second 'B' phase. An A-B-A-B design (and other derivatives) is fundamental to programme design if the effect of the intervention strategy is to be clearly demonstrated.

Multiple baseline

In the example above, concern was focused on one specific behaviour, i.e. alcohol consumption. However, there are occasions when programmes are aimed at more than one behaviour; when this occurs we have a situation in which a multiple baseline is required.

Figure 3.2 shows a multiple baseline for a social skills training programme. In this case, the programme was concerned with three particular aspects of social skill: the micro-skill of appropriate eye contact; the macro-skill of displaying appropriate listing skills; and the global skill of initiating and maintaining an interaction with peers. In the first stage, days 1 to 5, baseline frequency counts are taken for all three behaviours. (The system for making the counts obviously having been arranged in advance.) The first five programme sessions (days 6 to 10) are devoted to developing eye contact. During this period all three behaviours are continually monitored: as can be seen from Figure 3.2, appropriate eye contact increases, while the other two behaviours remain unchanged. In the next stage, days 11 to 15, the programme continues to reinforce the improved eye contact and begins to work at appropriate listening skills, while continuing to

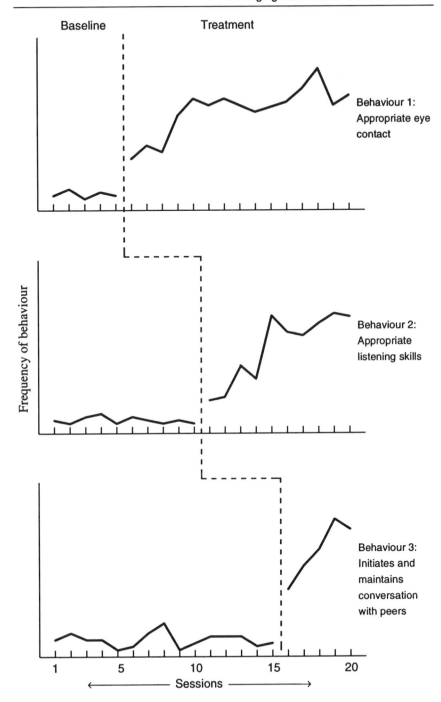

Figure 3.2 Multiple baseline (across behaviours) case design

monitor interaction with peers. The gain in eye contact is maintained, while listening skills improve, and frequency of interaction remains low. In the final stage, days 16 to 20, the programme continues to reinforce eye contact and listening skills, while introducing specific strategies for interaction with peers. The final result is a gain at the end of the programme in all three aspects of social skill.

There are several points to make regarding the above. First, sometimes it takes a long time to see gains in one behaviour; however, as long as monitoring continues as at baseline, it is perfectly permissible to move to another target behaviour to introduce variety into sessions. Second, behaviours do not have to be taken one by one: programmes can work on two or more behaviours at a time, one would simply expect a different pattern of change. Third, sometimes behaviours change before being specifically worked on during the programme; this, of course, is generalization of the effects of the intervention and a sign that the programme is having a strong effect. Finally, multiple baselines are not limited to behaviours. There are *multiple baselines across situations*, in which a specified behaviour is monitored in different settings; and *multiple baselines across people*, in which the programme is delivered sequentially to different individuals.

In summary, there are three key areas that require good management if assessment is to be conducted properly. First, a system must be constructed to make maximum use of pre-intervention information. Second, whenever possible baseline information should be collected and used to inform programme planning. Third, the baseline information should be used in the context of a single case design to inform monitoring of programme effectiveness.

RELIABILITY AND VALIDITY IN ASSESSMENT

Behavioural practice relies in large part on non-inferential, objective measures of behaviour. Decisions about intervention will be based on behavioural measures and therefore these measures have to be both *reliable* and *valid*. These two terms are inextricably linked to the practice of behavioural assessment and therefore their meaning warrants clarification in this chapter.

Reliability

A reliable measure is one that will consistently produce the same results when measuring the same thing. For example, suppose two trained observers are recording elements of a person's behaviour, such as physical proximity and words spoken in social situations, over a given time. With training, observers should produce assessments that are the same, or at least very similar, if the measure is reliable. If the assessments are dissimilar, it suggests that something – i.e. the observer or the assessment method – is unreliable. Reliability therefore refers to the difference between *actual* behaviour and *recorded* behaviour: the bigger the difference, the less reliable the measure. Checks for reliability are discussed later in this chapter.

Table 3.2 Important principles in behavioural assessment

- Behaviours under examination should be objectively measurable.
- Deviant behavour, unless there is a known organic pathology, is due to inappropriate learning.
- The presenting behaviour is held to be *the* behaviour for assessment, not some underlying cause.
- The aetiology of the behaviour, in terms of the events present at the time of the occurrence of the behaviour, together with the maintaining events in the environment, are taken as the main ingredients for treatment.

Validity

A valid measure records exactly what the investigator wants to measure. For example, a teacher may wish to know how much time a child spends 'on task', and decides to record the amount of time the child spends sitting at his or her desk as the measure of being 'on task'. This measure of time sitting may or may not be a valid measure of 'on task behaviour'. The child might well be on task while sitting at the desk but may leave it to sharpen a pencil or consult a book, activities that are task-related behaviours but would count as 'off task' according to the measure. In other words, the chosen measure may not be fully valid as a measure of the specified behaviour. A point to note here is that two observers recording the behaviour according to the defined measure may get similar results, suggesting good reliability, but this is not a guarantee of validity.

CONDUCTING THE ASSESSMENT

Assessment and treatment implications

There are several principles that inform the practice of behavioural assessment and treatment. The most important of these are highlighted in Table 3.2.

The main message from Table 3.2 is that it is highly desirable, if not essential, that reliable and valid measurement instruments are used by trained practitioners. It follows that management of the data collection procedures must be considered.

Table 3.3 Main sources of information for assessment

- Archival information
- Informal observations
- Assessment interviews
- Direct observation
- Self-report

Data collection procedures

Information about a young person's behaviour can be obtained in a multitude of ways from a variety of sources, each of which will have its own strengths, weaknesses, and specific uses in the overall assessment battery. We have identified five main sources of data, as shown in Table 3.3, and their use is considered later in this chapter. Before doing so, however, it is useful to address the question 'How much assessment is needed?'

How much assessment?

As noted previously, the task of the behaviour analyst is to attempt to sort out critical from trivial information, and thereby concentrate his or her efforts on *relevant* information. To achieve this goal, many writers have proposed the idea of multi-modal assessment as essential to a complete behavioural analysis (e.g. Herbert, 1987b). Multi-modal assessment refers to collecting information about several elements of the individual's behaviour. For example, data may be collected about overt behaviour, about thoughts and beliefs, and about physiological responses to a particular event or set of circumstances. This 'multi-response' assessment is necessary because individuals may differ on their responsiveness in each modality, depending on environmental circumstances and their learning histories. A full assessment of this type is important because there is no guarantee that the various elements of behaviour will correspond in any given circumstances. Therefore, without full assessment an intervention programme might appear to have been effective in modifying one element of a person's behaviour, such as social skills, but without any beneficial effect on other behavioural modalities such as, say, self-esteem. While there is not unanimous agreement among practitioners about the utility of multi-modal assessment, we suggest that not to attempt a multi-modal assessment is to stand the risk of missing valuable information.

In the section below, which discusses sources of information, we cover not only the main management issues, but have also included several pointers to good practice. This mixture will help in highlighting both the important areas and giving a substantial basis to inform, for example, monitoring and training procedures.

Sources of assessment information

Archival information

There are probably very few young people who come to the attention of the helping agencies for whom there will not already be information on file that will be relevant to assessment. However, there is often a massive amount of information that is not relevant to the immediate assessment. When dealing with archival data it is beneficial if the information-sifting process is managed in a

Table 3.4 Brief profile format for the organization of archival and other information

---

- *Demographic* details including date of birth, age, sex, address, telephone number, and information about relevant others, e.g. social worker, probation officer
- *Family* information with details about parents, guardians, siblings, and other important family members
- *Historical* information including problem history, offence history, educational institutions attended and attainment
- *Medical* information giving relevant details of past or current medical problems, such as the results of hearing and sight tests, past illnesses, current drugs, dental and inoculation record, and EEG tests
- *Psychological and psychiatric* reports, giving details of findings from previous reports

---

way that focuses attention on what might be relevant pieces of information, so avoiding lengthy duplication. The advantages to management of using a standardized information retrieval system are that it gives a consistent format across cases, it can save valuable time, and information is readily available. To this end the initial information sort can be speeded up by standardized information retrieval sheets that give a skeleton profile of the client. Information can be usefully sorted into reasonably discrete blocks and subsequently accessed with considerably more ease and utility than by continually wading through the original files. For example, it might be useful to organize the collection of information under a number of separate headings as shown in Table 3.4.

Establishing a profile of this sort can greatly *aid* the assessment and analysis of problematic behaviour, but it must be remembered that this is not *the* assessment. The profile serves first to inform in a structured, unambiguous way, and secondly to advise as to the initial areas in which assessment may be needed. The profile from the files can serve several functions: it can act as a guide to structured assessment interviews and therefore serve as a cross-reference for the subsequent information; it can give information about the behaviour that may need to be the focus of early observation; and it can show where there might be the need for self-report questionnaires. A profile also gives the opportunity both to acknowledge any previous work that may have been undertaken with the client, and allow any previous ideas to be thoroughly tested.

One of the greatest management advantages to profiling is that once the practice is established it takes very little management. Profiles need not be viewed as one-off 'snap shots' of the young person, but can be regularly updated as the programme progresses, providing a running record of the programme and its progress, so aiding programme management.

Informal observation and anecdotal information

During the early stages of an assessment there will probably not be the time or opportunity either to define operationally behavioural targets for assessment or to specify the type of measure to be used. During this opening period, anecdotal reports and informal observations are often the only information available to add to archival information. While we would not advocate reliance on casual observation or informal information, it is possible to 'manage' the recording of day-to-day reports to give relevant and useful assessment information. In many settings it is not unusual to have written 'logs', either on a daily or an event basis, about the young person's behaviour. Often these logs are unstructured, and represent little more than a diary of events. This may have some value to the running of an institution or community unit, but such diaries generally are of little use to the behaviour analyst. However, this can be changed by asking the reporters to structure their comments towards reporting what *happened* (i.e. report on behaviour), rather than giving their *interpretation* of what happened. Similarly, by noting the circumstances that led up to the event(s) (i.e. the antecedents), and recording what happened afterwards (i.e. the consequences) valuable information can be gathered. Thus information can be gathered in a form that has relevance to the overall assessment. Such a method does not reject or negate the opinion of those involved with the young people: they can report what they felt about a specific incident or behaviour and interpret it as they wish, providing the facts are noted. All too often the observed information is lost in a wealth of interpretation and opinion.

It is important to note that this style of A:B:C reporting is not restricted to any specific setting. It can equally well be used in settings as diverse as parents keeping diaries of their child's behaviour, or teachers of their pupils' classroom behaviour, or staff in secure settings. Thus careful management of the early stages of the assessment period can not only help to gain information that may otherwise have been lost or forgotten, but also help practitioners to record behaviour in a way that will become increasingly important as the assessment and intervention stages get fully under way.

In summary, good initial data collection will use a multi-modal assessment rather than just one method of gathering information. This assessment will inform the using of individual profiles to aid identification of relevant material. But throughout, the emphasis will be to concentrate on facts not on interpretation, conjecture, and opinion.

Assessment interviews

An interview can be defined as a meeting of two people, face to face, to accomplish a specific purpose by discussion. In this definition, it is the reference to *purpose* that is important; an interview is essentially a conversation where one party is seeking specific information. For example, the purpose of a job interview is to inform the employer whether the prospective employee has the necessary knowledge, experience, technical ability, and attitudes, to perform the job that is on offer.

Assessment interviews should be similarly purposeful. The interviewer is seeking specific information about the interviewee's behaviour and learning history to inform a subsequent analysis. In a behavioural interview the interviewer might be seeking information about overt behaviour, asking about what the person does in certain situations; or the focus might be on covert behaviour, what the person thinks, feels, and believes. Similarly, questions might be asked about the setting conditions (antecedents) for the behaviour, and the events (consequences) that maintain, increase, or decrease the behaviour. Selecting the target behaviours for intervention can be greatly aided by good assessment interviewing (Hersen and Turner, 1985; Kanfer and Grimm, 1977). Indeed interviewing is probably the most frequently used method of behavioural assessment.

Assessment interviewing is a highly skilled undertaking, and should not be carried out without either the necessary training or supervised experience. If conducted incorrectly it at best might be a simple waste of time for all concerned; at worst it can lead to a wrong analysis, inappropriate or misapplied treatment, and a continuation of the long-term problems.

With this in mind, it is important that managers ensure that those involved with assessment interviewing should be given adequate training and supervision and adhere to good practice guidelines. For the benefit of those reviewing their own organization, some guidelines are given below which might serve as a checklist against which to gauge current work. This might, in turn, be beneficial in informing managers of targets for change. With regard to time management, it is worth remembering the caution given by Peterson (1968) that about three-quarters of the material exchanged in a traditional interview is redundant in terms of its eventual impact on the formulation of an intervention programme.

Training in interview skills

Effective training of assessment interviewers can be carried out using techniques commonly employed in skills training, such as modelling, role-play, discussion, feedback, and practice. The use of videotaped recordings of actual or mock assessment interviews can be helpful during training. Supervision of the novice interviewer should also be an integral part of the training. Discussion of the interview, both of its structure and strategy and its information content, can effectively shape up the interviewer's skills, reinforcing the positive elements and eliminating errors. Training on these lines is time-consuming, but essential if the assessment is to be carried out effectively and professionally.

Planning and preparation

Assessment interviews should in part be formal and highly structured, the interviewer having control over the proceedings at all times and having specific aims to be achieved (Murphy *et al.*, 1985). For this to occur, it is essential that the interview is carefully planned and the aims and objectives of the interview session clearly understood. Possible objectives may include obtaining information about a particular event, testing feelings and attitudes towards specific events or people, and sorting out the chronological order of significant events. During the interview many factors should be balanced; some young people will respond openly and willingly, others will be more reticent or even silent; the subject matter to be covered may be distressing (for either interviewer or interviewee); and the young person's concentration span my be limited. A balance therefore needs to be struck between obtaining the required information and putting undue pressure on the young person. The length of each interview should be planned to take account of the factors associated with both the subject matter and the needs and welfare of the young person.

In planning an interview session the practitioner should also consider the setting in which it takes place. Having previously said that the interview should in part be structured, this does not mean it has to be conducted 'across the table' in an interrogatory manner. The interviewer must choose the setting conditions for the interview carefully to get the best results. Some practitioners will inevitably be limited in the range of settings they have available, but most furniture can be rearranged temporarily to suit the needs of an individual interview session. Gauging the most appropriate setting is usually a combination of interviewer experience, trial and error, and available resources.

Assessment interviewing, therefore, normally calls for preparation by the interviewer such as obtaining relevant background information from files and records, and reading any existing assessment reports. While some people profess to prefer to interview 'blind', we believe there are many advantages to 'doing one's homework' before interviewing. After completion of the interview a detailed evaluation and scrutiny of the new information are vital. To aid this process, the use of video or audio recording, with the client's consent, can be an extremely useful adjunct to written notes in some instances.

By undertaking careful preparation and planning of each session, the interviewer can be in a much better position to determine the degree of consistency or discrepancy between different accounts of the same situations. This may then either prompt further questioning at another interview, or confirm opinions regarding specific issues. A skilled interviewer can save him- or herself a great deal of time and effort by concentrating on relevant issues.

Conducting the interview

When carrying out an assessment interview two important features need to be borne in mind – structure and the strategy.

Structure

Both before and during the interview you should consider the form it is going to take: ideally, there should be a distinct beginning, a middle, and an end, with a smooth transition between the various stages. The first stage should be welcoming and warming, a time to relax the interviewee and relax yourself. At this stage the aim of the session should be clearly explained, focusing the attention of both parties on what is trying to be achieved. The topic(s) for discussion should also be outlined to give the interviewee some thinking time, and confidentiality issues can be reiterated. You may also wish to give the interviewee the opportunity to ask questions and voice concerns before the interview starts in earnest.

The middle section, the information-gathering stage, is where the careful planning of the interview comes to the fore. There should be a tight discussion of the main issues, with the interviewer checking the reliability of the answers. This checking can be done, for example, by posing the key questions in a different form. It is up to the interviewer to keep the information flowing and not to be distracted by irrelevances or be led off the topic. If something new or interesting is revealed which the young person wishes to discuss but is not on your agenda, make a note of it for later discussion. Stick to your plan unless you feel that this new information is unlikely to be revealed ever again. This is, in our experience, rarely the case. We have all been lead astray by verbose clients taking charge of the interview and 'hooking' the interviewer into discussing what initially appeared to be a 'revelation' but ends up, an hour later, as 'irrelevant'.

The final section of the interview should be a winding-down stage when a summary of the proceedings is offered. This can help to reduce any tension on the part of the interviewee and clarify and confirm issues for the interviewer. Generally an outline of the next session should be given, unless you think that this might be detrimental to the young person or lead to a refusal to attend the next session.

Strategy

The interviewer can change the parameters of the interview and in so doing change the behaviour of the interviewee, either for the better or (unfortunately) the worse. It is important, therefore, to decide what strategy you are going to employ during the interview. Clearly the degree of empathy and warmth of the interviewer can affect the behaviour of the interviewee (e.g. Chamberlain *et al.*, 1984). The much preferred strategy is to be warm and friendly towards the interviewee, and to be totally non-judgemental. Whatever information is revealed – however distressing, shocking, funny, or stupid it appears – it should be treated with respect and this conveyed to the young person. It is important that the interviewer encourages the interviewee to talk by responding with appropriate verbal and non-verbal cues. The aim is to get the young person to work with you rather than against you. One of the best ways to do this is to encourage the young person's sense of partnership and joint control of the proceedings. Use plenty of reinforcement for his or her efforts; use an approach that stresses collaboration, explaining that both of you must work as a team to sort out the issues. When difficult topics are covered in the interview you must recognize signs of stress and acknowledge that you have done so. Effort towards building a working relationship can pay big dividends in terms of a successful outcome.

Self-report and self-monitoring assessments

Self-report measures are an important part of behavioural assessment. Self-report procedures and their application to behavioural assessment have received increased attention in recent years. There are assessment procedures for covert 'private' events such as thoughts, feelings, emotions, and beliefs (Parks and Hollon, 1988), as well as physical feelings such as headaches and tachycardia (Kallman and Feuerstein, 1986). In addition, there is an increasing awareness of the reactive effects – i.e. the behavioural change properties – associated with self-monitoring, which increases its potential as an effective intervention technique (Kanfer and Gaelick-Buys, 1991). However, the phenomenon of *reactivity* (discussed in detail below) also has implications for the use of self-report as an assessment measure that poses important issues for supervisors and managers.

Self-report can provide an accurate measure of pre-intervention levels of behaviour, including frequency, duration, antecedent and consequential events; as well as produce qualitative information via reinforcement inventories and social interaction questionnaires. This self-reported information can be subsequently used in the intervention and follow-up phases of a behaviour change programme. There can also be an educational component to the use of self-report measures: they may increase the young person's awareness of his or her own behaviour, their understanding of the effect this behaviour has on others, and their appreciation of environmental influences on his or her own behaviour.

Self-report as a method of both assessment and intervention has been applied in diverse settings and across many populations and environments, including children, adolescents, and adults, and institutional, community, and family settings. As with any other assessment method, the selection of an appropriate measure is of paramount importance, and depends to a large extent upon the target behaviour in question. Rating scales, narrative accounts, frequency and duration measures, product of behaviour measures, attitude and belief recording, and diaries are among the most widely reported self-report methods. All self-report measures, however, can be affected, sometimes adversely, by reactivity.

Reactivity

The term reactivity refers to the behaviour change brought about by using an assessment method, as distinct from change directly attributable to a specific intervention. The target behaviour may be either increased or decreased because of the assessment, depending on the interaction of a number of important factors described below. In the same way that an observer visibly recording someone's behaviour during the assessment period may change that person's behaviour, so self-report questionnaires can have similar effects on the individual's covert and overt behaviour. It is important, therefore, to manage the potentially reactive effects of behavioural assessment if the information from the assessment is to be as reliable and valid as possible.

Several factors have been identified as possible causes of reactivity (Haynes and Wilson, 1979). The likelihood of these should be gauged and counter-measures put in place where possible.

1 *Obtrusiveness*   Certain types of assessment methods are more obtrusive than others and are therefore more likely to produce reactive effects. For example, like all self-report devices, assessments using diaries and question-naires are obviously obtrusive in that they cannot be completed without the person being aware of them. Thus, depending on the behaviour being monitored, some self-report instruments may need to be completed regularly and others seldom, some publicly and others in private. The assessor needs to judge care-fully what assessment instrument to use and under what conditions to maintain control over the reactive effects produced by that instrument.

2 *Valence*   The valence – i.e. the positive or negative attributes that the individual attaches to the behaviour being monitored – can affect not only the *amount* of reactive effect that takes place, but also whether an *increase or decrease* occurs with the target behaviour. For example, if the target behaviour is seen by the person as positive or desirable, such as an increase in social inter-action, then self-monitoring of the behaviour may well lead to an increase in it. Conversely, a target behaviour that is judged by the individual concerned to be negative or undesirable, for example smoking, may well decrease in frequency as an effect of self-monitoring.

3 *Behaviour or product of behaviour*   The monitoring of either a behaviour, for example worrying, or the product of the behaviour, such as social withdrawal, can both have reactive effects.

4 *Temporal relationship*   The reactive effects of assessment can be affected by the temporal relationship between the behaviour and the monitoring of the behaviour. If the monitoring takes place before the occurrence of the behaviour this has a greater reactive effect than monitoring after the behaviour has taken place. In other words, to ask 'How much are you going to worry about tomorrow's interview?', is liable to have a greater reactive effect than asking 'How much did you worry about yesterday's interview?' The relative advantages and disadvantages of both strategies need to be considered before asking the question in the context of an assessment.

5 *Social contingencies*   All self-monitoring methods are obtrusive to a greater or lesser extent, but the social contingencies attached to the self-monitoring of a particular behaviour can greatly influence reactivity. If the behaviour is monitored publicly this can act to either increase or decrease the

behaviour (depending on valence) to a greater extent than private monitoring. However, for some individuals public monitoring may cause embarrassment or anxiety and cause undue distress.

6 *Contiguity* Contiguity refers to time that passes between the behaviour occurring and the monitoring taking place. As might be expected, there is a greater reactive effect when the monitoring is close to the actual behaviour.

7 *Monitoring schedules* The monitoring schedule itself can increase or reduce the reactive effects of self-monitoring. As a rule the more frequent the self-monitoring becomes, the more likely it is that a reactive effect will occur.

8 *Nature and characteristics of the behaviour* In common with observational measurement, the more discrete the behaviour(s) being self-monitored the more accurate and reliable the assessment is likely to be. It follows therefore that there is potentially a greater reactive effect present when clearly defined and discrete behaviours are monitored.

9 *Motivation and expectation* The more motivated the person is towards the self-monitoring task, which may be closely linked with his or her expectations of the outcome of the task, the greater the reactive effect.

In total, the reactive effects associated with self-report measures are important because of their influences on the assessment information. Additionally, self-report measures may give an accurate measure of current behaviour but nonetheless inaccurately reflect behaviour before the measure was applied or behaviour when self-monitoring is not occurring. While it is important to be aware of these limiting factors, self-report has an important role to play in the assessment of a wide variety of both covert and overt behaviours. Standardized self-report measures have usually been evaluated by concurrent observation of the target behaviour but, as with any other type of measure, the use of self-report needs to be backed up by training in both observational skills and in the use of any specific assessment protocol.

Direct observation of behaviour

The direct observation and assessment of overt behaviour is a feature which distinguishes behaviour analysis from other, more traditional, psychological change techniques. However, the actual practice of direct observation is not, as commonly believed, a simple exercise. If observation is to be carried out effectively – by which we mean that some credence can be given to the resultant information – then, as detailed below, several conditions have to be met (Foster *et al.*, 1988). Effective management should seek to provide these conditions for good practice. Further, as these conditions make up the general observational 'system', they not only require setting up but also close monitoring and supervision.

First, the observer(s) need to have a sound knowledge of the strengths and weaknesses of observational recording methods. Second, the target behaviour needs to be exactly defined. Third, the correct type of observational measure has to be chosen. Fourth, the selected measuring device – checklist, rating scale, etc. – needs to be capable of accurately measuring the target behaviour.

Assuming these conditions are met, the final part of the 'system' is to ensure that observations are carried out correctly. As this relies on human behaviour it should not be assumed that it will 'just happen' because it is deemed as necessary or important. Observational systems are only as good as their weakest link, and it is our experience that the link is often the human element, and therefore requires the greatest management attention.

The essence of managing observational systems is to cut down on error and produce information that accurately reflects the behaviour of the target individual. (Direct observation can be carried out without individuals being aware that their behaviour is being monitored. If this is the case there would be no reactive effect from the assessment procedure. However, this raises the question of ethics with respect to informed consent. There are no right and wrong answers to this question, but it must be fully debated within an organization before any assessment work is started.) The following guidelines cover the key components for an observational system that will alert managers and practitioners to pitfalls, and help strengthen the use, reliability, and validity of observational assessment data.

Observational training

It is essential that observers are trained in direct observation including the points discussed below.

Operational definition of the target behaviour

The first step in managing the process of assessment is to decide what behaviours need to be observed and by what method(s). However, a feature of human language is that we tend to describe things, including other people's behaviour, in general terms. While we all recognize terms such as 'aggressive' or 'depressive', we do not always agree on exactly what they mean; therefore, for the purpose of behavioural observation, such terms are too general and too global. Defining the behaviour in terms that are more specific is not difficult. What is required is to translate the global terms into observable behaviours that can be seen to occur at specific times. Thus, in the case of aggression, we may wish to note the number of times a young person hits other people or throws an object across the room. These might be component behaviours subsumed under the global term 'aggression', but both these behaviours are observable and measurable in some way. An operational definition of the target behaviour must, therefore, specify exactly the behaviour to be assessed. This definition must be understood and agreed by all those involved in the observation. To ensure that this is the case – understanding and agreement in theory may not translate into practice! – it is essential that reliability checks are performed on the measure chosen for the assessment. These checks need not be complex or time-consuming; a simple but effective method is shown below.

Inter-observer agreement

An essential part of collecting information about an individual's behaviour by direct observation is to establish how reliable the observers are at actually recording the occurrence or non-occurrence of the target behaviour(s). Inter-observer agreement is established by comparing the results of information gathered from two or more observers measuring the same target behaviour at the same time. Ideally, 100 per cent agreement between the observers would be found; however in practice this is rarely the case. In order to work out the percentage agreement between observers a simple formula can be used:

$$\frac{\text{No. of agreed events}}{\text{No. of agreed events + no. of disagreed events}} \times 100 = \% \text{ agreement}$$

Managers should aim to achieve 85 per cent or greater agreement between the observers. Failure to reach this figure would suggest a problem with either (or both) the physical or human components of the measurement 'system'.

Choice of measure

Information from archival sources together with that from 'casual' observation should have suggested specific observable behaviours as the initial focus of the assessment. To allow collection of the assessment information, decisions must be made about what characteristics of the behaviour – including frequency, intensity, and duration – are most appropriate and how they might best be observed.

The exact method used will usually be a trade-off between the expense in terms of time and difficulty involved in gathering information and the accuracy of a given method. Ideally, the data collection method would provide a complete picture of the target behaviours, i.e. a quantitative continuous measure. In practice, however, less accurate measures are often an inevitable compromise. It is important, therefore, to select a method that will provide reasonably accurate information in a manageable way.

Having reached an operational definition of the target behaviour(s) it should be possible for an observer to return reliable and valid data across a range of settings. Obviously some behaviours are much more amenable to being measured using observational systems than others. In essence, the more discrete in nature the behaviour under consideration, the more easily it can be observed. Very high frequency or short duration behaviours (such as eye contact) can be difficult to measure without the use of video playback. Similarly, asking observers to return some form of qualitative measure of observed behaviour, as opposed to quantitative measure, relies on interpretation and subjectivity, and the subsequent information should be treated with caution.

TYPES OF MEASURE

There are several different types of measure that can be used when carrying out direct observation of behaviour. The type of measure used to assess the problem behaviour is very much determined by the general goals of the intervention programme. For example, suppose we are faced with the problem of a young person in a residential setting who calls out persistently and regularly at night after going to bed. Having checked the possibilities, it may be that he or she is calling out and asking for various things in order to draw out the amount of time taken to settle each night, and you may wish to note *how often* the child calls out each night. However, the aim of an intervention programme might be to reduce the amount of delaying tactics each night, so a more useful measure would be to note *how long* the calling lasts each night. Hence the assessment strategy of choice, a duration count, is decided by the overall aim of the programme. Planning prior to the main assessment phase can often save a great deal of time and effort, ensuring that helpful information is obtained at the first attempt, rather than having to repeat the operation, or try to make the data fit the problem!

Frequency counts

A frequency count is a measure of the number of times that a target behaviour occurs in a given period, which is usually averaged to produce an understandable measure, for example 8 times per day, or 56 times per week. This means we can discover whether a particular behaviour occurs episodically or consistently. It also gives rise to information regarding the clustering of behavioural events, which might prove valuable alongside other information such as specific locations, people, or events. There are several derivations of the straightforward frequency count that are important to mention.

Time sampling

This refers to the observation of the target behaviour(s) at specified periods throughout the young person's day. These times can be evenly or randomly spaced, but should be clearly specified to ensure that the observations are carried out. The advantage of this type of observation is that it tends to keep the observer 'on task' by concentrating his or her efforts into fixed periods of time, thus reducing bias problems such as observer drift (see below). It can also ensure that the observations are carried out at times when the behaviour under scrutiny is most likely to occur. There are several important factors to consider when managing assessment programmes that use time sampling.

First, it is important to realize that the sampled information is only a 'sample' and should not necessarily represent the 'true' level of behaviour. It may be that the target behaviour occurs at a much higher or lower level outside the monitoring periods. Second, sampling means that during the intervention period monitoring of the target behaviour should take place during the same periods as the initial assessment took place if an accurate comparison of behaviour is to be made. Third, to complete a functional analysis, it is important to get an accurate account of the situational factors (antecedents and consequences) relevant to both the occurrence and non-occurrence of the target behaviour during the assessment periods.

Interval recording

This is a type of frequency count with the focus of attention not on the total number of responses or events over time, but rather on whether a particular behaviour did or did not occur during specified equal intervals of time. For example, you may want to measure whether a young person uses offensive language (however defined). This can be carried out using interval recording such that any offensive comment in a specified period, say 5 minutes, counts as an event; more than one profanity in the same time block is not recorded. The benefit of recording only the occurrence of the behaviour in specific time blocks is its simplicity: the observer only has to record once per time period. This can be of great advantage when the frequency of the target behaviour is at a high rate, making recording all instances of the behaviour difficult if not impossible. Its disadvantage is the lack of accurate information regarding the exact frequency of the behaviour. Again it will be the aims of the subsequent intervention programme that will determine whether interval recording is the best method of assessment for any particular behaviour.

Duration and proportion recording

Duration recording, as its name suggests, is a measure of the period over which a particular behaviour is performed. For instance, you may wish to know how long a young person spends watching television. To measure time you could use a stopwatch, or mark off minutes on a devised checksheet. Either of these would give you an indication of the duration of the behaviour; the difference between the two provides an estimate of their accuracy and precision.

Proportion recording is very similar to duration recording but establishes the proportion of time, usually expressed as a percentage, the person spends engaged in one behaviour relative to another. For example, a teacher might be interested in measuring the relative amount of time a young person spends 'on task', i.e. engaged in work related behaviour, as opposed to 'off task'. This adds an additional dimension to the information that may be important during the intervention stage.

Both duration and proportional measures rely on the fact that the target behaviours are of sufficient duration to be able to be timed in some way – events lasting only milliseconds prove problematic! – and are sufficiently discrete to enable the observer to know when the behaviour starts and finishes.

Intensity or severity measures

Measures of the intensity or severity of a particular target behaviour are not easy to make, often having to rely on subjective opinion rather than objective measurement. For example, if an observer wished to gain some measure of a young person's volume of speech, he or she may have at their disposal a decibel meter which could give them fairly accurate objective measurement of the volume intensity. However, most of us do not have access to this type of technology, and will therefore have to rely on more subjective measurement. This is often done by asking the observer(s) to complete a rating scale, say asking observer(s) to indicate how loud they considered the person's speech to be. While this may not be as accurate as using an objective measure, providing some form of reliability check is carried out, the information from this type of assessment can be used with some confidence.

Categorization measures

Categorization measures, sometimes called discrete categorization, are commonly used as a measure of dichotomous behaviour. For example, a member of staff might be asked to record instances of appropriate as opposed to in-appropriate behaviour, or correct versus incorrect actions. This type of measure is easy to apply to a wide range of behaviours because it involves an assessment of only two clear options. It follows that categorization measures are often used to assess performance over a range of independent tasks that put together to form a particular skill. A simple example of this would be a young child dressing, where each article of clothing is assessed in terms of being put on correctly or in-correctly, the completed tasks forming the overall skill level. The individual tasks may be totally dissimilar but still form part of the complete performance. The information from this style of assessment can give a clear indication of which particular aspects of an individual's performance need attention and which are already present. This distinction can be very important in the overall management of an intervention programme in that it can focus attention on appropriate areas, saving time and effort in unnecessary work. It also points to 'asset behaviours' that can be built upon during intervention.

Information-gathering methods

Having examined the types of observational 'systems' that are available and of the most use, the next step in managing the process of assessment is to decide what behaviours need to be observed using what method(s). Information from archival sources with that from 'casual' observation may well have indicated specific observable behaviours that will be the focus of the initial assessment procedure.

Ideally, the assessment will provide a complete picture of the target behaviours, but in practice less accurate measures are often an inevitable com-promise. It is important, therefore, that the system can select an assessment method that will provide reasonably accurate information in a manageable way. In order to facilitate the collection of information, decisions must be made about what behavioural dimension – frequency, intensity, duration, etc. – is most appropriate. The assessment tools must permit easy, accurate collection of information about specific defined behaviours without undue inference and with minimal subjectivity. The final style of assessment used will usually be a managed compromise between the 'expense' involved in gathering information, in terms of time and difficulty, and the accuracy of a given method.

To guide managers, the following section briefly examines the types of assessment tools most commonly used in behavioural assessment, together with implications for their use in practice.

Checklists and ratings scales

Alongside interviewing, behaviour problem checklists and rating scales are the primary means of gathering information in child and adolescent behavioural assessment (e.g. Herbert, 1987b). The popularity of checklists and rating scales can be attributed to several factors. Such measures are economical and easy to administer and to score, in contrast to behavioural coding systems, which require expensive and specialized training (and sometimes equipment) for administration and scoring. Rating scales are also seemingly easy to construct, although this is deceptive unless factors such as the accuracy, reliability, and validity of the scale have been addressed. The multi-dimensional checklists (e.g. Herbert, 1993) survey a wide range of behaviours, thus enabling identification of problem behaviours that might be missed in an interview. Finally, checklists have also proved to be sensitive measures of treatment effects and can therefore be used as a measure for evaluating interventions.

In utilizing checklists and rating scales, those staff conducting the assessment are typically asked to assign a rating to one or more traits or behaviours. Behavioural checklists and rating scales vary with respect to both the number of items included and the range of behaviours sampled. The shorter checklists and scales tend to be uni-dimensional, for instance, assessing specific problem-solving skills (e.g. problem recognition, alternative solution generation). The longer checklists and scales, on the other hand, often sample a range of potentially problematic behaviours (e.g. sexual behaviour, social skills, life skills, classroom behaviour). Checklists also vary with regard to the specificity and objectivity of the items included in the scale.

While rating scales may aid in the identification of problem behaviours, information relevant to antecedent and consequent conditions that elicit and maintain target problems are not generally assessed in this way. Thus, behavioural assessment should include, but not be restricted to, the use of behavioural checklists and rating scales. However, it should be noted that checklists and rating scales can be affected by situational and contextual bias and errors, so detrimentally affecting the reliability and validity of the resultant data.

In order to manage assessment effectively it is important to understand how these errors can be avoided or at least minimized.

Errors in ratings

Ratings can be affected by many sources of error. A well-known example of the source of an error is the 'halo effect', that is, the tendency for staff completing the ratings to be unduly influenced by a single favourable or unfavourable trait, which then influences their judgement of the individual's other traits. One way to reduce the possibility of a halo effect is, as noted earlier, to ensure that the target behaviours being assessed are clearly operationally defined.

Another source of error in assessment ratings is the 'error of central tendency', this refers to clustering of ratings in the middle of a scale, avoiding the high and low ratings. Yet another rating error is the 'error of leniency', as when raters show a reluctance to assign low or unfavourable scores. An 'error of severity' can also occur – 'Nobody gets an "A" in my class!' – although this is generally less common (Anastasi, 1982).

Overall, training is probably the best strategy for eliminating, or at least reducing, rater bias and error (Ivancevich, 1979).

Rater training

Rating procedures and the subsequent assessment can usually be improved by training raters to use the specific instrument(s) in question. Research in various settings has demonstrated the effectiveness of rater training in both increasing the reliability of ratings data and in reducing common judgemental errors (Bernadin and Pence, 1980; Landy and Farr, 1980). However, many different types of training have been included in rater training programmes, and their effects vary in kind, amount, and duration. Training may involve familiarization with the use of a particular rating format; strengthening rater knowledge of job requirements; analysis of common rating errors and ways of minimizing their influence; or improvement of observational skills. Any combination of these types of training could be appropriate, depending on the particular context in which the rating is conducted. In most situations, however, enhancing the raters' observational skills is likely to yield favourable results (Anastasi, 1982). Finally, the design of the rating sheet can have specific effects on the quality of the resultant information, with both trained and untrained raters (Kendrick, 1984).

FUNCTIONAL ANALYSIS

Functional analysis is the framework used in behavioural analysis to describe the relationship between the environment and the person. Functional analysis views current behaviour in relationship to both antecedent, setting events, and the environmental consequences of the behaviour (see Chapter 1). These environ-

mental conditions are thus directly related to both the learning and the modification of learned behaviour. In the functional analysis of a particular behaviour,
both the antecedent and consequential environmental conditions should be identified, together with any changes over time in the relationship between environmental factors and the behaviour. In simplest terms, functional analysis is an
attempt to answer the question 'Why?'. Why does the person behave as he does?
In what settings does the behaviour occur? Why is a particular behaviour being
maintained? Further, any individual's behaviour is not static, but rather reflects a
dynamic, shifting interchange between the person and his or her environment.

The focus of functional analysis should be not only to specify topographical
descriptions of a person's behaviour (i.e. what he or she does), but, more important, to specify functional descriptions (i.e. what he or she *gets* in terms of pay-offs
for what he or she does). In practice, the assessment is not simply focused on
target behaviour(s) but also on the examination and analysis of 'clusters' of
behaviour, together with the identification of the interrelationships between
behaviours in terms of antecedent and consequential events. The quality of a
functional analysis is clearly affected by the accuracy, reliability, and validity of
the assessment methods. Therefore, as previously stated, it is important to control
sources of variability in gathering assessment information.

From a practical standpoint, the emphasis must be on a person-centred
analysis that recognizes individual differences in young people's behaviour and
the causes of their behaviour. The focus must be on understanding the behaviour
from the young person's point of view, understanding the function of the
behaviour for him or her personally, rather than from the point of view of the
member of staff conducting the assessment. It is this aspect of practice that often
calls for the closest management when constructing a functional analysis. Those
conducting the assessment must examine, compare, and cross-reference information, rather than offer their own favourite interpretation. Many experienced
and proficient therapists are used to making clinical judgements of a person's
behaviour based on their own 'theory' of human functioning. While not dis-
counting this expertise, functional analysis does demand the rigour to apply a set
of theoretical principles to reach an understanding of the assessment information.

The A:B:C model (see Chapter 1) is the essential building block for functional
analysis. Determining A:B:Cs for discrete behaviours is often not too difficult,
but with more complex behaviours it can be a demanding task (e.g. Gresswell and
Hollin, 1992). An analysis of behaviour in terms of the functional relationship
between individual behaviours, groups of behaviours, and the environment can
take a great deal of time, effort, skill, and practice and will profit from close
supervision.

On some occasions a functional analysis is comparatively easy to formulate.
For example, suppose a child is trying to gain his or her parent's attention when
the parent is otherwise engaged. The child may pull the parent's clothing, shout,
stamp, throw an object across the room, or lie back and kick. A simple A:B:C
analysis reveals the following picture as shown in Table 3.5.

Table 3.5 Simple A:B:C analysis of functionally similar inappropriate behaviour which may be displayed by a child to gain parental attention

A Parent occupied
   Child wants something (e.g. food, attention)

B Temper display (e.g. cries, screams, shouts, throws object, stamps, pulls parent's clothing)

C Gains parental attention
   Gets given desired object

If we now examine the basic theoretical premises that underpin functional analysis, it should be possible to reach a working hypothesis that offers an account of the behaviour(s), and so informs the most likely effective intervention strategy.

Theoretical premises – the basis for practice

There are two premises at the foundations of the whole model.

1 The rate or frequency of behaviour is governed by the consequences of that behaviour; i.e. the frequency of future behaviour is related to the pay-offs that behaviour gains from the environment. For example, if a child gets rewarding attention by exhibiting inappropriate behaviour, then the next time he or she wants attention the child is likely to behave in a similar manner. In other words, the A:B:C sequence in Table 3.5 exemplifies a positive reinforcement contingency.

2 The immediate environment at the time the behaviour occurs – the antecedent or setting conditions – will play an important part in determining whether a given behaviour will occur again. Simply, setting conditions come to predict for the person concerned the availability (should they behave in a particular way) of consequences that will maintain, increase, or decrease behaviour. This establishes a very important point: the consequences of a current behaviour can serve as antecedents to future behaviour. See Hollin (1990a) and Gresswell and Hollin (1992) for worked case examples.

Putting the theory into practice

The A:B:C format has been established as the basic building block of functional analysis, and the associated theoretical premises above give us a framework for understanding behaviour. With the assessment completed and information available, what steps are needed in practice to make 'sense' of the behaviour? There are certain features that the behavioural practitioner can look for and identify in a person's behaviour that will greatly aid analysis (Herbert, 1987b).

Table 3.6 A:B:C analysis of temper loss by young person illustrating antecedent and consequential variables

A Young person wishes to go to friend's house
   Parents demand he or she tidies their bedroom before going

B Temper loss (may include) actual assault, property damage

C Parents allow young person to go to friend's house
   Bedroom not tidied

The *ratio of behaviours to consequences* is not always constant in that several behaviours may have one consequence, or one behaviour may have several consequences. For example, any one or any combination of the behaviours noted in Table 3.5 may be successful in gaining parental attention. To that extent all the behaviours are functionally *similar*, that is, they serve the same purpose. However, they are all topographically *dissimilar* in that the form of the behaviour is different, the structure is different, and the severity is different. Thus a range of dissimilar behaviours is being maintained by a single set of consequences. In this style of analysis a single A:B:C arrangement will serve the purpose of making sense of the case information.

However, it is also true that *consequences may change over time* in that the environmental factors currently maintaining a behaviour may be different from those prevailing at the onset of that same behaviour. This suggests we need to look for changes over time in the consequences maintaining the same behaviour. This in turn may lend itself to a style of analysis based on multiple sequential functional analyses. For example, assume that the hypothetical child in the above example has reached adolescence without earlier problems having been resolved. Despite growing older, the temper outbursts are still cause for concern in that while less frequent, they are generally more violent in nature. An A:B:C analysis might reveal something along the lines shown in Table 3.6.

Table 3.6 shows a similar behaviour pattern to Table 3.5, but note that the consequences have changed: attention is no longer the prime consequence – although that is not to say it does not still play a part in the maintenance of the behaviour. The key consequence now maintaining the behaviour is the gain in control over the behaviour of other people, thus displaying inappropriate behaviour is positively reinforcing, while avoiding work and reducing adult pressures is a negative reinforcement contingency.

Finally, the point should be made that *behaviour may change over time* yet may still be governed by the same set of consequences. To follow our example, suppose the adolescent is now an adult, married and working, and, for this example is a male. His behaviour is still cause for concern. His partner reports that he is 'idle' and 'very demanding', refusing to do anything except the most basic jobs around the house, yet expecting her to do everything. If she fails to

Table 3.7 A:B:C analysis of adult work avoidance behaviours

A General maintenance needed around house
   Has full-time employment
   Spouse complains of incompleted work

B Complains of illness
   Complains about work stressors

C Avoids working on house
   Avoids further negative comments from spouse
   Avoids full-time employment

meet his expectations or requests help, he will often become very angry, then calm down and complain about how hard he has to work and how unfair life is. This develops into his complaining about how ill he feels, followed by periods of silent, morose behaviour. Things are not good at work either: his attendance record is poor, and he is frequently absent owing to reported headaches. The standard of his work has led to several reprimands, often followed by a period of absence, and he is generally considered lazy.

Now we can look at the behaviour pattern in terms of an A:B:C analysis (Table 3.7). The consequences for the behaviour are very similar to those in the previous analysis. However, there has been a change in the behaviour pattern from aggressive to passive attention-seeking and work-avoidance behaviours.

Our analysis of behaviour over time has revealed that there have been many changes in antecedent conditions, behaviour patterns, and associated consequences. We are left, however, with a clear indication of the present problematic behavioural repertoire and the current maintaining factors for these behaviours. We also have a picture about how the current difficulties may have developed. This may be interesting and may help us to understand current issues, but should not be seen as causal. Parental indulgence or inability to handle temper outbursts does not necessarily explain the current behaviour. It simply informs us that the person has a long learning history of inappropriate behaviour. Current behaviour has to be explained in terms of the current situation, and this should be the basis of any subsequent treatment programme. After all, to follow the fictitious case example, it would be ridiculous to introduce for the adult an intervention to reduce the amount of aggressive attention-demanding behaviour directed at his parents, although twenty years ago that was precisely what was needed.

In summary, we have tried to explain in this section how, using stated theoretical concepts, human behaviour can be analysed and understood in terms of its function for the individual. As we have further tried to show, this does not mean that historical factors are unimportant; they may be crucial to both our understanding and plans for intervention. Conversely, historical factors may be

Table 3.8 Key issues in assessment

- Pre-intervention assessment should take place
- Baseline data should be collected
- Programmes should be of single case design
- Use multi-modal assessment
- Concentrate on facts rather than opinion
- Always train interviewers
- Use a strategy and structure in interviews
- Self-report measures are usually affected by reactivity
- Reactivity should be kept to a minimum during assessment
- With observation, operationally define the target behaviour(s) and train the observers
- Check reliability of observer data and alter the 'system' as necessary
- Use the A:B:C format to identify behaviours

of interest but irrelevant to the present issues. This is for the practitioner to decide in formulating a testable hypothesis that offers an account of the current behaviour pattern.

A workable model?

We have presented an analysis using a chronological sequence of individual A:B:C formulations. We believe that this format provides a workable model for analysing an individual's behaviour pattern because it focuses attention on specific behaviours and the associated antecedent and consequential conditions. It allows the practitioner to see the interrelationship between individual behaviours, and to identify both commonality and differences in the controlling variables. It also simplifies the explanation of the problem to others by high-lighting only the relevant information.

The written assessment

In most cases a single or sequential A:B:C analysis needs to be complemented by a written report, but this only needs to report the major factors of the analysis. A common presentational style with functional analysis is to construct a flow diagram. There are three problems inherent in this form of representation of case information. First, the flow diagrams themselves are surprisingly difficult to construct, primarily because of the complexity of the interaction between the behaviours and the relevant As and Cs. Second, in analyses of complex behaviour patterns it is often found that the person who drew the flow diagram is the only person who can make any sense of it! This inevitably leads to an additional explanatory narrative account having to be written, which not only offers an account of the analysis but also an explanation of the flow diagram. Third, flow diagrams with their linking lines and arrows are often read as implying causal relationships between the factors contained in the boxes. Although there may be links between parts of the diagram, they do not need to be causal in nature.

The final point we would like to make concerns the integrity of the process of assessment, analysis, and design of the intervention programme. To ensure consistency of approach, to optimize the collection of assessment information, focus the analysis, and train and maintain staff performance it is essential to keep the 'system' as simple as possible. By concentrating everyone's attention, at all stages of the programme, on the identification of both behaviours and their controlling As and Cs, the 'recipe' remains stable and all concerned understand what they are meant to be doing. This is good management. In this chapter we have pointed to a number of key issues that need to be addressed to conduct a successful behavioural assessment. We have taken a pragmatic approach in an attempt to offer guidance to supervisors and managers. As stated in Chapter 1, it is a mistake to assume that the behavioural approach is essentially simplistic or just common sense. Practitioners need to be well trained in both the theoretical and practical aspects of their work (see Chapter 5). Equally important is the need to be well supervised and managed if they are to carry out the task properly.

This chapter has covered a great deal of important information, Table 3.8 highlights the major management issues discussed in this chapter.

Finally, it must be remembered that although good assessment and analysis do not ensure good programmes, it is difficult to see how good programmes can be designed without good assessment. The management of behavioural intervention is considered in the following chapter.

Chapter 4

Designing and managing the treatment regime

Having looked at various factors that have a bearing on the shape and structure of an organization dealing with difficult and delinquent young people (Chapter 2), and having considered the role of assessment in the development of effective behavioural programmes (Chapter 3), we now turn our attention to the design and management of treatment programmes. It is important to state at the outset that no organization can afford to leave to chance the question of what techniques to adopt to bring about behaviour change. An overriding concern must be to identify those factors that will enhance the chances of success and minimize programme failure. The aim of this chapter is not so much to outline what methods and techniques are most effective in producing change (see Chapter 1), but to suggest how the process of treatment should be managed to maximize effectiveness and efficiency of resources.

THE CONCEPT OF TREATMENT IN RELATION TO DELINQUENCY

Before moving on to look at how best to approach the behavioural treatment of difficult and delinquent young people, it is worth examining some assumptions relating to the treatment of delinquents. As explained in the Preface, in many ways the word 'treatment' is unsuitable: it is closely associated with a medical model, with the implicit assumption that the behaviour being treated is the manifestation of some underlying organic (or psychological) disorder or pathology. A psychopathological approach can also reinforce the notion held by many behaviourally disordered young people and their parents that their problems are beyond their control and have a physical cause. Many delinquent young people entering treatment programmes expect something to be done *to* them so that they will be cured, and assume that their role is a passive rather than an active one. Nevertheless, it is difficult to find a suitable substitute for the term 'treatment' and so we do use this word here, acknowledging openly all the problems inherent in its use.

It is also necessary to justify the treatment of difficult and delinquent young people. Why not leave them alone? Some, after all, may leave their adolescent problems behind as they mature into adulthood. Further, what proof is there that treatment can be successful? If something has to be done, why not simply contain and manage their behaviour?

There is neither the space nor the intention here to review in detail all the outcome studies that have looked at the effectiveness of behavioural treatment of difficult and delinquent young people, whether in residential or community settings. As discussed in Chapter 1 with regard to the recent meta-analytic studies, there is substantial evidence that structured, focused, skill-based interventions can help to produce significant and long-lasting changes in the behaviour of delinquent young people (Andrews *et al.*, 1990; Garrett, 1985; Lipsey, 1992a, 1992b). There is also evidence that many difficult, disturbed, and delinquent young people do change without specialist intervention, perhaps through natural developmental processes such as psychological maturation and changes in social circumstances. This in turn suggests that if left alone young people might grow out of crime (Rutherford, 1986).

Both sides of the argument have a grain of truth. Some, perhaps most, young people will grow out of crime; however, some young people do not change and will continue to experience problems into adulthood, also inflicting damage to others (e.g. Millham *et al.*, 1989). Although some of these young people may refuse the opportunity to be helped, some actually ask for help, and many others can be encouraged over time to participate in treatment programmes, in the context of a supportive relationship based on honesty and trust.

It should also be remembered that the aim of working with delinquent young people is not always directly concerned with the reduction of reoffending rates. Many delinquent adolescents are tormented and troubled by their personal difficulties and the consequences they produce for themselves and their families. For example, young people with poor social skills may be marginalized by their peer group, find it difficult to form meaningful and lasting relationships, and suffer further damage to their self-esteem and confidence that, in turn, may increase the risk of reoffending (Calabrese and Adams, 1990). The question of whether treatment does reduce recidivism is an empirical one, and is rarely the sole *raison d'être* for treatment. However, it is important that any evaluation of treatment outcome should clearly distinguish between *clinical* (or *personal change*) and *criminogenic* outcomes (Hollin, 1990a; Hollin and Henderson, 1984). For example, it is reasonable to assume that training a young person in assertion skills should lead to improved personal performance in situations requiring assertive behaviour (i.e. clinical or personal change); it does not necessarily follow that this will reduce the risk of further offending behaviour (although this would obviously be a very desirable outcome).

SETTING THE SCENE FOR TREATMENT

Chapter 2 outlined some important factors that need to be considered when creating an environment and ethos that facilitates and promotes behaviour change in difficult and delinquent young people. There are, however, additional factors that have a direct bearing on the behavioural treatment of young people. Three sets of factors can be identified: (1) adolescent developmental processes; (2)

legal and ethical considerations; (3) the treatment setting. Each of these factors helps to set a limit on the extent to which behavioural change can be brought about. It is important that practitioners working with young people have a good understanding of each of these areas. It follows that they should be addressed in staff training (see Chapter 5). Before moving on to look at the design and management of behavioural treatment programmes, it is worthwhile looking at each of these areas in more detail.

Adolescent developmental processes

As shown in Table 4.1, there are four main sets of processes that can be identified and that help to differentiate adolescence from other developmental periods (Coleman and Hendry, 1990). Needless to say, adolescence is a time of change, and each of these four sets of processes have extensive effects on the lives of young people. It is important to place behavioural treatment within this overall context of change.

There are, in particular, two factors that have important implications for treatment: *behavioural instability* and *psychological denial and avoidance.*

Behavioural instability

While most adolescents survive until adulthood relatively unscathed, without the need for professional psychiatric or psychological intervention (Rutter *et al.*, 1976), many young people do experience some difficulty in adjusting to the

Table 4.1 Developmental processes during adolescence

Process	Consequence
Puberty	growth spurt; increase in weight; increased muscle development/strength; body proportions change; increase in sex drive and sexual activity; acne; body hair
Cognitive	increase in hypothetical thinking; increase in arithmetical and logical reasoning; increased self-awareness; interest in moral, religious, political ideas; educational demands
Social	increased social expectations and competence; peer pressure; formation of social and sexual relations; cultural and personal identity formation
Family	increased freedom and autonomy; family conflict; becoming independent; leaving home

demands of adolescence. Feelings of misery and self-depreciation, for example, are relatively common during adolescence (Rutter *et al.*, 1976). There are also important social changes during adolescence that place extra demands on young people's social functioning. For example, there is usually the transition from a protective primary school environment to a larger and more complex secondary school, which can affect adversely self-esteem and self-consciousness (Blyth *et al.*, 1978; Simmons *et al.*, 1979). These disruptions in psychological and social functioning can give rise to new behavioural problems or, as is probably more commonly the case, exacerbate existing difficulties.

Psychological denial and avoidance

The successful treatment of difficult and delinquent young people is often a complex and arduous task. A frequent complaint among practitioners working with young people is the problem of engaging the adolescent in the treatment process. Behavioural practitioners certainly require a degree of creativity and flexibility in adapting particular methods and techniques to the needs of this client group. Adolescents are often ambivalent about the need for personal change, and this ambivalence can be expressed in a variety of ways: failure to attend treatment sessions; reluctance to talk about themselves, or specific aspects of their lives; denial and avoidance of specific problems; failure to complete homework assignments (e.g. self-report diaries); and dropping out of treatment programmes.

Many of these difficulties are exacerbated in delinquents, who often have poorly developed verbal and social skills, and frequently lead chaotic and disordered life styles where stability and predictability have not been significant features. In this light it is not surprising that some behavioural practitioners are reluctant to work with young people. It can be a punishing experience to work with a client group who are resistant to change, and present obstacles when efforts are made to help.

Sanson-Fisher and Jenkins (1978) looked at the effects on staff behaviour of negative social interactions in a study of interaction patterns between inmates and staff in a maximum security institution for delinquent young people. This study found that staff responded to most inmate behaviour, no matter whether that behaviour was appropriate. Only a small proportion of staff behaviour involved the creation of constructive opportunities for inmates to learn and to exhibit appropriate behaviour. Sanson-Fisher and Jenkins suggested that this low rate of desirable staff behaviour may have been the result of a pattern of coercion: since the inmate group behaved negatively towards therapeutic opportunities but gave positive attention to other staff behaviours, the delinquents shaped the style of staff behaviour. This process of negative coercion is similar to that described by Wahl *et al.* (1974) and by Patterson (1982) through which antisocial children control their parents' behaviour.

Clearly, any programme attempting to increase pro-social behaviour in difficult and delinquent young people must attend to these patterns of social behaviour.

Failure to do so will almost certainly guarantee programme failure. Throughout this chapter various techniques and strategies will be suggested to overcome client resistance and to develop a social environment conducive to behavioural change. Staff training is also essential: staff must learn to discriminate between appropriate and inappropriate behaviour, and to control their own responses.

Legal and ethical considerations

As emphasized in Chapter 2 and as covered in Chapter 6, it is important to recognize the significance of legal issues in the behavioural treatment of young people. The legal framework surrounding work with young people is complex and serves many different functions: one function is to protect the rights of young people from abuse and violation, and the rights of others who have an interest in the young person, such as parents or guardians. The legal framework also helps to make clear who – parents, the local authority, the organization offering treatment, or the young person – has legal responsibility for the care and treatment of a young person. It is important to clarify issues of responsibility before treatment begins. Young people are often referred for treatment without being consulted, and it is therefore not surprising that they are sometimes poorly motivated and uncooperative. Where young people enter treatment under a legal restriction, such as a section of the 1983 Mental Health Act, or on a probation order, it is equally important to be clear where responsibility lies, and to monitor the conditions attached to the restriction order.

Managers should be aware of the need for long-term planning to ensure that sufficient time is available to achieve treatment targets. There is little point in setting ambitious treatment objectives if the young person is likely to be discharged or relocated after a few weeks.

The use of behavioural techniques with young people has often aroused suspicion that the very use of such techniques means that rights are being violated. These views are often held by people with a limited understanding of behavioural theory and practice, who associate behavioural work solely with classical conditioning and aversive techniques, and see behavioural approaches as cold, mechanistic, and non-humanistic (Clements, 1992). This could not be further from the truth. The emphasis in a true behavioural approach is on individuals and their relationship with their physical and social environment. This is entirely consistent with the 1989 Children Act, which stresses the need for individualized child-care planning and treatment. Further, it is only right that young people are fully consulted about their involvement in treatment programmes of any type, and that they have the right to complain to an independent representative. When used properly, behavioural approaches, like any other approach, will respect the rights of the individual. For example, the need for individual consent to treatment is stressed, and effort should be devoted to ensuring that clients understand what treatment entails, including the possibility of any deleterious or adverse consequences.

Behavioural approaches also have the advantage of making explicit any ethical problems surrounding the use of particular techniques. Ethics committees are commonly found in organizations operating behavioural methods of treatment. Behavioural work with difficult and delinquent young people occasionally produces ethical dilemmas and the presence of an ethics committee consisting of both professionals and lay people is essential.

Particular problems can arise, for example, when using intrusive assessment or treatment techniques. For example, penile plethysmography (PPG) is frequently used to measure sexual arousal in recidivistic adult sex offenders (Simon and Schouten, 1991). PPG is a technique used to measure male sexual arousal. An electronic device called a penile transducer is attached to the penis by the client. It detects changes in the size of the sexual organ from a state of no sexual arousal (flaccidity) to a state of complete arousal (full erection). If stimuli of both deviant and non-deviant content are presented to a client while measuring his sexual response, the associated degrees of erection can provide an indication of his sexual interests, preferences, and inhibitions.

The use of PPG with young people is controversial, partly because of the intrusiveness of the technique and partly because assessment may involve exposing the client to pornographic material. It may be the case, however, that treatment of some sex offenders requires the use of the PPG. If this is so, one could argue that young people have the same right to this form of treatment as adults. The task of a professional ethics committee would be to decide whether this kind of technique is permissible even when the young person fully consents to its use and, if so, what are the conditions of its use. Clearly, these kinds of issues cannot be resolved by individual practitioners, and neither should they be. It is important to recognize that those who have responsibility for the treatment of particularly disturbed and dangerous young people often feel under pressure to produce changes in the behaviour of their clients. Indeed, a failure to do so is sometimes condemned in public, especially when a young person is released from an institution and reoffends in a serious way. It is our firm contention that the issue of what constitutes an acceptable form of treatment should not be the sole province of individual practitioners, or even organizations, but should be an issue for public opinion and debate. An ethics committee can be the first forum in which to test out ideas in the presence of non-specialist lay people.

The treatment setting

The third and final factor that helps to determine treatment outcome is the setting in which treatment is conducted. Again it is worth emphasizing some of the main points made in this respect in Chapter 2, particularly with respect to the way that they influence the management of the treatment process.

Generalization

Behaviourally disordered and delinquent young people are treated in a variety of settings, ranging from residential secure facilities, to outpatient psychiatric clinics, to community-based probation programmes. Each of these different settings has advantages and disadvantages that determine the extent to which behaviour change takes place and can be maintained over the long term, that is, the degree to which new behaviour can be generalized to the real world (see Figure 2.3).

Highly structured settings, such as secure facilities and open residential units, can have a greater impact on behaviour in the short term. Such settings have several advantages, including: the potential to set up structured daily routines; continuous observation of clients' behaviour; easier control over reinforcement contingencies; higher levels of staff and client interaction; and greater control over the implementation of treatment programmes, through staff supervision and monitoring.

Outcome research into the residential treatment of delinquency suggests that significant changes in behaviour can be brought about in residential settings (Braukmann *et al.*, 1985; Kirigin *et al.*, 1982). However, the residential programmes that stand the greatest chance of long-term success are those that plan for the careful reintegration of young people into the community as early as possible, and maintain close links with family members and other significant people for the young person.

Managers should aim to promote and facilitate the process of generalization. The allocation of specific tasks to members of the multidisciplinary team responsible for planning the care, management, and treatment of the young person needs to be carefully decided. For example, it needs to be agreed who should work with the family and who should identify and investigate potential future placements. In addition, the use of goal-planning helps to promote forward thinking, such that long-term aims and objectives can be clarified and appropriate action taken to meet those objectives. For example, some possible future placements can be discounted at an early stage, enabling efforts to be directed into other possibilities. Less than successful residential programmes return young people to the community with little in the way of preparation, planning, support, and after-care. The importance of maintaining family and community links is made clear by the findings of several studies. Children and young people who are separated from their parents often become isolated, and find it difficult to preserve a relationship with their parents (Millham *et al.*, 1986), or to develop strong links with substitute parents (Berridge and Cleaver, 1987). Such children may also fail to establish close relationships with their peers (Tizard *et al.*, 1975), and are likely to be educationally disadvantaged (Jackson, 1987).

There is no room for complacency: it cannot be assumed that positive behaviour change that takes place during a programme will generalize back to 'real world' settings when residents are discharged. Even the most highly regarded programmes, such as the Achievement Place projects in the USA, have struggled to produce long-term behaviour change (Kirigin *et al.*, 1982). In truth, more research is needed to show which factors help to promote generalization.

Relevancy

One of the keys to success lies in making programmes *relevant* to the young people involved. We have already seen earlier in this chapter that certain developmental and psychological processes associated with adolescence create obstacles to treatment. Treatment programmes frequently emphasize targets that are perceived by *staff* as the most important areas for behaviour change. Little or no account is taken of the young person's point of view, while assessment is non-existent. It is not unusual, for example, to find delinquent adolescents participating in social skills training or anger management groups but with little idea of why they are attending or what relevance the group has for them personally. If behavioural programmes are to be successful then it is essential that close attention is given to the young person's own agenda, and that all those parties involved agree on the targets for change.

The issue of relevance assumes particular significance within residential contexts. Admission to a residential setting is disruptive and unsettling and can demand a considerable amount of readjustment and adaptation, especially if the young person has never lived away from home. Occasionally the move is a traumatic life event, especially for young people with a history of poor peer relationships. It can take weeks or months for young people to adjust to new settings, during which time their personal agenda may be very different from that of the staff. Some key points regarding relevance are shown in Table 4.2.

Table 4.2 Factors that enhance treatment relevance

Young people should be:
- fully involved in the selection of treatment goals and objectives;
- made aware of the time-scale within which treatment will take place;
- helped to understand the likely outcomes of treatment;
- kept informed of likely placement options upon leaving the treatment programme.

Those responsible for organizing and delivering programmes should:
- be aware of stresses and life events that may undermine treatment objectives;
- try to timetable treatment initiatives to coincide with relevant life experiences;
- try to ensure that new behavioural skills are heavily reinforced in the natural environment.

In contrast to highly structured settings, the strength of diversion and community-based programmes (Davidson *et al.*, 1990; Preston, 1982) lies not in their ability to bring about behavioural change in the short term, but in developing a long-term working relationship. Community-based treatment programmes avoid many problems inherent in residential treatment, with the additional advantage that they can be cheaper. Further, once young people are engaged in such programmes their progress can be monitored over time and additional support offered at times of stress and crisis. Unfortunately, many delinquent adolescents are reluctant to take part in such programmes, or are judged to be so difficult and dangerous that community treatment is not an option. The use of probation orders that specify the need for treatment is one way to encourage young offenders to attend regular treatment sessions.

Ideally, a range of settings should be available for the behavioural treatment of difficult and delinquent young people. Some delinquent adolescents who are too disruptive to be involved in community-based programmes may profit from a short period of stabilization and containment in a safe, structured setting, where they can be engaged in treatment before moving to a less restricted setting. Unfortunately, there is often a mismatch between the sentencing practices dictated by the juvenile justice system and the treatment needs of many young offenders. This is not to say that all delinquent adolescents need treatment. We have already seen in Chapter 1 that crime in young people is the result of a complex interaction of influences operating at a variety of levels. It is true to say that many difficult and delinquent adolescents are not given the opportunity to be involved in individualized, structured, systematic programmes aimed at reducing the risk of reoffending.

DESIGNING BEHAVIOURAL MANAGEMENT SYSTEMS

The distinction between management and treatment is in many ways an artificial one, but one that nevertheless serves a useful purpose. One aim of behavioural management is to ensure that adequate resources are available to contain and cope with behaviour on a short-term basis. Failure to manage difficult behaviour may mean, at worst, the young person being discharged or expelled from the programme, thus denying him or her the opportunity of treatment and personal change. At best it may mean the young people being reluctantly tolerated, with so much time and energy spent trying to cope with their behaviour that there is little left to engage them in the treatment. The extent to which behaviour is successfully managed will be decided in the main by two factors: (1) the amount and quality of available resources (e.g. number of staff, staff skills, building design and structure); (2) the demands made by the young person to be managed, in terms of the frequency, intensity, and seriousness of his or her behaviour. When deciding whether to admit a young person into a treatment programme, it is essential that the programme director or manager has access to information about both these factors.

Resources

We have already seen in Chapter 2 that it is possible to monitor and evaluate the working of a programme for delinquent and behaviourally disordered adolescents. At any time the programme director should be able to specify with reasonable accuracy the amount of spare capacity available in the programme. It should also be possible to plan ahead, so that fluctuations in available resources – e.g. staff absences due to planned sick leave or annual leave, staff turnover, and building work – can be anticipated. The availability of money to buy equipment and reinforcers is another important consideration that has been frequently related to the failure of behavioural programmes (Repucci and Saunders, 1974; Tharp and Wetzel, 1969).

Behavioural demands

Young people enter treatment programmes for a variety of reasons. The use of admission criteria, of the kind described in Chapter 2, often defines the kinds of young people who enter particular programmes. With respect to management there are two types of problems that need careful consideration: as shown in Table 4.3 these are *behavioural excesses* and *clinical problems*. Often these types of problems determine whether a young person can be managed successfully, regardless of whether they were the main reason for referral and admission to the programme.

Assessment of the young person before admission is always desirable. Information should be gathered from as many sources as possible, including caregivers and professionals previously involved with the young person.

A successful behavioural management system is one that achieves the following goals.

1 *It establishes a calm, relaxed living environment for the young people and the staff.* The aversive features frequently found in the social environment of delin- quent young people, such as threats, bullying, and racist and abusive

Table 4.3 Behavioural management problems

1. *Behavioural excesses*

Physical violence to staff/other young people; verbal aggression and swearing; bullying other young people; non-compliance; damage to property; fire-setting; sexual assaults on staff/other young people; sexual misbehaviour (e.g. indecent exposure, public masturbation); self-injurious behaviour (e.g. self-cutting, head-banging, self-strangulation, overdoses); absconding

2. *Clinical problems*

Enuresis/encopresis; faecal smearing; obsessive/compulsive problems (e.g. washing/dressing routines); depression; anxiety/phobic disorders; substance abuse; social withdrawal; attempted suicide; hyperactivity language, often serve as antecedents to further behavioural problems. For example, young people frequently abscond from residential settings to avoid further bullying and violence from other residents. The removal of aversive 'setting events' helps to reduce incidents of this kind, and creates a more relaxed, tension-free living environment. Dean and Repucci (1974) describe how the introduction of a token economy programme helped to restore equilibrium during a time of crisis at the Connecticut School for Boys in the USA.

By the same yardstick, staff are more likely to be pleasant and helpful if the young people with whom they work do not abuse them and each other; this reduces the risks of staff burn-out (Corcoran, 1988). Staff who perceive themselves as in a caring role, yet are exposed to harassment, threats, and abuse on a daily basis may find themselves becoming emotionally exhausted and depersonalized. Depersonalization serves to distance the member of staff from the source of stress, namely the young person. This emotional and psychological detachment may be perceived by others, especially the young people themselves, as indifference and disregard. Inevitably, staff who are depersonalized are unlikely to provide an effective service, which in turn can result in low self-esteem, depression, or other problems associated with burn-out.

2 *It sets clear behavioural limits.* Many delinquent adolescents come from backgrounds characterized by disorganization, instability, and unpredictability. An effective behavioural management regime should make the environment predictable, so that there is structure and routine in daily life, and the consequences following specific behaviours are both foreseeable and justifiable. Many young people with a history of delinquency often have a strong sense of justice, though their idea of what is right or wrong may be at odds with that of most other people! A management system that explicitly sets out the rules, and the consequences that follow rule-breaking, therefore has a certain appeal. An example of a management rule is shown in Table 4.4. This kind of system removes the mystery from a world that often appears to deliver random, unjust, and unpredictable consequences. It also provides a forum in which rules can be challenged verbally, giving young people a feeling of participation and control: they may not agree with the rule but they come to understand why it exists and the underlying rationale. This openness and sense of 'fair play' help to minimize the suspiciousness and hostility often found in delinquent young people, who themselves have frequently been the victims of neglect, abuse, and rejection (Burgess *et al.*, 1987).

3 *It provides performance feedback.* It is well established that many delinquent young people, especially those who exhibit disturbances in behavioural and emotional functioning, come from backgrounds characterized by physical and emotional deprivation, poor parenting, abuse, and rejection (e.g. Burgess *et al.*, 1987; Stein and Lewis, 1992; West, 1982). One consequence of such abusive experiences is an impaired sense of perceived social and cognitive competence, and a lowered level of self-worth (Cole *et al.*, 1989). Many delinquents lack confidence and tend not to set goals or plan ahead. Often they have had little in

Table 4.4 Example of a management rule

Rule: No smoking in security
Management policy: Smoking in security is considered a breach of security regulations.
Consequences: If a young person is found smoking in security, or in the possession of cigarettes, matches or lighters, he or she will:
1 Have their room searched by a member of staff. Young people can be present while the search is undertaken.
2 Have all cigarettes, matches and lighters confiscated. These will be returned upon leaving security.
3 Lose all privileges for 2 nights.
4 Lose access to late night television for 2 nights.
5 Have no social contact with young people from other units for 2 days.
The incident will also be reported to the Centre Manager.

the way of consistent feedback or the encouragement from parents, teachers, or peers that, in Harter's (1981) view, is important for the development of self-competence. Frequently, delinquent young people fail to plan or to set realistic goals. The use of external social reinforcement and feedback, and help in planning and organizing activities, is therefore important for the effective management of this group of young people.

TYPES OF BEHAVIOURAL MANAGEMENT REGIME

Before discussing some significant factors involved in setting up behavioural management systems, it is necessary to describe briefly the two most frequently used types of system: these are the *token economy* and the *level system*.

Token economies

Most of the earliest behavioural programmes for delinquents were conducted in restrictive environments with populations of convicted delinquents (Burchard, 1967; Burchard and Tyler, 1965). On the one hand, these programmes were dealing with the most difficult groups of delinquents in terms of management or treatment, yet on the other they were carried out in settings in which a high degree of control of environmental contingencies could be achieved. Many of these early behavioural programmes employed a token economy (Ayllon and Azrin, 1968).

The token economy is a motivational system in which large numbers of consequences and many set behaviours can be targeted. In essence, in a token economy some token, such as coins, tickets, stars, or points, is earned for meeting previously agreed standards of behaviour. These tokens, which operate as generalized reinforcers, can then be exchanged for a variety of rewards commonly called 'back-up reinforcers'. These back-up reinforcers may include tangible rewards such as chocolate and other consumables, or access to extra activities and privileges. The rate at which tokens can be exchanged for back-up reinforcers must be specified, so that it is clear how many tokens are required to purchase various reinforcers. It is also important that the target behaviours are made explicit, along with the number of tokens that are administered for their performance.

Perhaps the best-known programme for delinquent young people that incorporates a token economy is at Achievement Place (Kirigin *et al.*, 1979). This programme was successful in bringing about a range of positive changes in behaviour, including social interaction skills, vocational skills, and contributions to residential life (Burchard and Lane, 1982). Young people participating in the programme also committed fewer criminal offences in the community and had fewer contacts with police than did delinquents placed on probation or in settings where the programme was not in effect (Kirigin *et al.*, 1979, 1982). However, the positive effects on offending are largely lost at a one-year follow-up (Braukmann and Wolf, 1987).

The token economy has been used in several British residential programmes for young people; the list includes the Aycliffe Children's Centre in Durham (Hoghughi, 1979); Feltham Borstal (now a Young Offender Institution; Cullen and Seddon, 1981); Glenthorne Youth Treatment Centre, Birmingham (now part of the Youth Treatment Service; Reid, 1982); and the Unit One programme, developed at Orchard Lodge in London (Brown, 1985, 1987).

While all the above programmes were residential, there have been attempts to extend the use of token economies into community settings. The SHAPE Project (Reid *et al.*, 1980) and the BAY Project (Preston, 1982), both developed the use of the token economy programme with young people in the community.

There has been surprisingly little research into the design and operation of token economics for young people, despite their widespread use. However, several factors can be identified as having an important influence on their effectiveness.

Relevance and availability of back-up reinforcers

The extent to which a young person will strive to achieve behavioural targets, and earn tokens or points, will vary according to the desirability of the back-up reinforcer. Back-up reinforcers should reflect the interests and hobbies of young people in the programme. These often change over time. It is not unusual, however, to find programmes that have not reviewed their back-up list for over a year. Ideally managers should ensure that this is done about every three months. Similarly, young people are often not consulted about their preferences. Thus, back-up lists are more likely to reflect staff opinions and assumptions about the likes and dislikes of young people rather than the interest of the young people involved in the programme.

It is also important to ensure that advertised back-up reinforcers are readily available. Young people who have worked hard over a period of days or weeks to achieve specific behavioural targets are obviously disappointed and angry when they are informed that they cannot have agreed rewards. Adequate funds must be available for the purchase of material back-up reinforcers, such as sweets or magazines. Similarly, staff must be available to carry out planned activities that are used as back-ups, such as trips to the cinema or to sporting events. Programme managers should plan the staff rota well in advance to avoid disappointed and angry young people.

Staff training and supervision

A strength of the token economy is that it helps to structure staff–client interaction. Good token economies are those in which staff and individual young people meet several times each day so that tokens or points can be allocated. This social contact can become a powerful source of secondary reinforcement. It is important that the staff training programme includes training in relevant interpersonal skills, such as the use of constructive verbal feedback and criticism. Programmes that pay too little attention to feedback may become impersonal and mechanical in their operation and so reduce their effectiveness. Examples of bad practice include token economies in which tokens or points are allocated with little or no social contact or verbal communication. Such programmes fail to make effective use of staff time and skills. They provide fewer opportunities for staff to model appropriate social behaviour or for giving regular verbal feedback on behavioural performance. The token economy may also become boring and uninteresting, doing little to enhance the motivation of the young people.

Programme monitoring

Activity within the token economy should be carefully monitored. It is not uncommon for young people to find 'loopholes' or design faults that can be exploited. After all, it is the young people not the staff who have a vested interest in developing a detailed understanding of the workings of the economy. For example, young people may learn how to forge signatures on points cards, gamble with tokens, steal tokens from other residents, or set up an 'underground economy' in which points are traded 'illegally'. It is similarly important to monitor the performance of each young person. Some individuals may consistently perform badly, whereas others do well. Ideally, behavioural targets should be tailored to the needs of each individual so that all young people fare the same.

Level systems

Level systems, of the kind described by Ostapiuk and Westwood (1986), give young people a structured and graded access to increasingly higher levels of privileges contingent upon their behaviour. The system is standardized and young people are aware that their progress through the system is dependent upon their performance in several areas related to daily routines. For example, the system currently in operation on Snowdon Unit at Glenthorne Centre involves each young person being rated twice daily by a member of staff according to their performance in seven different areas (see Table 4.5). Staff make ratings on a scale from 1 to 4, in which a rating of 2 represents the expected level of performance. At the end of each week the average rating for each young person is calculated, and it is this score that determines their level of privileges for the following week. Young people on level 4, for example, have no restrictions in a range of activities and reinforcers, such as pool, computer games, swimming, access to the music room, table tennis, and late nights. In contrast, young people on level 1 have the highest level of restrictions, including early bedtimes and restricted access to television.

Another element of this system is the use of weekly rating feedback meetings. These seem to create an atmosphere of peer reinforcement and competition, and help to create a culture in which young people strive to achieve the highest ratings. Further, young people who achieve consistently high ratings and remain on level 4 for a specified number of weeks can move off daily ratings and the level system on to a personalized behaviour contract.

Many design and operational problems associated with the use of token economies apply equally to level systems. Staff require proper training and the system needs to be closely monitored and reviewed about every three months. It is especially important that young people are rated consistently by different members of staff. This can be achieved through staff training and supervision, ensuring that staff are rating according to the same criteria.

A common problem is for some staff to rate according to effort while others rate according to performance. This can result in inconsistencies, by which a young person whose behaviour falls well below the expected level of performance gains access to a higher level than another young person whose behaviour is above the expected standard. Such inconsistency can cause friction and disruption in the peer group. The use of written guidelines for administration of the level system, backed up though training and supervision, can help to improve consistency across team members. This point is discussed in more detail later in this chapter.

MAKING BEHAVIOURAL MANAGEMENT SYSTEMS WORK

From experience and research into structured behavioural management systems for disturbed and delinquent adolescents, both in the United States and Britain, several important design and operational features have come to light that influence the effectiveness of such programmes.

Table 4.5 Glenthorne level system

Area	Room	Hygiene/ appearance	Unit/centre responsibilities	Physical behaviour	Verbal behaviour	Problem-solving	Night-time
Brief description of area	Bed Desk/floor Shelves Cupboards Lights Switches Windows Clothes Possessions	Clothes Hair Face and hands Teeth/breath Smell/bath Personal laundry	Security Keeping unit tidy Use of equipment Chore Cooking/dishes Movement around centre	Good use of leisure time Physical interactions Gestures Posture Eye contact Habits Use of rooms Eating	Listening skills Conversation content Tone/volume Appropriateness Clarity/rate Language to staff Language to peers	Response to prompts Accepting praise Respect for others Information giving Cooperation Gratitude Apology	Settling down Socializing Ablutions Dress Departure on time Interaction with night staff Remaining in bed

NAME:

Complexity

It is important that behavioural management systems are simple and easy to administer. Often those who design the systems are not those who administer them on a daily basis. Consequently, the designers may not fully appreciate the amount of time and effort needed to administer the system as intended. This can result in care staff feeling burdened by the system such that it diminishes rather than enhances their ability to work with the young people. Further, at times of staff shortages or when staff are under particular pressure from difficult clients, short cuts may be made in programme delivery that then become established over the longer term. As a result, the programme is not delivered as intended, leading to low treatment integrity, and making it impossible to evaluate the programme in a meaningful way.

Staff training

If behavioural management systems are to be administered consistently and effectively it is essential that staff receive training, both in relation to the implementation of the system and in behavioural theory. It is a mistake to assume that staff can administer such systems simply as a result of reading the programme manual. Staff not only need the personal skills required for work with difficult and delinquent young people, but also the skills for effectively carrying out behavioural programmes and an understanding of the theory that underpins the programme. It is important not to neglect theory; ignorance of the principles that underline behavioural change programmes has been related to programme failure (Bernstein, 1982; Emerson and Emerson, 1987). Staff should be encouraged to monitor programme delivery and performance, and to give feedback to improve the programme.

Aims and objectives

As noted above, behavioural management systems have been adopted in a range of different settings, including secure units, penal institutions, residential homes, community settings, and schools (Hollin, 1990a). Each of these settings imposes particular constraints and limitations on the use of behavioural systems of management and it is important to bear these in mind when designing programmes. Specifically, clear aims and objectives must be formulated for the programme.

Programmes can be considered along two main dimensions: (1) the extent to which the programme is intended to promote behaviour change, rather than simply maintain and contain behaviour; and (2) the degree to which the programme can be tailored to the needs of individual clients, rather than applied in a fixed and rigid way regardless of individual differences. Table 4.6 shows the extent to which different methods of behavioural management are individually, as opposed to institutionally, oriented.

Table 4.6 Extent of orientation of behavioural management systems

Method	Institution	Client
Tokens/points	High	Low
Level systems	High	Low
Behavioural contracts	Medium	Medium
Natural contingencies	Low	High

The conflict between individual and institutional aims and objectives are seen, for example, in the extent to which young people are rewarded if their behaviour meets a specific *performance* target (i.e. an absolute criterion), or according to how much *effort* they make in meeting that target (i.e. a relative criterion). While the latter system is one that will motivate and encourage young people to improve their behaviour, and can help to improve the rate of learning (Masters *et al.*, 1987), it can appear unfair to those whose performance is satisfactory but who exert little effort. This can give rise to a situation in which some young people in a programme may receive less reinforcement although their behavioural performance is superior. Not surprisingly, this can result in feelings of injustice that, in turn, may lead to a deterioration in behaviour. One solution to this state of affairs is to have two different systems: one performance-based that sets out the minimum standards of expected behaviour that apply to *all* the young people in the programme such as those shown in Table 4.7; and another that is determined by effort so that young people who try hard to meet *individualized* behavioural targets are rewarded, despite level of performance. Of course, some kind of intervention is needed to help a young person achieve specific individual targets. Indeed, such a system should alert staff to a young person's need for such help.

Responding to emergencies

On occasion situations arise that are unusual, extreme, or potentially serious; this includes physical or sexual assaults on other young people or staff; serious or persistent self-injurious behaviour; hostage taking; the use of illicit drugs; fire-setting on the premises; and, in secure facilities, absconding or other breaches of security. Within the behavioural programme it is necessary to have specific policies and procedures to deal with these kinds of situations, as described in Chapter 2. These procedures usually operate above and beyond the day-to-day systems of behavioural management, although there may be some degree of overlap. A young person who threatens another young person could, for example,

Table 4.7 Example of programme expectations

Young people are expected:
1   not to threaten or physically assault staff;
2   to be friendly and pleasant to each other;
3   not to swear or use foul language;
4   to attend all programme activities and be on time;
5   not to use racist or sexist language;
6   to do all their chores as shown on the weekly rota;
7   not to abscond;
8   to ask for staff permission before leaving the building;
9   not to bring drugs, solvents, or pornography into the building;
10 to keep themselves and their room clean and tidy.

be removed temporarily from the token economy so that he or she is denied the opportunity to earn points. Alternatively, the young person could be returned to the system immediately after the crisis, but be fined a fixed penalty (response cost). If strategies for managing extreme situations are not given adequate attention before the management system is implemented, the result will be confusion and uncertainty in decision-making and hence inconsistent and arbitrary practice.

Ethical and legal considerations

Ethical and legal consideration must take the highest priority when designing behaviour management programmes. There are two main aspects of programme design to consider: first, what can be *given* to young people to reinforce behaviour; second, what can be *taken away* to punish behaviour. Examples of situations where the ethical, or indeed legal, position is uncertain include: the use of cigarettes as reinforcers; restricted access to television; insistence on early bedtimes; and forcing young people to eat alone as a punishment for unacceptable behaviour. Managers and staff who take responsibility for the design and running of behavioural programmes must always respect the individual's dignity and basic human rights. It is important that these issues are given a high profile, perhaps in the context of an ethics group or committee in which lay people and legal advisers are represented.

Monitoring and evaluation

If a behavioural management system is to survive then it is crucial that its implementation and performance are carefully monitored. Monitoring enables the system to be 'fine-tuned' and adjusted to meet the needs of a changing client group. Monitoring also helps to ensure that the system is carried out as intended, thereby reducing the risk of 'programme drift' (Johnson, 1981). It is not uncommon for programmes to be carefully designed and set up, then left to develop and evolve of their own accord. Drift away from the original programme can result in gross distortions in practice. At best the programme fails to meet its objectives and is unhappily written off as a failure; at worst the programme becomes unethical and abuses the people it was designed to help.

If programmes are to be effective it is essential that they are properly monitored and maintained. This, in turn, means defining the information that will be routinely collected; deciding who should collect this information; and how the information should be recorded. Further, programmes should be overhauled regularly, at least once every six months; for example, changes in popular trends and fashions among young people can affect the salience of particular reinforcers.

DESIGNING AND DELIVERING INDIVIDUALIZED PROGRAMMES

The previous section was concerned with the design and management of behavioural regimes, with the purpose of creating a social environment that will help to promote pro-social behaviour and create an atmosphere of control and stability. This section deals with the task of the management of the design and delivery of programmes tailored to the needs of individual young people. The aim here is not to describe the kinds of behavioural or cognitive interventions that can be used with difficult and delinquent young people (Hollin, 1990a; Ross and Fabiano, 1985), but to outline the ways in which the design and use of these techniques can best be achieved.

The first question managers should ask themselves when designing individualized intervention programmes for difficult and delinquent young people is 'What is the purpose of this intervention?' While the assessment of the young person's needs, using the techniques described in Chapter 3, will help to identify possible areas for intervention, it is necessary to give careful consideration to several other important issues.

What are the goals of treatment?

It is vitally important that managers set realistic short- and long-term goals, and then set the time-scale within which the programme will run. In practice, the long-term goals within the time-scale create the framework within which short-term goals can be set. These short-term aims are reviewed more frequently and help to keep the programme on target. Generally speaking, long-term goals are normally concerned with helping the young person adjust to the demands of life in the community. Such goals may include, for example: improving the young person's ability to form and maintain interpersonal relationships; helping the young person to manage his or her anger more effectively, to reduce the risk of subsequent violence; and improving the young person's social problem-solving skills and life skills, such as the ability to handle money, shopping and cooking, and applying for jobs.

Table 4.8 Examples of good and bad programme goals

Poorly defined goals	Well-defined goals
John will be less aggressive.	Over the next 4 weeks the staff team will aim to reduce the frequency of John's physical assaults on staff (i.e. punching, kicking, slapping, biting) from an average of 14 per week to under 6 per week.
Samantha should keep her room clean and tidy.	Within 3 weeks, through appropriate modelling and prompting, the staff team will help Samantha to achieve a consistent Level System rating of 3 or above for the 'Condition of her Room'.
Dean should mix more with his peer group.	Dean will spend no more than 2 hours each day in his room. He will also participate in all organized unit activities.
Judy should relate better to staff.	By the end of the 8 week programme Judy will use appropriate eye contact and body language when talking to staff; she will stand at an appropriate distance and not physically touch staff.

Programme goals should be explicit, precise, and stated in behavioural terms. Examples of good and bad programme goals are shown in Table 4.8. This clarity of definition is important for three reasons: (1) the process of defining goals ensures that all those involved in managing and treating the young person understands what it is they are trying to achieve; (2) it is easier to monitor the progress of the programme and make changes when needed; and (3) it is easier to evaluate programme outcome.

What are the expectations of the programme?

While it is important to aim towards specific long-term goals, it is equally important to be realistic about the extent to which those goals can be achieved, given the available time and resources. Many delinquent young people are already chronically disadvantaged with a host of long-standing difficulties, some of which may have their origins in constitutional deficits, such as low intelligence or temperamental instability, which are difficult to change. Sometimes it may be unrealistic to expect the young person to survive independently without a great deal of support in the community. In this instance a goal of treatment may be to prepare the young person for long-term support, whether in an institution or in the community.

If goals are not realistic then failure will be the inevitable result, which is demoralizing both for the young person and the staff involved in carrying out the programme. There may be other casualties: for example, families who have been led to expect that the young person will return to them will be told that this is no longer possible. Programmes that consistently fail to meet their stated aims and objectives may, ultimately, be threatened with closure.

Which problem areas are most important?

One advantage of the functional analytical approach described in Chapter 3 is that it helps to identify those areas that contribute most to the young person being referred for treatment and which are amenable to change. For example, consider the case of Mark.

Mark was a 17-year-old young offender with a long history of antisocial behaviour and criminal offences for which he had already spent one period of six months in youth custody; he was referred to a treatment programme because of his continued offending. His most serious offences involved several indecent assaults on women. Assessment showed that Mark had many different problems: a dysfunctional family living in poverty; a history of educational failure; low self-esteem; poor social skills; no significant peer relationships; poor social problem-solving skills, expressed in impulsivity and a lack of thought; and a history of alcohol and substance abuse. Given this daunting set of problems, it was difficult to know where to start in trying to help this young man. However, a functional analysis, outlined in Table 4.9, showed that his alcohol abuse played a central role in his offending behaviour. All of his sexual offences had occurred after he had been drinking, and he also admitted to having committed several burglaries and car thefts, and a robbery to fund his drinking. An intervention programme was therefore designed, along similar lines to that described by Baldwin et al. (1988), aimed at helping Mark to reduce and control his alcohol consumption. At follow-up eighteen months after leaving the programme Mark was still controlling his use of alcohol, and although he had been involved in car theft had avoided other serious offending. He also had developed a steady relationship and moved into his own flat with the help of social services.

Is the young person motivated to change?

Young people, especially those who are delinquent and behaviourally disordered, are sometimes difficult to engage in individual work, and often poorly motivated to change. In other words, they see little reason to change or have little belief in their ability to behave differently. Frequently they have led unsuccessful lives, having been rejected, excluded, and marginalized since childhood, which often results in their having a sense of alienation from mainstream society (Calabrese

Table 4.9 Main elements of sequential functional analysis

Age: 0 to 12 years

A: Lack of physical and emotional stimulation
Temperamental factors: poor concentration, impulsivity
Poor peer relationships
Education failure
Exposure to hard-core pornography
Sexually abused at age 11 by older boy

B: Thoughts about own inadequacy
Low self-esteem
Concerns about homosexuality

C: Alcohol and substance abuse (alcohol freely available in house)

Age: 13 to 15 years

A: As above

B: Increased use of alcohol and solvents, usually alone
Offending to fund substance abuse (e.g. burglary, car theft)
Expulsion from school
Sexual and social isolation
Anger at own abuse
Masturbation to rape-fantasies

C: Repetitive thoughts about forcing women to have sex with him
No structure to daily activities

Age: 15 years 6 months, first sexual offence

A: As above

B: All day drinking binge
Feelings of enhanced confidence and power
Determination to act out sexual fantasy of forced sex

C: Shortly after leaving the pub late in the afternoon attacks woman, pulling
her to ground, attempts to remove her clothing, forces her to masturbate
him

---

and Adams, 1990). Often they have little experience of personal success and consequently have little intrinsic motivation (Harter, 1982). Indeed, Cole *et al.* (1989) suggest that school failure combined with lack of social status and social rejection all contribute to delinquents' self-perceptions of inadequacy and failure. Given this, it is not uncommon for such young people to feel that they have little control over their own lives and future. The association between delinquency and an external locus of control (a belief that one's behaviour is controlled by outside forces such as powerful others or luck) is well documented in the research literature (Kumchy and Sayer, 1980). Indeed, for many young offenders their offending behaviour is the only thing they are good at: 'It [offending] is a skilled behaviour that brings tangible and social rewards – not a problem to be removed. It follows that the therapist must have a strong set of arguments as to why the young offender should engage in a process of change' (Hollin, 1990a, p. 135).

Strategies to overcome resistance to change should be incorporated into the design of treatment programmes. The *idea* of treatment and personal change needs to be sold to such young people, and they need to feel confident that they can change their behaviour. These are not easy tasks, especially if the young person does not enter treatment voluntarily but is coerced into it, either by parents or through legislation.

The issue of reluctance to change is one, of course, seen in many fields of work with people. Miller and Rollnick (1991) describe the use of the technique of motivational interviewing to prepare people for behavioural change. It seems that much can be taken from this development and applied to work with delinquent young people.

One strategy to engage young people is to make the treatment on offer appear relevant and thus become more attractive to the young person in question. It is often worthwhile targeting a problem that is less important to the overall goals of treatment, but is more salient from the perspective of the young person and easier to overcome. This helps to draw the young person into the process of behaviour change. The resolution of the problem may also serve as a powerful reinforcer and provide the necessary motivation for participation in more complex and challenging interventions. For example consider the case of John.

John was 15 years old with a long history of antisocial behaviour and learning difficulties. Between the age of 13 and 15, when he was arrested, convicted, and referred for treatment, he carried out a series of serious indecent assaults on women. When he came into treatment he was reluctant to discuss his sexual offending behaviour, and little progress was made in this area for the first six months. However, he was keen to have treatment for a spider phobia that he found embarrassing and difficult to reconcile with his tough image and large stature. Consequently, a behaviour change programme was started involving desensitization and *in vivo* exposure. Over a period of four months he overcame his fear of spiders and could touch and handle small spiders. More important, however, he developed a trusting relationship with his therapist such that he agreed to discuss his sexual offences. He was thus able to disclose distressing personal information concerning his own sexual development, including childhood sexual abuse.

Are the resources available to meet treatment needs?

The treatment of disturbed and delinquent adolescents is without doubt a demanding and challenging task. Effective work with this client group requires multidisciplinary team work and close collaboration between a daunting range of professional groups: the list includes behaviour therapists, child abuse counsellors, child protection agencies, clinical and forensic psychologists, educational psychologists, family therapists, forensic and child and adolescent psychiatrists, magistrates and judges, police officers, probation officers, psychiatric nurses, social workers, solicitors, and teachers. It is likely that many of these professionals will have at least some involvement in the most difficult and demanding cases, although most difficult and delinquent young people in treatment will have contact with only a smaller core group of professionals.

The complexity of the treatment task gives rise to two important consequences. First, few, if any, professionals will possess all the knowledge and skills necessary to deal adequately with all cases. Second, it follows that effective interdisciplinary communication is vital if the treatment programme is to run smoothly.

Methods of intervention

The second issue that should concern managers in the design of individualized behavioural programmes is the selection of appropriate techniques for achieving the desired behaviour change with the young people. A wide range of methods is available to the behavioural practitioner working with children and adolescents (e.g. Herbert, 1991). For the purposes of this chapter, however, the emphasis is on the implementation of these techniques. Broadly speaking there are four main options, as shown in Table 4.10, each with its own particular advantages and disadvantages.

Individual sessional work

Most treatment work with young people usually begins with individual assessment interviews, conducted by one or two practitioners (see Chapter 3). This individualized style of working may be continued throughout the treatment programme, and can be especially useful in helping to develop trust and motivation. Young people who respond well to individual attention may also benefit from individualized work. Where issues of a personal or confidential nature need to be addressed, as for example with disclosures of sexual abuse, there may be no suitable alternative to individual sessions. However, as the *only* approach to promoting and maintaining behavioural change individual work is somewhat limited. As described later in this chapter, individual work is most often used as an adjunct to other behaviour change strategies.

An important consideration when designing programmes that include substantial amounts of individual work is whether to use a key worker system, in which one person carries out most of the work. The use of a key worker can be advantageous in that it promotes the development of an exclusive relationship or attachment that can foster the development of trust. This can be especially important for young people who have no consistent experience of care – a situation that frequently results in suspiciousness and a distrust of adults.

However, there are also serious potential disadvantages with the key worker approach. The young person may become too dependent on the relationship with the key worker, so that it becomes unhelpful in the longer term when it is time to

Table 4.10 Advantages and disadvantages of various treatment modalities

Advantages	Disadvantages
Individual	
Easier to address personal issues	Intensive in cost and time
Maximizes individual attention	Difficult to overcome resistance
Easier to respond to individual needs	Difficult to generalize behavioural gains
Group work	
Use of peer pressure	Difficult to address individual needs
Facilitates the use of role-play	Difficult to address personal issues
Cost and time efficient	More vulnerable to disruption and sabotage
Unit-based	
Promotes generalization	Difficult to achieve consistency of approach
Cost and time efficient	Difficult to address personal issues
Behavioural family work	
Helps to prevent further problems	Requires commitment and cooperation from family members to both the young person and the treatment process
Cost and time efficient	Less able to contain and manage difficult behaviour
Can address long-standing family difficulties	Demands highly specialist practitioner skills

move on. The young person may become jealous of others who receive attention from the key worker, which can result in disharmony or even physical violence. Similarly, the absence of the key worker owing to annual leave or illness can leave young people feeling isolated, rejected, or abandoned, unwanted feelings with which they may already be all too familiar. The premature end of the relationship, perhaps as the result of the key worker moving to a new job or the young person having to leave the programme, can also cause difficulties for the young person.

It is often not possible for managers to plan to avoid these occurrences: staff may leave at short notice and young people leave programmes because of a variety of factors including unacceptable behaviour (e.g. serious offending), a lack of funding, poor motivation to change, family relocation, or serious illness. Careful consideration must be given to all these factors before embarking on a programme in which key-working is adopted. If this style of working is to be used, the guiding principle must be that at all times the needs of the young person are paramount. It is *essential* therefore that the key worker is experienced in long-term individual work and has access to regular supervision and support. Where this does not occur there is a greater risk of key workers feeling isolated and perhaps anxious about how to proceed with their work. They may also feel weighed down by the enormity of the task and exposed to criticism should things go wrong.

The alternative to the key-worker approach, and one that we recommended where possible, is to engage several workers, working alone or in pairs, in carrying out the programme. This approach retains many of the advantages of individual key-working but focuses the work on two or three members of staff. This approach gives the young person more *choice* in his or her relationships, while interruptions because of holidays or sickness are less of a problem. In addition staff members can also learn from and support each other through sharing skills and knowledge.

Group work

The use of small groups as a forum for therapeutic intervention is common practice in most mental health services. Group work is not only effective in terms of cost and time, it also helps to broaden the available range of therapeutic strategies in two main ways. First, interactions and relationships between group members provide a rich source of information about how individuals function in a social context. It is generally acknowledged that the peer group is an important influence on the behaviour of children and adolescents (e.g. Hartup, 1983; Patterson *et al.*, 1992), and peer pressure can be an effective mechanism for changing behaviour. Second, small groups provide a venue for structured techniques such as role-play and skills training. Indeed, the use of structured small group work features in many programmes for young offenders, especially those programmes devoted to building social skills (e.g. Hazel *et al.*, 1981; Hollin, 1990b; Serna *et al.*, 1986) and managing anger (e.g. Feindler and Ecton, 1986; Feindler *et al.*, 1984). A potential disadvantage of group work is the opportunity it gives for attention-seeking and disruption. However, assessment for suitability for group work can help to reduce the risk of this happening.

Unit-based programmes

This approach is concerned with constructing the young person's social environment so that it responds in a predictable manner. This style of work can be used in any environment where staff have contact with the young person over an extended period, such as residential or institutional settings, and day centres such as Intermediate Treatment (IT) units. The basis of this approach is that all staff respond in the same way to the young person's behaviour, so that there is consistency with respect to the contingent social reinforcement and punishment. This does not mean that staff have to act like robots; stereotyped staff behaviour would be unhelpful and unnatural and young people need to see different adults with different interpersonal styles. Rather, this approach requires that staff members reflect on their own behaviour and the consequences it produces for the young person. As the goal is consistency in the young person's social environment, the staff must therefore agree to work to an agreed set of rules. The 'teaching family' model developed at Achievement Place (Braukmann and Wolf, 1987; Phillips *et al.*, 1971, 1972) referred to staff as 'training parents' and construed each individual interaction with the young person as a 'teaching interaction' that gave the opportunity to provide the young person with an experience that could promote behavioural change. The 'teaching interaction' consisted of ten components involving the expression of affection, praise for work already accomplished, descriptions of inappropriate and of appropriate behaviour, the rationale for the appropriate behaviour, a request for an acknowledgement of understanding, practice, feedback, and finally reward for a job well done (Phillips *et al.*, 1972). The 'teaching interaction' was a central feature of the teaching family model and was seen as essential to the successful operation of the behaviour change system used in the Achievement Place programme. Phillips *et al.* proposed that, 'Most of the youths need to learn new interpersonal skills so that they can improve their relationships with their parents, teachers, and other significant adults. The point system *alone* will not do a very good job of teaching these *new* behaviours' (p. 11).

Unit-based programmes, if properly managed, can operate across a variety of settings, and hence can facilitate generalization of behaviour change. For example, within residential settings programmes can be extended to educational and work groups. Similarly, programmes can be extended into completely new settings, to ease a young person's transfer from an institutional to a community setting.

Behavioural family work

The two main strands of behavioural family work are parent management training and systemic family work.

Parent management training (PMT)

There are several advantages to training parents and other care-givers to manage the behaviour of their children more effectively. First, this approach helps primary prevention by helping parents to respond effectively to new behavioural problems without recourse to professional help (Hawkins, 1972). Second, it can help promote generalization of behaviour from residential to family and community contexts (Wells *et al.*, 1980). Third, it is effective in terms of both cost and time (Christensen *et al.*, 1980). Finally, it can be effective in tackling long-standing behavioural difficulties within the family (Topping, 1986).

Although PMT was developed for use with parents of younger children, it has been used successfully with parents of older children, including delinquent adolescents (Bank *et al.*, 1987; Morton and Ewald, 1987; Serna *et al.*, 1986). Certain parenting skills have been found to be particularly important in helping to prevent further offending: these include the use of effective methods of discipline to control antisocial behaviour; monitoring the young person's whereabouts; reinforcing appropriate behaviour; and applying effective problem-solving strategies to manage family conflict (Loeber, 1990; Patterson, 1986; Patterson and Stouthamer-Loeber, 1984; Snyder and Patterson, 1987).

Family systems approach

Whereas parent management training focuses primarily on the parent–child relationship, the family systems approach is aimed at changing interactions between all members of the family. One of the main advantages of this approach lies in its ability to promote generalization. An example of this approach is the 'triadic model', developed by Martin Herbert (e.g. Herbert, 1987b), in which the young person, his or her parents (or other family members), and the family worker make up the triad. All members of the family, but especially the parents, are the main mediators of change (Herbert, 1988). The programme itself combines a variety of techniques, depending on the outcome of the assessment, and is tailored to the needs of each family (e.g. Welch, 1985).

Careful consideration should be given to the organization and delivery of behavioural family work. This is especially important if this approach is used in addition to other methods of intervention, such as a residential programme. Family work needs to be integrated into other aspects of the programme to ensure two-way communication and feedback. This helps to prevent the development of a split between family workers and residential staff and wherever possible residential staff should be included in family work. Examples of daily behavioural difficulties can then be recreated in the family work forum, through role-play for instance. This also helps to promote generalization of new behavioural skills from the residential to the family setting, with residential staff acting as a form of stimulus-control.

Programme managers need to ensure that adequate facilities are available for family work. This should include a good-sized well-lit room in a quiet part of the building, comfortable seating, access to refreshments, and the availability of toys and books for younger family members. Families of delinquent young people often need encouragement to attend family sessions. Before formal family work begins it is often worthwhile paying the family a home visit. This helps to establish rapport and allay any fears or concerns they have about family work. Some parents may be concerned that they will be blamed for the child's problems. Others may have previously experienced family work that they found unhelpful or too intrusive. Where families have to travel a reasonable distance, programme managers may consider offering free travel as an incentive to attend.

Similarly, the availability of on-site overnight accommodation may not only encourage families to attend but can also be used as a means of re-creating the 'natural' family environment. This enables intensive parent-training programmes to be carried out, over the course of a weekend for example.

It is perhaps worth noting in conclusion that family work has been identified in a recent meta-analysis as an essential ingredient for a successful behaviour change programme with young offenders (Roberts and Camasso, 1991). In particular, family work nested with other methods of behaviour change appears to be particularly powerful in work with delinquent adolescents (Henggeler *et al.*, 1992).

DELIVERING PROGRAMMES

Even the best designed behavioural programmes will fail unless they are delivered correctly: the terms *treatment integrity* (Quay, 1987b) and *treatment fidelity* (Moncher and Prins, 1991) have been coined to describe the extent to which the treatment programme is delivered as planned. That the effectiveness of an intervention is dependent upon the rigour with which that intervention is conducted is an obvious, if often overlooked, fact. Clearly the most effective programmes with young offenders have high treatment integrity: they are carried out by trained practitioners, and the programme planners are involved in all the operational phases of the programme (Lipsey, 1992a).

Goal-directed treatment programmes produce important consequences for the way in which the treatment process is managed. Specifically, treatment teams themselves need to exhibit goal-directed behaviour; they need to know how to respond to specific situations so that they operate in a consistent manner. In order for this to occur, the team needs to be carefully managed. Successful management is the key to programme success, whatever the setting in which treatment occurs. The processes of management influence staff behaviour in various ways.

Defining target behaviours

The task of identifying and defining problem behaviours requires discussion among team members, so that each person feels part of the treatment process and is given the opportunity to express his or her views. It is only through this process that individuals can come to a unified view of the behaviour and an agreement about how the behaviour should be defined. If the discussion is to be constructive and goal-directed, however, it needs to be charted or eased by an experienced behavioural practitioner. Failure to do this can result in long, irrelevant discussions about trivial behaviours, and sometimes arguments that are destructive to the cohesiveness of the team. Effective facilitation of team discussion is a skilled task, often ignored in much of the literature on behavioural programmes. Treatment meetings should be structured, with a prepared agenda. Minutes should be taken of decisions made, specifying *what* action needs to be taken, the *person responsible* for each task, and the *time* by which it needs to be completed.

It is also important to involve young people in this process. Their views need to be considered and respected. The aim should be to develop a programme in *partnership* with the young person. Young people who feel involved in their programme design and delivery will be more interested and motivated to see it succeed. Conversely, programmes that fail to achieve involvement risk excluding and alienating young people, and substantially reduce the chances of success.

Feedback and support

Those staff responsible for programme implementation need critical and positive feedback on their performance. They need to know how they are doing and whether they could do better. Managers should be supportive and encouraging wherever possible and aim to help individuals reflect on their work. This support will encourage staff learning and development, and promote confidence and a sense of self-efficacy. In the longer term, support may help to prevent staff stress and burn-out in residential settings (Corcoran, 1988).

Team-building

Desired behaviour change is more likely to occur, and at a greater speed, if the social environment responds in a consistent, contingent manner. Managers of behavioural programmes should aim to develop effective teamwork, so that each person knows how and when to respond to particular situations. Team-building exercises can be employed to enhance this process (Woodcock, 1979). These can be especially useful at times of particular stress or change, for example when there is staff reorganization. In the *Team Development Manual*, Woodcock describes several useful team-building exercises, each aimed at different aspects of team functioning. For example, the 'Highway Code', outlined in Table 4.11, explores information-sharing and consensus-seeking activity within a team.

Programme planning and monitoring

Managers can help treatment teams to set realistic short- and long-term goals for young people; monitor the performance of the team in helping the young people to meet these goals; and ensure that the team has sufficient time and resources to meet the goals. Performance indicators can be used to monitor certain aspects of programme delivery. For example, if interventions are planned properly, it should be possible to evaluate programme delivery in terms of the discrepancy between what was planned to occur and what actually took place. For example, if only nine out of twelve individual sessions were delivered as part of an anger-management programme, this represents a discrepancy of 25 per cent in quantity of service delivery. It should be possible to identify factors – such as staff sickness and shortages, emergencies, and holidays – to account for this difference. Over time it should be possible for programme managers to set

Table 4.11 The 'Highway Code' team-building exercise

1 Any number of groups of 5 to 8 participants may take part in the activity. Approximately 90 minutes should be allowed.

2 The facilitator distributes 'Highway Code' question sheets and individual answer sheets to each participant.

3 Up to 15 minutes are allowed in which individual answer sheets are completed. Participants may not discuss questions or answers but should work privately.

4 The whole group meets together to complete the group answer sheets. As far as possible the group should discuss the possible answers and reach consensus on group answers. Voting should be avoided. Thirty minutes are allowed for this stage.

5 The facilitator distributes the model answer sheets and both individual and group answer sheets are scored.

6 A score sheet is distributed to and completed by each group.

7 The facilitator leads the group in a discussion of the results of the activity, focusing particularly on the issues listed on the review sheets. At least 30 minutes should be allowed for this stage.

Source: Woodcock, 1979

realistic targets for programme delivery. For example, if over a six-month period the mean discrepancy between planned and actual programme delivery is 15 per cent, an improvement on this figure could be used as a target for the next six-month period. With careful thought similar targets can be generated for the quality of programme delivery.

Programme managers have a particularly important role to play in ensuring that the staff team stays 'on task' in its efforts to meet short-term goals, and in reviewing the appropriateness of long-term goals. The latter may have to be reformulated according to progress in achieving short-term goals, or in the light of other unforeseen factors. Managers should ensure that goals are reviewed and discussed regularly and that record-keeping is accurate and efficient. These points become especially important if complex multi-modal intervention programmes are carried out over long periods of time. All too often the original aims and objectives of the programme are forgotten, or become obscured by other, more recent events. Similarly, record-keeping can become disorganized and inaccurate, resulting in important information being overlooked or making it difficult to assess the effectiveness of current programmes. An important task for programme managers is to decide which method of record-keeping to adopt and to ensure that routine records are completed in a comprehensive, accurate manner. Particular attention should be paid to confidentiality and the use of derogatory or discriminatory language. It can be the case that the daily records in residential programmes for delinquent adolescents are littered with conjecture about *why* certain events occurred at the expense of a more detailed account of *what* actually happened. The use of specially designed systems of record-keeping are important, such as that described in Chapter 2 for recording incidents of violence.

A useful management strategy is to conduct regular programme 'audits'. At regular intervals, say monthly, selected programmes are reviewed in depth, checking that each programme is being delivered as originally intended. Programme audits serve three useful functions: (1) they remind staff to keep on task; (2) they allow for the early identification of problems so that action can be taken to put the programme back on course; (3) they provide programme managers with an overview of service performance and how this relates to any performance indicators that have been set.

Managers also have the responsibility of reviewing programmes. Reviews are different from audits in several ways. Whereas audits are narrowly concerned with service delivery and performance, reviews are an opportunity to consider both programme design and delivery. They also aim to include a wider range of individuals involved in the programme, such as family and other professionals, giving them the opportunity to air their views and opinions. Unlike audits, reviews are concerned with the development of new treatment initiatives, as well as the continuation of those presently in operation. Finally, reviews often serve a statutory function. For example, Regulation 2 of the Children Act 1989 places a specific statutory duty on the responsible authority to review the case of a young person who is looked after or accommodated.

Decision-making

Finally, programme managers have an important role to play in ensuring that information is used effectively to improve decision-making about the management and treatment of young people. Some of these decisions can have important consequences and are best not left to chance. For example, decisions often have to be made concerning the risk a young person, such as someone with a history of violent or sexual offending, poses to other people. We have already seen that the behavioural treatment of delinquent adolescents is a complex task, demanding involvement from a diversity of professionals. One of the tasks of programme managers is to make the best use of the information generated by these individuals. The aim should be to make programme decisions that are *clinically defensible* (Marra *et al.*, 1987). So that managers can make defensible decisions, it is important that they know *what* information can be used, as well as *the source of the information*. If the rationale for decision-making is understood, it becomes possible to argue for one decision against another. Further, it allows for the decision-making process to be refined and developed so that better decisions are made.

This is not to say that programme managers should be responsible for all decision-making. Rather, it is their task to identify the decisions that need to be made, and then to ensure that the appropriate individuals are asked to provide the required information. The management of sexual offenders is one area in which this work is relatively well developed (Kain and Chambers, 1991; Loss and Ross,

1988). Research and clinical work with adolescent and adult sexual offenders has identified several factors that need to be considered when assessing the risk to others posed by sex offenders. The risk factors to be considered should include the degree of aggression in offences, the frequency and duration of offences, offence characteristics other than sexual aggression, victim selection characteristics, other abusive or addictive behaviours, honesty and self-initiated disclosure, personal responsibility for offending behaviour, family system functioning, non-offending sexual history and past victimization, and motivation for treatment. Clearly the list is long and complex, providing a challenge for managers and staff alike.

In conclusion, this chapter has raised a number of issues that are fundamental to the effective design and delivery of programmes for managing and treating behaviourally disordered and delinquent young people. It is difficult to avoid the conclusion that programme success depends above all else on the ability effectively to organize and manage the staff responsible for carrying out the programme. However, the extent to which programmes are delivered correctly also depends on staff having sufficient understanding of what they are being asked to do, and having the necessary skills to carry out complex, multi-modal programmes. So it is to the issue of staff training that we now turn in the next chapter.

Chapter 5

Staff training and development

In the opening chapter we looked at the conclusions of the meta-analysis studies of rehabilitation programmes with delinquents. One of these conclusions was that the most effective programmes have high 'treatment integrity', that is, the intervention with the young offenders is conducted by trained staff alongside management of the programme. It is therefore not enough to devise highly sophisticated and complex programmes; the staff responsible for delivery of the programme have to carry out exactly what is planned. At one level this is a management issue, and management strategies for ensuring integrity at the stages of both assessment and intervention have been discussed in Chapters 3 and 4. At another level, however, this is a matter for staff training and development; it is unrealistic to expect untrained staff to operate treatment programmes that demand knowledge and skills they do not possess. This is particularly pertinent in behavioural treatment. We made the point previously that many people, including the writers of some textbooks, say that behavioural theory and practice are simple and undemanding. Indeed, as trainers ourselves, one problem we frequently encounter is the assumption held by some practitioners that they know all there is to know about behaviourism.

A study by Donat and McKeegan (1990) investigated behavioural knowledge among direct care staff. The test of behavioural knowledge consisted of an inventory made up of 44 items presented in a multiple choice format devised by the same researchers (McKeegan and Donat, 1988). Examples of the inventory items are shown in Table 5.1.

This inventory was given by Donat and McKeegan to separate groups of direct care staff in an American psychiatric hospital. Across the 146 staff who participated in the study, there were significant differences in knowledge. The psychologists scored highest on the inventory with an average score on the inventory of 39.8 – which is high but short of the maximum score of 44. The next highest scoring group were the social workers, followed by the mental health workers (paraprofessionals); the nursing staff scored lower still, with the psychiatric aides returning the lowest score of all. It is important to note, as do Donat and McKeegan, that these findings do not mean that any participant in the study or any professional group has a less than adequate knowledge and understanding of

Table 5.1 Examples from a 44-item inventory of behavioural knowledge

A resident has just torn up a new magazine. Of the following choices which is probably the *best* way for the staff to respond?
1   Tell him that he will be spoken to by the Treatment Team at the next progress rounds.
2   Punish him immediately by making him clean up the torn magazine and then have him clean the ward's furniture. (correct choice)
3   Explain to him the wrongness of his behaviour.
4   Angrily yell at him so that he will learn that such an act is wrong and upsetting to staff and other residents.

Which of the following is *not* an important step in a behaviour change programme?
1   Try to make certain that the resident feels shame for misbehaviour. (correct choice)
2   Decide on a particular behaviour that you wish to change.
3   If necessary, break the selected behaviour down into smaller steps.
4   Select the proper time and situation for measuring the behaviour.

Source: after McKeegan and Donat, 1988

behavioural principles. The results should be seen as reflecting differences between individuals and professional groups; it should not be assumed, from these findings at least, that knowledge correlates positively with practical ability. Nonetheless, it is far from ideal that the care staff with probably the greatest amount of client contact have the lowest level of knowledge of behavioural principles. The point has been made by other writers, such as Gardner and Cole (1987), that the majority of direct care staff are probably poorly equipped to conduct behavioural programmes. The findings of Donat and McKeegan do not give any cause to disagree with that view. This, in turn, reinforces the frequently made point (e.g. Knowles and Landesman, 1986), that there is an imperative need to train staff at all levels in the principles of behavioural practice. However, despite the identified need, surveys consistently discover low levels of consistent training in behavioural principles (e.g. Boudewyns *et al.*, 1986).

To achieve a high level of treatment integrity, it is therefore essential that *all* staff – but especially staff who work for the bulk of their time directly with clients – receive appropriate training. As we believe firmly in the importance of training, this whole chapter is given to that topic. We will cover the design of training courses, the evaluation of training, the maintenance of training gains, and resistance and pitfalls the trainer is liable to encounter. The discussion that follows raises, as we see them, the most salient points; there is such a vast literature on training generally and behavioural training specifically that it is impossible to cover it in one chapter. We have therefore selected from the training literature representative studies to make particular points; however, for further reading several recently published reviews are available, including those published by Bootzin and Ruggill (1988), Davis (1985), Gardner (1981), Harchik *et al.* (1989), and Milne (1986). After this discussion of the literature we offer a framework for the development of a training course in applied behavioural theory and practice with delinquents.

TRAINING: THE CRUCIAL ELEMENTS

When thinking about training there are several issues that merit careful consideration: these are the level at which the training is to be delivered; the training methods to be used; the evaluation of the effects of training; and resistance and pitfalls to be aware of and avoid. Drawing on the training literature we discuss each of these issues and look in more detail at some of the finer points in organizing training.

Levels of training

As hinted above, there are several levels at which training might be pitched: Gardner (1981) has identified five such levels – *applicator, technician, specialist, generalist,* and *consultant* – ranging in sophistication and complexity from the most basic to the most highly advanced. As Gardner suggests, the training must be tailored to an appropriate standard to meet the trainee's needs and abilities.

Applicator

At this level behavioural programmes and techniques are used under very limited conditions and with an extremely high degree of supervision. An example would be in training parents how to reward a specific behaviour of their child's by supplying exact instructions on the procedures to follow and by monitoring the parents' behaviour.

Technician

In this case trained individuals use specific techniques for specified aims; while monitoring of performance is necessary this is not of the same intensity as at the applicator level. Monitoring may be achieved by 'built-in' checks such as data sheets and checklists rather than through personal supervision. One example is to be found in behavioural programmes in which there is an explicit goal for clients to attain such as reading skills or personal hygiene.

Specialist

The specialist is an individual trained to a high level of proficiency in a specific area of work; such a practitioner would be capable of applying principles and techniques to solve problems within his or her particular specialist field. For example, some practitioners work exclusively with parents and children and become highly skilled at applying behavioural principles to the issues encountered when working with families. Other examples include practitioners who specialize in working with anxiety disorders, or classroom difficulties, or delinquents. Practitioners working at this level are, of course, a valuable resource for their colleagues working in the same specialist area at the applicator or technician level.

Generalist

Unlike the specialist, the generalist is trained to apply behavioural principles and methods to a diverse range of areas. Gardner suggests that schoolteachers are an example of the need for generalist training: teachers have to manage a range of problem behaviours in the classroom, encourage and develop their pupils' academic skills, deal with social problems, and cope with school problems such as bullying and absenteeism. As with the specialist, the generalist can be a valuable resource for colleagues working at the applicator and technician levels.

Consultant

The behavioural consultant is the individual responsible for the training of the other groups. Consultants are generally professionally trained – psychologists, speech therapists, nurses, social workers, and so on – to a high educational level. However, this in itself does not make a *behavioural* specialist; Poser (1967) made the important distinction between two skills levels for the behavioural consultant. At 'level one' the trainee acts as an apprentice to an experienced behavioural practitioner: through guided experience and reading the trainee masters the necessary basic principles and skills. At 'level two' there are greater academic demands to increase the trainee's appreciation of theoretical issues in the field of learning theory, to further his or her understanding of psychopathology, and to develop research and evaluation skills. An individual working at this level could make a contribution by 'pushing' the behavioural model both theoretically and practically in new and exciting ways.

Gardner's five-level classification is informative, but there are other ways to consider matters. The distinction can be made, for example, between *non-professionals*, such as parents; *paraprofessionals* without specialized training or extensive educational qualifications who are employed to administer direct care to a given client group; and *professionals* with appropriate training and educational qualifications. Alternatively, rather than thinking in terms of groups of people, the 'career' of an individual can be considered in developmental stages from raw beginner to seasoned practitioner. No matter how it is considered, it is important at the outset to judge the abilities and requirements of trainees and so deliver the relevant level of training.

Training methods

A variety of training methods has been used to increase knowledge and skills of behavioural theory and practice. In this section we will look at what has been attempted and, using the research literature, make suggestions for effective training programmes.

Didactic approaches

It is easy to confuse giving information with training, in other words, to assume that simply telling people what to do will change and improve their practical skills. Several studies have looked at the effectiveness of traditional teaching methods on training courses in behavioural techniques. Adams *et al.* (1980) compared the utility of lectures versus role-plays in training non-professional aides in the use of positive reinforcement. They found that the aides whose training consisted simply of a lecture on the principles of reinforcement failed to show any marked change in their practice. However, the aides who were trained using role-play and contingent feedback showed a significant improvement after training in their use of positive reinforcement with their clients.

Watson and Uzzell (1980) reported the effects of a training programme for paraprofessional staff in a residential institution. The programme was designed to train the staff to develop self-help skills in their client group. The study was designed to assess the impact of two phases – academic input and practitioner skills – of the training programme. It was found that academic training primarily influenced academic performance but had little or no practical pay-offs. The practitioner skills training, however, had a clear beneficial effect in increasing the ability of the staff effectively to teach self-help, recreational, and language skills to the residents.

A study reported by Bouchard *et al.* (1980) evaluated two approaches to teaching the technique of social skills training (SST) to qualified, professional therapists. One group of therapists was trained using a structured learning approach; thus the therapists participating in this style of training participated in a training programme that used verbal instruction, modelling, role-play, and performance feedback to encourage skill acquisition. Another group of therapists took part in a programme with the same aim, teaching SST, but delivered in a seminar format; thus this group joined in discussions about the use of SST, including presentations of case material. The outcome of the study was somewhat mixed: on some outcome measures of skill acquisition relevant to the ability to conduct SST there was a clear superiority of the structured learning format over the seminar approach. However, on measures concerned with SST performance in real therapy situations, there was no clear advantage of either training format: therapists trained with both methods showed equally proficient abilities in the practice of SST. Bouchard *et al.* suggest this unexpected finding may be due to variability across clients; or it may be due to a lack of generalization of acquired skills by the therapists trained using the structured learning format. Another study by Wright *et al.* (1981) explored further this issue of different approaches to training professionals how to carry out SST. In this study three groups of mental health professionals received a reading package and videotaped modelling on how to conduct SST. As in the Bourchard *et al.* study noted above, one group participated in a seminar programme; a second group received a structured learning format consisting of instructions, rehearsal, and feedback; while a third group took part in a workshop, receiving precise instructions on how to carry out SST. As in the Bouchard *et al.* study the results were mixed and while advantages had been predicted for the structured learning format this was not generally the case. Wright *et al.* suggest that *too* much might have been attempted using a structured learning approach, and these high expectations may have swamped any advantages it might have had as a training method. Edens and Smit (1992) reported positive effects of a skill training approach to enhancing group-work ability among residential child care workers.

Finally, Milne (1982) compared 'active' and 'passive' methods of training nursing staff in behavioural skills. The active course consisted of role-play, lectures, and live and videotaped modelling; the passive course used much more traditional methods such as lectures, discussion, reading, and demonstration. The group trained using active methods did considerably better than the group taught using passive methods as assessed by tests of both knowledge and practice of behavioural principles. At a six-month follow-up, the nurses trained using the active approach reported using behavioural methods more frequently in their work than the nurses who participated in the passive training course.

In summary, traditional didactic teaching does not appear to be the optimum method for training in behavioural practice. However, this is not to say that there is no role in a training course for this traditional form of passing information. Welch and Holborn (1988) found that paraprofessionals' skills at writing behavioural contracts with delinquents improved after didactic teaching in the form of subscribed reading. The benefits of a didactic approach, the literature strongly suggests, are enhanced by active learning methods such as role-play and modelling, and by the inclusion in the training course of the chance to practice the skills. Having said that, it is important to add the caveat stemming from the studies by Bouchard *et al.* and Wright *et al.*, that while this might be true for paraprofessional and inexperienced staff, it does not appear necessarily to be the case for experienced therapists.

Performance feedback

While the provision of formal training courses is one way to shape up behavioural practice, the use of contingent feedback on performance offers another means by which to train staff. An attractive feature associated with feedback is that it does not demand a great deal of resources. What it does require is a clearly specified target for feedback; a well-defined method for giving feedback; and a supervisor who can assess performance and so provide accurate feedback. The literature on performance feedback (Balcazar *et al.*, 1986) shows that there have been many different targets for feedback, some therapeutic in nature, others managerial or organizational; indeed, *any* behaviour of any member of any organization can be included in a feedback programme. The methods of giving feedback include written feedback, verbal feedback, and tangible feedback such as refreshments and monetary prizes; the feedback can be given privately or publicly; and with or without accompanying praise. The role of the supervisor is crucial: it is essential to train this person to administer the feedback programme in a consistent and cogent manner.

Several studies have examined the effects of feedback on performance. Brown *et al.* (1981) looked at the effect of verbal feedback on the performance of staff in a residential establishment. They considered two aspects of staff performance: 'off-task' activities such as reading a newspaper or magazine, chatting with other members of staff, or just plain daydreaming; and 'task' activities such as social interaction and direct care activities with the clients. The introduction of verbal feedback into the organizational routines precipitated a reduction in off-task activities, but only temporary or no positive changes in task activities. However, when the procedure for giving feedback was modified to include statements of approval, off-task activities remained low but task activities increased markedly.

Fleming and Sulzer-Azaroff (1989) used performance feedback, in this case both verbal and written, to equip direct care staff with the skills to teach self-care to developmentally delayed adolescents. After a brief training package consisting of written instructions and demonstrations, staff began to receive the feedback on their performance. The results clearly showed that providing contingent performance feedback led to significant improvements in the teaching skills of the newly trained staff. However, a two-month follow-up suggested that there was some tailing off in staff performance. This issue of performance feedback and maintenance of improvements in staff behaviour has been discussed by Arco and Birnbrauer (1990). They make the distinction between *process feedback*, that is, feedback to staff about their performance; and *outcome feedback*, that is feedback to staff about the effects of their actions on their clients' behaviour. Arco and Birnbrauer suggest that both types of feedback will be important with respect to maintenance of changes in staff behaviour, but that they may need to be applied in different ways. Process feedback may be important during training and in the early stages of maintenance to inform staff that what they are doing is correct, and to determine that new procedures are being implemented in a competent and safe manner. If continued for too long, however, process feedback may become unnecessary and even detrimental as staff become more experienced and outgrow the need for this type of feedback. Indeed, some studies have suggested that staff can begin to compete for rewards for their performance, leading to resentment and fragmentation of staff teams (Iwata *et al.*, 1976). Outcome feedback, on the other hand, may be the optimum long-term feedback strategy as it informs about their success as practitioners, thereby reinforcing high standards of practice.

Balcazar *et al.* (1986) conclude their review of performance feedback with three observations: (1) feedback *per se* is not guaranteed to improve performance in a steady consistent manner; (2) adding rewards such as praise can improve the consistency of the effects of feedback; (3) immediate feedback, given at daily or weekly meetings, is more effective than feedback delayed for a month or more.

Self-management

In the previous section feedback was considered as something delivered by another person, a 'supervisor'. However, another approach is for the members of staff each to provide their own feedback and so self-manage their own performance: self-management itself is a time honoured behavioural technique (Kanfer, 1975). The essential components of a self-management approach are the clear definition of target behaviours, negotiation and setting of performance goals, self-recording of behaviour, self-evaluation of progress, and self-reinforcement for achieving goals and targets. This approach, used either alone or with other management strategies, has been applied in both residential and community settings.

Burg *et al.* (1979) used a self-recording and supervision programme to increase the number of interactions between direct care staff and residents in an establishment for people with learning difficulties. After taking a baseline assessment, staff were instructed in the use of a self-recording form to count their (defined) interactions with clients. The forms were returned on a daily basis, and staff were praised for self-recording, whatever the actual number of interactions recorded. The results showed that the self-recording and supervision were effective in increasing the numbers of staff–client interactions. It was significant that other staff duties, such as maintaining cleanliness, were not affected; while slight decreases in the levels of undesirable client behaviours such as aggression were found. As Burg *et al.* note, the programme was successful with a minimal amount of disruption in its implementation and at low financial cost. Other studies have reported similar successes with programmes of this type (e.g. Burgio *et al.*, 1983), with the common denominator being that publicly agreed goals are very important predictors of success. As Arco and Birnbrauer (1990) suggest, it is probably true that publicly set goals have a much greater potential for social reinforcement than private, individual goals. This, in turn, suggests that staff trained to use self-management procedures will profit from performance feedback, at least in the early stages of a self-management programme.

Doerner *et al.* (1989) reported the findings from a study of the effects of a staff self-management programme in two community-based group homes for clients with learning difficulties. The self-management programme involved goal-setting, self-monitoring, self-evaluation, and self-praise. The staff were given appropriate training and, as in other studies, were praised for self-managing but not for the frequency with which they achieved their targets. The findings showed that self-management produced an increase in the number of positive interactions between staff and clients. However, there was no such improvement on other measures such as frequencies of aggressive behaviour and negative interactions. Doerner *et al.* suggest that the gains were not all they might have been for several reasons. Some baseline levels were at a favourably high level, leaving little scope for improvement (i.e. a 'ceiling effect'); other baselines, such as the aggression, were at such low levels that the programme could not be expected to have a marked effect (i.e. a 'floor effect'); and the lack of specific performance-related feedback may have been a disadvantage. Nevertheless, this study clearly shows that self-management procedures can be effective in community as well as institutional settings.

Evaluation of training effects

Evaluation methods

There are two sides to the evaluation of training: the selection of the target for change following training; for example this might be knowledge, behaviour, or attitudes measured before and after training; and the identification of the target group for the evaluation: the staff, the clients, or both. To help the process of evaluating training a number of instruments have been published. Alevizos *et al.* (1978) devised a 'Behavior Observation Instrument' (BOI) for recording behaviour in treatment settings, such a measure being often part of the evaluation of a training programme. As shown in Table 5.2, the BOI codes observable behaviours under three discrete headings: (1) mutually exclusive classes of behaviour; (2) concomitant behaviours; (3) the location in which the behaviour is observed. Thus by simply recording observations by reference to codes, it is possible for trained observers to record quickly, easily, and accurately what and where behaviour is taking place. Alevizos *et al.* present data to show that the BOI is sensitive to changes in client behaviour following organizational change.

Other evaluation instruments are designed to test knowledge of behavioural principles rather than record behaviour. For example, O'Dell *et al.* (1979) devised a 50-item multiple choice inventory to assess understanding of basic

Table 5.2 The format of the 'Behaviour Observation Instrument'

- Coding category 'mutually exclusive behaviours', e.g. walking, sitting, lying down

- Coding category 'concomitant behaviours', e.g. drinking, eating, conversation, inappropriate behaviour, group meeting

- Coding category 'locations', e.g. day room, corridor, dining-room, kitchen

Source: after Alevizos *et al.*, 1978

Table 5.3 Typical items from the 70-item 'Knowledge of behavioural principles as applied to children' inventory

Read each question and each of its four possible answers. Sometimes more than one answer could be correct under certain circumstances; however, you should select the *best* answer or the answer that is most generally true. Select only one answer for each question.

Desirable and undesirable behaviour are most alike in that they are:
1 The results of emotions and feelings;
2 Habits and therefore difficult to change;
3 Ways the child expresses himself;
4 The result of learning?*

Which of the following is most important for parents in controlling their child's behaviour?
1 The rules the parents make about behaviour;
2 The parents' understandings of the child's feelings;
3 The behaviours to which the parents attend;*
4 Being strict, but also warm and gentle.

A good rule to remember is:
1 Do not reward with money if possible.
2 Catch a child doing something right.*
3 Reward good behaviour and always punish bad behaviour.
4 Punishment is always unnecessary.

*correct response
Source: after O'Dell, Tarter-Benlolo and Flynn, 1979

behavioural principles in the field of child care. Typical items from this 'knowledge of behavioral principles as applied to children' inventory are shown in Table 5.3.

While typical examples of evaluative instruments have been given, both for behavioural observation and assessment of knowledge, a wide range of such instruments is available in the literature.

Outcome studies

As discussed by Milne (1986), there are literally hundreds of studies of the effects of training; indeed, many of the studies we have discussed in this chapter have had an evaluative component. To focus attention on the evaluation we have selected a few representative outcome studies; these can be read with the outcome findings cited previously.

Gardner (1972) evaluated the effectiveness of two instructional techniques, role-play and lecture, in teaching behavioural principles to non-professionals. The assessment of trainees' performance was carried out using a standardized observation scale, the Training Proficiency Scale (TPS); and knowledge was assessed using the 229-item Behaviour Modification Test (BMT). The TPS and the BMT were both given pre-and post-training. The findings showed that role-play was a more effective training method for behavioural practice, while lectures were to be preferred for imparting knowledge of behavioural principles. Another study by Schinke and Wong (1977) evaluated the effects of a training programme by comparing two groups of residential staff. One group took part in a training course while the other simply carried on with its work in the usual way. Schinke and Wong found, as would be expected, that after the training the trained group showed an increase in knowledge of behavioural principles and displayed more positive behaviours towards clients than the untrained staff group. However, the training had further advantages: the trained staff showed a more robust job satisfaction and more positive attitudes towards their clients; and the clients began to respond in a more positive manner with the trained staff. As Schinke and Wong point out, there is every indication of a high degree of reciprocity in the improvements of both staff and clients: training increases staff ability, leading to improved client behaviour, so reinforcing the staff changes, further improving client behaviour, and so on.

Zlomke and Benjamin (1983) also assessed the impact of training but with a much sharper focus on client behaviour change for judging the effectiveness of training. They found that their training programme was effective in increasing knowledge of behavioural principles. However, this gain in staff knowledge was followed by beneficial changes in client behaviours such as self-abuse, property destruction, and non-compliance. Rosen et al. (1986) also assessed the effectiveness of training by monitoring changes in client behaviour. They reported a similar pattern of results as in the Zlomke and Benjamin study, with the important addition that a follow-up over a twelve-month period showed good maintenance of behavioural gains. Seys et al. (1990) similarly reported good maintenance effects following a staff training programme in communication skills.

In conclusion, while there are good grounds for optimism, it is important to make the point that short-term gains do not necessarily translate into long-term changes. In their review of therapist training Alberts and Edelstein (1990) suggest that the maintenance of training gains is one that, in the main, researchers and trainers have been reluctant to tackle. In the next section we consider some problems that can hinder and inhibit trainers and the effectiveness of training.

RESISTANCE AND PITFALLS

The trainer's lot in life is not always a happy one: as any one who has been responsible for training will testify, there are problems to be faced.

Resistance

Goisman (1988) has identified three sources of resistance to learning about behavioural theory and practice.

Role conflict

Goisman uses this term to refer to the conflict between the role of the practitioner in behavioural work and in the more widespread and accepted psychodynamic approaches. In behavioural intervention the practitioner may be directive and performance oriented; in psychodynamic approaches the client does the talking and the clinician is mostly non-directive. Further, behavioural approaches may be seen as the province of a particular group of psychologists, and therefore not to be accepted as part of the professional culture by, for example, members of the medical, nursing, and social work professions. It is almost as if adopting behavioural methods of practice stands in violation of unwritten professional rules.

Model conflict

As discussed in the opening chapter, there are clear points of disagreement between a behavioural model and traditional psychodynamic models. The behavioural model looks to behaviour in relation to the environment; the psychodynamic model looks to behaviour in relation to inner forces and conflicts, probing the mysteries of the unconscious. As Goisman notes, behavioural theory can appear mundane and ordinary when placed alongside 'the grander philosophic vision of psychoanalysis' (p. 68). It is probably true that a book on how to understand the hidden symbolism of dreams is a more entertaining read than a text devoted to the topic of schedules of reinforcement. However, models of human functioning do not stand or fall according to their appeal on the grounds of offering mystery and intrigue. A (probably apocryphal) anecdote makes the point. A well-known behavioural researcher was giving a talk and, when taking questions, the point was put from the audience that behavioural theory was unacceptable as it lacked both sparkle and metaphysical appeal. The reply from the stage was that the speaker, the behavioural researcher, preferred not to believe that his ancestors had lived up trees; however, if Darwin was right, then whether he liked it or not was of little consequence.

Disparagement

It is paradoxical that behaviourists often come under the most vicious attacks from those who profess to espouse more 'caring and person-centred' approaches. Skinner writes poignantly about the personal abuse directed at him:

Why is discussion in the behavioural sciences so often personal? I do not believe that Einstein, finding it necessary to challenge some basic assumption of Newton, alluded to Newton's senility. I do not think that Mendel and the other early geneticists, discovering facts that Darwin needed so badly, then accused him of 'totally ignoring' the genetic basis of evolution. I do not think that those who propounded the gas laws for the so-called ideal or perfect gases were condemned for their prejudice against the individual gas molecule. Why has it been tempting to say, as one commentator does, that I am 'strangely provincial' or that something else is a 'tragic irony'? Are points of that sort relevant in a scientific discussion?

(Skinner, in Catania and Harnad, 1988, p. 486)

Even Skinner's obituaries were cruel: 'Fanatical Guru of Behaviourism' was the headline extracted from a quite savage obituary in a 'quality' daily newspaper. Of course, as Skinner would have realized perfectly well, the debate is anything but scientific: behaviourists might wish to look to the data, but this style of debating does not have universal appeal. It is easy to disparage a theory by attributing to it motives and intentions it does not have; this style of disparagement 'often relies on the stereotyped portrayal of behavior therapy as mechanistic, inhumane, or somehow totalitarian' (Goisman, 1988, p. 69). Of course, the implication of such a stereotype is that a theory of this type would attract some extremely dubious types; for example, Nahem (1981) suggests that behavioural practitioners are 'unquestioning servants of a system which thrives on a petty reign of "law and order"' (p. 57). While Nahem does not have a good word to say for any therapeutic approach – which is hardly surprising given the number of basic theoretical errors and miscomprehensions in his book – there is one particularly nasty piece that obviously aims to damn by association:

Although not part of the behaviour modification movement, the forced steril-ization of welfare mothers to prevent 'reproductive behavior', the restriction of education of Blacks . . . forced cultural assimilation – 'Americanization' – of national groups, and the huge numbers of programs of human experi-mentation without consent and through deceit – all are part of an overall reactionary offensive to modify, repress, or eliminate behavior unwanted by monopoly capital. The smell of the ovens hovers around behavior modification.

(1981, p. 58)

It would be interesting to formulate a behavioural analysis of such offensive and distasteful remarks but, tempting as it is, that is probably best set aside for the present. It is enough to note that disparagement and hostility may be encountered at some stage by behavioural practitioners. There are no right and wrong ways to deal with disparagement; education, training, and reasoned argument might help but, as in many walks of life, some people refuse to listen and there is little to be done. Where hostility is evident within a staff team, the management system should ensure that such individuals are not in positions where they can sabotage the efforts of other practitioners.

Pitfalls

One pitfall that may be encountered is the view that training will solve all the problems. If a service is encountering problems – such as high levels of disruption of programmes, poor staff performance, and low rates of success – it is too easy to make the assumption that the cause of the poor organizational performance is that staff do not have the skills to do better and so staff training is the answer. As Ziarnik and Berstein (1982) point out, this assumption is not invariably correct, there are many other reasons why staff do not give their optimum performance. It may be that there are no clear criteria by which staff and management can judge performance; or that poor staff performance is reinforced either socially by the staff culture, or organizationally by the award of incentives such as pay rises and promotion on criteria other than performance skills; or that performance skills are extinguished by a lack of feedback from supervisors and managers; or by an organizational structure that places greater importance on other areas such as security. Ziarnik and Berstein neatly sum up this line of thought:

> If environmental conditions maintain poor staff performance, then it logically follows that no amount of in service training will remediate the problem. The appropriate methodology for remediating performance problems maintained by environmental conditions is to alter those conditions. Similarly, no matter how skilled staff are, the environment must support the exhibition of those skills for performance to be satisfactory.
>
> (1982, p. 111)

The importance therefore of 'setting events' cannot be underestimated with respect to the effectiveness of staff training: there are several relevant analyses in the literature (e.g. Paul and Lentz, 1977; Wahler and Fox, 1981). Burdett and Milne (1985) considered the views of nursing staff about what affected their performance as behavioural practitioners after a training course in the principles of behavioural practice. They found that factors typically offered as obstructing practice – lack of previous success, shortage of time, priorities having to be given to other duties, too many work routines, too few staff – were not seen by the nursing staff as problematic. The difficulties in putting into practice what had been learned on the course were much more to do with receiving support from nursing officers and specialists such as psychologists, a lack of feedback on their work, and a shortage of equipment.

Thus a potential pitfall for the trainer is to be cast in the role of the person who is going to solve all the organization's problems which, as shown above, is highly unrealistic. It follows from this that training should be used in a planned manner, directed at areas in which it can have a maximum impact as a strategy *within, not instead of*, a coherent organizational structure.

However, even when training is being used properly, there are still pitfalls that can trap the unwary trainer. In an admirably brief paper, Mealiea and Duffy (1980) have drawn a list of nine pitfalls for the training and developmental specialist. Although in this chapter we have already paid heed to and discussed several of these pitfalls it is worth commenting on all nine to provide an overall summary.

Pitfall 1: Training as a cure-all   The trainer as the panacea for an organization's ailments has been discussed above: the trainer should not be drawn into this game, but should first seek to establish whether a shortfall in staff performance is due to a lack of personal skills or whether the functioning of the organization is rewarding poor performance and punishing desired performance.

Pitfall 2: Ignoring the need to rank performance and organizational problems The need to rank performance and organizational problems is a means by which to provide a basis for deciding what action is needed within an organization. If a training solution is being sought, a ranking of requests on five dimensions – cost effectiveness, executive pressure, training population, immediacy of impact, and possible legal constraints – might set the proposed training in context and so make it less likely that the training will 'fail'.

Pitfall 3: Failing to give trainees the required time, support, and material to adjust to a new position   This refers to the need to allow new members of staff time to settle into a work routine before beginning to evaluate their performance and set agendas for training.

Pitfall 4: The unmotivated trainee   This pitfall typically comes about by individuals being instructed by their manager or supervisor that they need training to improve their performance. Thus little heed is paid to the individual's own views and attitudes towards his or her training needs and the implicit slight on performance to date. Mealiea and Duffy suggest three strategies to avoid the problems of unmotivated trainees: (a) develop *intrinsic motivation* by involving the individual in the assessment of his or her training needs; (b) provide *extrinsic motivation* by rewarding the individual on the successful completion of the training and its implementation in the organization; (c) *generate interest* by making the training itself interesting and rewarding.

Pitfall 5: Assuming that one training technique can be applied to all group and situations   This refers to the content and delivery of training programmes. The substance of the training must be of relevance: it would be of little relevance, for example, to conduct a training course on working in security with a group of community workers. Further, the training methods may have to be tailored to the level of the trainees: one interpretation of the findings on skills training for *experienced* practitioners (see p. 141) is that when the skills are already present, seminar and discussion may be the optimum training method. Conversely, if the skills have not been learned, then 'active' skills training methods may be preferable.

Pitfall 6: Inadequate evaluation of solutions   Assuming pitfall 2 has been avoided, it is necessary to evaluate the training. Mealiea and Duffy suggest three points at which evaluation can take place: (a) during the training programme; (b) at the conclusion of the training; (c) back at the trainee's place of work. The evaluation measures should be realistic and relevant: if the aim of training has been to improve practitioner performance in a specific technique, then performance of that technique should be the means of evaluation, not other practitioner skills or another aspect of organizational performance.

Pitfall 7: Failing to evaluate results for one trainee in the light of the results for all trainees   The conclusions about a trainee's performance after training may be misleading if judged solely on an individual basis. An uncooperative trainee or an untrainable individual might make a sound training programme appear ineffective. Mealiea and Duffy suggest that the preferred strategy is to consider the aggregated results for all participants in the training; then on this basis highlight the individuals who appear not to have benefited from the training.

Pitfall 8: Failure to evaluate long-term trainee performance   As we have already suggested, a failure to carry out a long-term follow-up after training leads to an incomplete evaluation. While long-term success is rewarding for all concerned, a failure to achieve long-term success is informative in that it might identify the factors, either personal or organizational, which inhibit staff performance.

Pitfall 9: Failing to gather the appropriate cost vs. benefit information   While cost-benefit evaluation is not easy, it is not something the training specialist can afford to ignore. To avoid training programmes being the first casualty in times of economic hardship, it is necessary to have the figures to hand on the financial advantages of training. The rule here is to be simple: it is preferable to generate a means by which to document the costs expended and the benefits gained rather than design complex experimental designs involving intricate tests of performance.

A FRAMEWORK FOR TRAINING

In this section we present a framework for the development of training based on the points covered in the preceding section. The term 'framework' was deliberately chosen as we would not wish to suggest that this is the only way or the best way to organize training. We hope, however, that it will provide at least a basis for the development and organization of training initiatives.

Trainee groups

Most organizations are made up of many different groups – such as administrators, domestic staff, and care staff – with various subgroups within each group: for example, care staff may include medics, psychologists, social workers, and teachers. While the focus here is on training care staff, those responsible for organizing training may well need to be aware of the specialist training needs of all these groups. From the point of view of treatment integrity, the decision must be made about the level of knowledge of theory and practice regarding treatment issues the non-care staff need to have. Clearly this cannot be dictated in advance as it will differ from location to location.

As in Gardner's five-level scheme discussed previously, the training of care staff may be organized around the educational attainment and training of the staff

Table 5.4 Stages in the professional career of a behavioural practitioner

Stage 1: Induction into the organization; day 1 to day 14

Stage 2: Development of basic knowledge and skills; from end of week 2 to end of month 6

Stage 3: Intermediate development of knowledge and skills; month 7 to year 2

Stage 4: Development of advanced, specialist knowledge and skills; year 2 and beyond

and their role within the organization. This system may be appropriate for large organizations with fixed professional roles and boundaries. However, the potential disadvantage with this way of thinking is that the system may become 'static', that is, individuals might be assigned to a level of competence and become stuck there with little opportunity for development to further levels. One way around this – which accords very neatly with a behavioural emphasis on the individual rather than on groups of people – is to consider the professional 'career' of a member of staff from the point at which he or she enters the organization. Of course this career analysis can be carried out in several ways; in our own work, on which we draw here, we have evolved a system that divides a career into four developmental stages, as shown in Table 5.4. The training task is then to decide the content of the four stages and devise the optimum means of delivery.

Curriculum

In our own training programme the curriculum is divided into three main areas: *residential practice, professional issues, treatment skills*. Again these will vary from setting to setting, so that *community practice*, or *working in high security* might replace residential practice. Thus what follows should serve as a model to inform the organization of training rather than being read as a definitive statement.

Induction training

It is important at the outset to make some firm statements about induction training: (1) new staff should *not* be counted as part of the treatment team during this two-week period; (2) the first two weeks should be devoted to the new member of staff becoming familiar with both the organization and the specific location in which he or she will work; (3) staff on induction training should meet individuals from across the whole of the organization, with the freedom to ask whatever questions they wish. Table 5.5 shows an example of a curriculum for induction training.

Table 5.5 Outline of areas to consider in developing a curriculum for induction training

New staff should meet representatives from a variety of areas to gain information about the work across the organization; a record of meetings should be kept. A number of topics for discussion are suggested where appropriate.

PEOPLE TO MEET

Senior management: organizational structure and philosophy, etc.

Administrator: organizational rules, confidentiality, pay and conditions, staff welfare, etc.

Domestic bursar: meals, supplies, accommodation, etc.

Advisers (e.g. psychologists and social workers): role of advisers, statutory obligations, family visits, liaison with other agencies such as probation, etc.

Trade union representative: role of union, meetings, etc.

ORGANIZATIONAL INFORMATION

Supervision

Shift pattern

Training requirements

Emergency procedures

Meeting structure

Security

Record-keeping

Treatment procedures

Basic training

Basic training has several aims: (1) to provide staff with the treatment skills to begin to work in a behavioural manner and to understand the work of colleagues already working in this way; (2) to foster residential skills (which might vary from organization to organization); and (3) to increase awareness of professional issues. We have devised a system of six modules, delivered at the rate of approximately one a month, to cover the essentials of basic training. As a point of policy, all new members of staff must complete the basic and intermediate training. Our own experience, with the findings from the studies reported earlier, tells us that self-reported ability and knowledge do not necessarily match the required levels and standards. For reasons discussed in the *Training methods* section below, there are advantages in organizing the delivery of training, at all levels, in self-contained modules. An outline of these modules is shown below.

Module 1: Core concepts in behavioural theory and practice This includes key concepts such as reinforcement and punishment, modelling and extinction; and an introduction to behavioural methods such as shaping and fading, and reinforcement programmes. These are related specifically but not exclusively to adolescent and delinquent behaviour. *Time required*: one-day workshop.

Module 2: Measuring behaviour 1   As behavioural assessment and practice depends in large part on the accurate recording of behaviour, a module is included to introduce staff to the appropriate methods of measuring behaviour. This is linked to the organization's working practices, both in terms of the use of specific measuring instruments such as checklists and rating scales, and how the information from such instruments is used on a day to day basis. *Time required*: one-day workshop.

Module 3: Passing on information   The ability to communicate effectively is a fundamental professional skill. This module is therefore concerned with verbal communication skills, particularly at staff change-overs, and with written communication skills for internal documents such as treatment logs, and in writing reports for outside agencies such as courts. *Time required*: one-day workshop.

Module 4: Working in teams   Many if not all of us work in teams and this demands particular professional skills: for example, communication within the team, supervision practices, team problems and problem-solving. *Time required*: one-day workshop.

Module 5: Working practices   Organizational issues as they affect staff such as pay and conditions, policies on a range of matters; and issues concerned with the client group such as adolescence and antisocial behaviour, children's rights, juvenile justice, and other ethical and legal matters. *Time required*: one-day workshop.

Module 6: Applied computer training   If your organization has the resource of computers it is important to familiarize new staff with their use: we include computers in education, in information and data handling, and word processing. Again, however, the importance of this topic will vary from setting to setting. *Time required*: one-day workshop.

At the end of their first six months, new staff will have completed their induction training and will have some basic knowledge and skills at their disposal. This should, in turn, serve a number of functions from the point of view of both the individual members of staff and the organization. The new staff member should begin quickly to feel 'at home' with both the organization and the treatment methods, not going through a prolonged period of feeling lost and having to discover everything by chance and individual initiative. The organization will benefit from bringing a new staff member quickly 'on stream' so that he or she begins to work effectively relatively soon after arriving.

Intermediate training

The aims of intermediate training are to build on and develop the knowledge and skills encouraged during basic training. Again we suggest the use of a module system, and we have devised a system of ten modules delivered at the rate of about one every two months. To repeat the point made previously, some of these modules may be redundant or may need amendment in other settings.

Module 1: Measuring behaviour 2   This module develops the topics introduced in the module *Measuring Behaviour 1*: it addresses issues such as the utility of different methods of measuring behaviour, the concepts of reliability and validity of measurement, reactivity, and basic skills in using descriptive statistics to summarize observational data. *Time required*: one-day workshop.

Module 2: Functional analysis   This module draws the distinction between *assessment* in the sense of gathering data and information, and *analysis* in the sense of applying a theoretical model to make sense of that information. This module is therefore concerned with understanding and applying the A:B:C formulation (see Chapter 1), with attendant theoretical constructs, to treatment work. From the point of view of treatment skills this is arguably the most crucial module of all. In our opinion, a behavioural practitioner stands or falls according to his or her appreciation of the implications and complexities of functional analysis and ability to use it. *Time required*: one-day workshop.

Module 3: Applied behaviour analysis   This module is concerned with the application of behaviour analysis to the assessment and understanding of specific issues concerned with delinquents: this includes *offence analysis, current behaviours*, and *family functioning*.

Module 4: Changing behaviour   This module is concerned with development of skills in techniques, such as reinforcement programmes, used to *increase behaviour*; and with techniques, such as response cost, used to *decrease behaviour*. *Time required*: two half-day workshops.

Module 5: Social skills training   The technique of social skills training, and associated methods such as assertion skills training and life skills training, are frequently applied methods of helping people to change their behaviour. This module considers the conceptual and practical issues involved in skills training. *Time required*: one-day workshop.

Module 6: Behavioural contracting   Contracts can be a highly effective technique, both in terms of detailing agreements (i.e. a service contract) and in changing behaviour (i.e. a contingency contract). This module examines the theory, practicalities, and rules in writing behaviour contracts. *Time required*: one-day workshop.

Module 7: Self-control training   The use of cognitive-behavioural techniques is becoming much more widespread in behavioural work and this module considers the theory and practice of the particular technique of self-control training. *Time required*: one-day workshop.

Module 8: Using video and audio equipment   Video and audio equipment can be valuable resources for assessment, intervention, and evaluation. This module considers the practical, ethical, and legal issues associated with the use of recording equipment. *Time required*: one-day workshop.

Module 9: Dealing with aggression   This module is concerned with the aetiology of aggression and the factors that can promote aggressive behaviour. Techniques for the assessment and change of aggressive behaviour are examined. *Time required*: a half-day workshop.

Module 10: Working with families   This module is intended to give an introduction to a highly specialized field of work. The topics covered include family assessment and changing behaviour, particularly delinquent behaviour, through working with families. *Time required*: a half-day workshop.

After completion of this level of training, along with eighteen months of supervised practice working as part of a team, the member of staff should be capable of working to a relatively high standard. The next stage therefore seeks to build on these gains by pushing the level of training input to very high standards.

Advanced training

To commit time and resources to advanced training can be expensive in financial terms; however, the potential dividend on the investment can make an organization rich in talent and level of service it offers. One avenue for advanced training is to move in the direction of recognized academic training at a post-qualification or even postgraduate level. Again to draw on our own experience, this was a move that our organization made in 1983. We set up a partnership with a university and established the Diploma in Social Learning Theory and Practice. The diploma, first mentioned in print by Reid (1982) and subsequently discussed by Hollin *et al.* (1987) and Hollin (1990a), is a part-time course with a multi-disciplinary intake – of nurses, psychiatrists, psychologists, teachers, and both field and residential social workers – lasting for one calendar year. Therefore those completing the course must be prepared to commit themselves to a year of hard academic study and supervised practice. The diploma recruits half its intake from Glenthorne Youth Treatment Centre and half on an 'open' basis.

To complete the diploma, trainees are required to complete five pieces of work to a pass standard. These five pieces of work are two short essays (approximately 2,000 words) and one long essay (approximately 4,000 words); a case assessment displaying the ability to carry out a functional analysis (approximately 4,000 words); and a single-case study to display both assessment and intervention skills (approximately 12,000 words). The latter two pieces of work are completed in the trainee's place of work and are managed by an on-site supervisor.

The core topics covered by the course are shown in Table 5.6: this is not an exhaustive or final list, as it is continually modified to meet some demands of different courses and to reflect changes in the field.

The progression of material over the first three terms begins with behavioural theory and practice, with particular note of assessment; then follows practitioner skills, with an emphasis on evaluation; and finally the application of assessment and practice skills to particular client groups and types of presenting problem. Full details about the diploma are available on request (write to CRH at the University of Birmingham).

Other advanced training avenues are encouraged. The following are examples of sponsored training and development: higher degrees by research; Open University courses and degrees; higher degrees and diplomas by taught courses

Table 5.6 Core topics from an advanced course in behavioural theory and practice

Behavioural theory	classical conditioning, operant conditioning, social learning theory, extinction, generalization, internal and external control of reinforcement, modelling, primary and secondary reinforcement, reinforcement and punishment, schedules of reinforcement
Behavioural techniques	anxiety management, assertion training, behaviour rehearsal (covert and overt), biofeedback, chaining, coaching, cognitive behaviour modification (anger management, problem-solving, self-control, self-instructional training), constructional approach, contingency management, contracting, extinction programmes, feedback, flooding, relaxation training, response cost, shaping, social skills training, stimulus control, time out, token economy programmes
Practical skills	assessing contingencies, establishing baselines, evaluation skills, functional analysis, identifying and defining behaviours, interview skills, measuring behaviour, phasing out a behavioural programme, single-case design and analysis, writing contracts
Ethical issues	client rights (legal and moral), confidentiality, the use of negative reinforcement and punishment, reinforcement control, treatment versus management issues
Applications of behavioural techniques	aggressive and violent behaviour, conduct disorder, delinquency, disruptive behaviour, family work, neuroses, self-mutilation, sexual problems, psychoses
Applications in a wider social context	in community work, in the classroom, in residential settings, in hospitals

in, for example, education for children with special needs; and attendance at conferences and short courses. One development that we are seeking to encourage at present is the formation within the organization of Special Interest Groups. Thus, for example, if professional staff wish to develop their expertise in single-case methodology or in working with adolescents who have been physically or sexually abused then resources will be allocated to facilitate this interest. Typically, this might take the form of six or seven members of staff requesting a training input for which it might be necessary to buy in expert training. However, once the initial training has taken place, these professional staff are encouraged to establish a Special Interest Group in their chosen topic. This Special Interest Group will act as a support group, a seminar group, and a training group in the sense of both offering training and identifying its own further training needs. These groups will therefore develop the expertise of their members, thereby delivering a better service to the young people.

Prescribed training

While most training is delivered in a sequential manner, there are other areas of which all staff need to be aware whatever the stage of their career. These areas of prescribed training include in the main professional issues such as techniques for the safe control and restraint of aggression, first aid training, HIV Positive/AIDS training, race awareness training, and equal opportunities training. Most, if not all, of these training areas require expert trainers to be 'bought in'.

Needless to say, this all costs money and should therefore be part of the budget when estimating the cost of setting up a behavioural programme (see Chapter 2).

Training methods

As was discussed previously, there are several training methods available, some effective for teaching theory, others for developing practitioner skills. As most training courses are seeking to increase both knowledge and skills, it follows that a multiplicity of training methods can gainfully be used. Knowledge of behavioural principles is probably best taught by didactic methods such as seminars and reading assignments. However, one method that we are developing at present uses a behavioural style of teaching called *programmed learning*. Programmed learning is a style of self-instruction in which the person, in a sense, acts as his or her own teacher. A programmed learning text is written and given to the trainee; this text contains the facts the trainee has to learn, subdivided into various sections. At the end of each section there are a number of true/false questions that the trainee answers and then checks against the correct responses: any errors are explained, while correct answers confirm that the material has been understood and the next section can be tackled. An example from our programmed learning text (mainly the work of DK) is given in the Appendix to this chapter.

The use of these programmed learning packages dovetails neatly with the modular approach described above. Several programmed learning packages have been written for each module, thereby allowing each module to be delivered as a discrete package incorporating its own compendium of knowledge and skills. The great advantage of this is that the training at both basic and intermediate levels can be organized as a 'rolling programme'. In other words, new members of staff simply slot into the training programme when they arrive, beginning with whichever module is next in line. This removes the problem of new members of staff having to wait weeks or even months until a complete cycle of training is complete and then following a set course from beginning to end. It is our experience that with careful thought and planning independent, self-contained modules can be designed and used successfully.

To encourage practice skills, activity-based workshops are arranged, including training methods such as role-play, practice, feedback, discussion, and case examples. To facilitate generalization, the structure of the organization should be such as to reinforce the gains, both academic and practical, made during training (see Chapters 2, 3, and 4).

Monitoring and evaluation

It is important for a number of reasons to keep an accurate record of training. From the point of view of monitoring the progress of individual members of staff it is necessary to know who has completed what training, especially if completed training is to be a criterion for qualifying for more advanced training. There are several computerized database systems that have the flexibility to be used for this purpose and so allow individual 'training profiles' to be developed. A cumulative record of training, perhaps as 'training hours', or numbers of staff trained, or numbers of courses delivered (we recommend the first as it produces bigger numbers!), can be a powerful tool when bartering for resources. In our experience administrators like numbers, so the more numbers and figures you can produce the stronger you can make your case for funds for training. The training figures should be delivered with cost estimates to sustain present levels of output in the market-place, or even to increase productivity and thereby maximize the chances of enhanced consumer satisfaction and consumption (you need the necessary jargon too!).

The evaluation of training, as intimated previously, is a more difficult task. Short-term evaluation is not too difficult in terms of, for example, pre- and post-training tests of knowledge and behavioural principles. However, long-term evaluation is much more difficult and can be pitched at several levels: staff satisfaction with training; generalization of changes in knowledge and skills; and changes in client behaviour. Clearly this is a specialist research task and to be done well probably demands the time of an individual with research skills, time, and resources. If designing training from scratch this might be worth building into costings, although it will prove an expensive item.

APPENDIX 1 AN EXAMPLE FROM A PROGRAMMED LEARNING TEXT

Using reinforcement and punishment

Within the behavioural model there are a number of different relationships or contingencies between behaviour and the environmental events which influence behaviour. Most of the principles of operant conditioning refer to these different contingencies. The major principles associated with the model are outlined below; the application of the principles is dealt with in later sections.

There are basically four terms used to describe the type of reinforcement and punishment which may be associated with operant behaviour. Great care should be taken when using these terms as they are often misused or misunderstood.

There are two main types of reinforcement: positive and negative. It should be remembered that by definition both processes increase or maintain the frequency of a particular behaviour occurring.

1 *Positive reinforcement* An increase in the frequency of a behaviour brought about by the consequences of that behaviour is called 'positive reinforcement'. The event which follows the behaviour is referred to as a Positive Reinforcer and can include food, water, sex, praise, money, points, privileges, activities, or *any* event which serves to increase the behaviour it follows.

2 *Negative reinforcement* An increase in the frequency of behaviour that is immediately followed by the removal of an aversive event is referred to as 'negative reinforcement'.

N.B. Reinforcement *always* refers to an *increase* in behaviour.

An example of this would be telling James that when he does his homework he will not have to go to Grannie's house (assuming that going to Grannie's is an aversive event to James!).

There are also two types of punishment:

3 *Positive punishment* This is the presentation of an aversive event following behaviour that leads to a decrease in the behaviour. For example a child may be reprimanded after calling out in class or leaving a room without permission. The idea is that the aversive event (reprimand) should decrease the behaviour it followed (e.g. calling out).

4 *Negative punishment* This is the removal of a positive event following behaviour that leads to a decrease in the frequency of the behaviour. For example, a parent may remove a toy from a child for a period following the child misusing it (e.g. scratching a table with it).

It is important to note that punishment is not necessarily painful. Punishment only specifies a relationship (i.e. contingency) between behaviour and the events that follow behaviour. If behaviour decreases after the presentation or removal of a stimulus, this is a punishment contingency.

The four principles discussed above are easily confused. The table illustrates the differences.

	Positive	Negative
Reinforcement	Give a 'goody'	Take away a 'baddy'
Punishment	Give a 'baddy'	Take away a 'goody'

Questions on reinforcement and punishment
Answer each of the following questions by writing true or false in the space provided.

————— 1 Punishment must always be physically painful.

————— 2 An example of negative reinforcement is sending a child to bed when he or she has been naughty in order to decrease the 'naughty behaviour'.

————— 3 An example of positive reinforcement is giving a child something he or she wants in order to stop misbehaviour.

————— 4 An example of negative reinforcement is a boy doing his homework in order to get out of doing any chores.

Now check your answers with those below. If you have made any mistakes you may need to read points 1–4 again.

Answers

1 FALSE. Punishment is not necessarily painful. Punishment only specifies a relationship between behaviour and the consequences for that behaviour. If behaviour decreases following the consequences then this is a punishment contingency.

2 FALSE. Reinforcement must, by definition, serve to increase the likelihood of behaviour occurring. Sending the child to bed is an example of positive punishment being applied in order to decrease behaviour.

3 FALSE. If the intention is to decrease behaviour then giving the child something he or she wants may bring about a temporary cessation of the misbehaviour, but it is likely to serve to increase the likelihood of future misbehaviour. In this case the misbehaviour has been positively reinforced.

4 TRUE. By avoiding the aversive event (chores) there is an increase in 'homework behaviour'.

Chapter 6

Legality and integrity

In this final chapter our aim is to look at two kinds of pressures that come to bear on administrators and practitioners responsible for setting up and maintaining programmes for working with young offenders. On the one hand there are the legal issues that must set the framework within which programmes operate. In this chapter we look at two highly relevant pieces of legislation, the Children Act 1989, and the Criminal Justice Act 1991. One the other hand, with respect to the delivery of programmes, there is the bottom-line issue of treatment integrity. Programmes can be set up, staff trained, and a real momentum achieved, but how can that momentum be kept on line? In the second part of this chapter we consider the issue of treatment integrity. However, we begin with the legislation and the Children Act 1989.

THE CHILDREN ACT 1989

The Lord Chancellor, introducing what was to become the Children Act 1989, described this piece of legislation as the most comprehensive and far-reaching reform of child law that has come before Parliament in living memory. After full consultation with relevant agencies and with cross-party parliamentary support the Children Act 1989 came into force in October 1991. The Act draws together and simplifies existing legislation to produce a more practical and consistent code of child care, with the overriding purpose of promoting and safeguarding the welfare of children and young people. The aim here is not to review the Act in detail; there are several useful publications that already do this (e.g. Dept of Health, 1989; White *et al.*, 1990). Rather, the aim here is to examine some of the main principles of the Act and the implications they may have for the care, management, and treatment of difficult and delinquent young people. It is the case, of course, that the Children Act 1989 has extensive implications for practitioners working not just with delinquent young people but with all children and adolescents (Herbert, 1993).

The main principles of the Act are summarized in Table 6.1. Practitioners familiar with working with young people will notice some immediate changes from previous legislation, some of which are listed in Table 6.2.

Table 6.1 Principles of the Children Act 1989

- Parents should be responsible for bringing up their children. Local authorities and other agencies, however, should be ready to help when this reduces risk of family breakdown.
- Services should be delivered in voluntary partnership with parents, in a way that promotes family relationships as fully as possible.
- Transfer of parental responsibility to a local authority should require a Court Order after due process of law. The court must be satisfied that this is in the child's best interests.
- Children and parents should have full party status and representation in such proceedings.
- Emergency powers to remove a child at serious risk should be of short duration and subject to court review if challenged.
- Where a local authority looks after a child away from home its powers and responsibilities, and those of the child's parents, should be clear cut.

Table 6.2 Main changes introduced by the Children Act 1989

- A single unified code of child care law.
- The new concept of parental responsibility that underpins the Act.
- Custody and Access Orders in family proceedings are replaced with four new types of orders known collectively as Section 7 Orders: Residence Orders; Contact Orders; Prohibited Steps Orders; and Specific Issues Orders.
- Matrimonial Supervision Order largely replaced by Family Assistance Order. This is limited to 6 months duration.
- Only one entry route into care: voluntary care is replaced by provision of accommodation; parental rights resolutions are abolished; and local authority access to wardship is restricted.
- Local authority responsibilities to children and their families are codified.
- New grounds for care proceedings include 'actual and likely harm'. This effectively eliminates warding children.
- New Education Supervision Orders for non-school-attenders.
- Child Assessment Order introduced as new non-emergency protective measures.
- Place of Safety orders are replaced by new emergency Protection Order. This is shorter in duration, open to challenge in court, capable of extension, and includes new powers with respect to contact and medical examination.
- The Criminal Care Order is replaced by the Supervision Order with a residence requirement.

Children in their families: the role of parental responsibility

The Children Act 1989 introduces the concept of 'parental responsibility', replacing the term 'parental rights'. This change in terminology is intended to shift the emphasis away from the idea of children as property, stressing instead the duty and obligation of parents to provide for the moral, physical, and emotional health of their children. The importance of parental responsibility is underlined by the fact that responsibility is not only unaffected by the separation of parents, but is also unaffected when the courts make orders in any legal proceedings, such as divorce. The only exception to this rule is in adoption, when birth parents lose their responsibility for their child. Thus, any action taken by the courts, where there is a family breakdown for example, should not be regarded as lessening the duty of both parents to continue to play a full part in their child's development.

It follows therefore that the managers of treatment programmes for difficult and delinquent young people will be expected to consult more fully with parents and involve them in decision-making about how their child is managed and treated. (The point concerning families is supported by the research findings on the ingredients of successful programmes with young people who commit offences.) However, as a consequence of the Gillick case,[1] the Act now also recognizes that parental responsibility diminishes as the child acquires sufficient understanding to make his or her own decisions. Yet further, a more recent ruling has indicated that a mature adolescent cannot necessarily say no to treatment; those with parental responsibility can in some cases say yes to treatment.[2] In addition to consulting with parents, therefore, the Act stresses the need to involve young people as fully *as possible* in decision-making. Again, all these changes in emphasis are consistent with good behavioural practice, as discussed in Chapter 4. Effective behavioural programmes have always stressed the need to work closely with clients to identify goals and objectives that are both realistic and desirable.

The Act rests on the belief that children are generally best looked after within the family, with both parents playing as full a part as possible. Generally speaking, reception into residential care is considered an undesirable option. Consequently, programmes for difficult and delinquent young people will need to become even more family and community-oriented, with residential care, and especially secure accommodation, being used as a last resort, and even then for as short a time as possible. The possible long-term implications of this shift in emphasis are yet to be seen. However, it seems likely that practitioners will need to develop community-orientated skills, while residential programmes will face an increasingly more difficult client group. On the positive side, family and community-oriented programmes avoid the problems inherent in institutionalization and the difficulties of generalizing behavioural changes back into community settings. On the negative side, however, is the likelihood that families and statutory and voluntary agencies will experience heightened stress in attempting to maintain difficult and delinquent young people in the home environment.

Under the Act, local authorities have a duty within their area to give support to children and families in need; this places pressure on social workers, who will have to assess continuously the risk of the young person to him- or herself and to other people. Schedule 2 (paragraph 7) of the Act emphasizes the need for local authorities to take reasonable steps to encourage children in their area not to commit criminal offences. They must also take steps to avoid the need for children and young people to be placed in secure accommodation. It is likely that this will result in social workers more often seeking advice from other specialized disciplines, such as forensic psychiatrists and psychologists. Further, given the emphasis on the family, some local authorities may decide to run down residential resources and concentrate their expenditure on family and community work. Those young people who are deemed to need a residential setting, perhaps because of extremely disruptive and delinquent behaviour, may consequently be placed much further away from home. This, in turn, may create further problems for social workers, who have an obligation under the Act to ensure that contact with parents is maintained whenever a young person is looked after away from home. Similarly, as residential treatment programmes become more centralized, effective family work becomes problematic. We have already seen in Chapter 4 that family work and residential work are difficult to combine at the best of times (Barker, 1988); over long distances such work becomes even more difficult. There is a danger that providers of residential treatment programmes will be under increasing pressure to return young people home as soon as possible, often before treatment objectives have been achieved, and with inadequate time to allow for generalization of behavioural change into the natural environment. Thus careful planning, implementation, and monitoring of programmes become even more important in that they can inform decision-making about when to terminate residential accommodation.

The protection of children: the role of the courts

The Act seeks to protect young people both from the harm that can arise from failures or abuse within the family, and from the harm that can be caused by unwarranted outside intervention in family life. The courts are given wider powers to intervene to protect children at risk of harm within the family. A variety of protection orders, including Emergency Protection Orders and Police Protection Orders, are available to the court, provided certain preconditions are met. For young people who are beyond parental control, perhaps because of persistent delinquent activity, or who are likely to suffer significant harm because of a lack of reasonable parental care, the courts can impose a *care* or a *supervision order*. There is a responsibility on all parents to seek help if difficulties occur in bringing up their children, whether this is due to changes in either the family situation or the behaviour of the child, or both. It is important to note that care orders may no longer be imposed as a sentence in criminal proceedings (Section 7(7)(a) of the Children and Young Persons Act 1969 is repealed by

Schedule 15). The fact that a young person has committed an offence, however, may be evidence that he or she is suffering or is likely to suffer significant harm. If there are grounds for believing that harm is likely, a local authority may apply for a care or supervision order. In this context, 'harm' includes impairment of behavioural or social development.

Supervision orders, however, may still be made in criminal proceedings, although the Act emphasizes the differences between criminal and civil supervision. It does this in two main ways. First, supervision orders under the Act may impose requirements on adults with parental responsibility for the child and other people with whom the child is living. For example, a condition of supervision may be that parents attend weekly behavioural family therapy sessions. Second, the Act introduces a further requirement that may be imposed under a criminal supervision order: that the young person will live in accommodation provided by or on behalf of the local authority for up to six months, termed a 'residence requirement'. Such a requirement may also stipulate that the young person will not live with a named person during that period.

The acquisition of parental responsibility by a local authority can only occur after a court order, that is, after the due process of law. As might be expected, the law places very strict limitations upon local authorities in their exercise of parental responsibility. The Act instructs the courts to treat the welfare of the child as the paramount consideration when reaching a decision about his or her upbringing. It is also important that parents and children have full party status and legal representation in such proceedings. A welfare checklist has been constructed (Children Act, 1989, Chapter 41, pp. 1–2, as shown in Table 6.3), which is to be considered in care proceedings. An order should be made by the court only if this would be better for the young person than no order at all.

Children away from home: the need for partnership

The Act recognizes the fact that because their parents are unable to meet their developmental, behavioural, and emotional needs some young people will need to live away from home. Sometimes the young person may be placed in respite care to give the parents a break. When a young person is looked after away from home, the Act emphasizes that, wherever possible, this should be under voluntary arrangements with the parents. Parents thus maintain their parental responsibility, acting as partners with the local authority and the substitute carers. Even when a young person is under a care order, the Act provides for the parents to retain parental responsibility, to be involved in local authority decision-making, and for them to have reasonable contact with the young person unless the court decides otherwise.

As noted above, some young people with a history of criminal behaviour may be subject to a 'residence requirement'. This order is intended to be available for a repeat offender who has committed a serious offence and whose criminal behaviour is attributable to the circumstances in which he or she is living. A residence requirement may not be imposed unless the young person has been convicted of an offence

Table 6.3 The welfare checklist

The courts must consider:
- the ascertainable wishes and feelings of the child (considered in the light of his or her age and understanding);
- his or her physical, emotional, and educational needs;
- the likely effect on the child of any changes in circumstances;
- his or her age, sex, background and any characteristics that the courts consider relevant;
- any harm that the child has suffered or is at risk of suffering;
- how capable each parent, and any other relevant person, is of meeting his or her needs;
- the range of powers available to the court under the Act.

that the court considers to be serious and which, if committed by a person over the age of 21 years, would have resulted in imprisonment. This offence must have been committed while there was in force an earlier supervision order (under the 1969 Act) which either imposed requirements under Section 12A(3) of the 1969 Act, or imposed a previous residence request under Section 12AA of the same Act. Further, except where the young person was already subject to a residence requirement, his or her criminal behaviour must have been due, to a significant extent, to the circumstances in which he or she was living.

Some difficult and delinquent young people may find themselves placed in residential homes of various kinds. Although the Act emphasizes the role of the family, it also recognizes that occasionally residential care will be the only available option. However, it stresses that residential care should be seen as part of the general network of services for children, used in a planned way and only when it is in the best interests of the individual young person. The major principles of the Act – including partnership with parents, involvement of young people and those with parental responsibility in decision-making, the right to legal representation – applies equally to young people in residential settings. These should help to ensure that the placement is not seen in isolation from the general services that seek to provide support to families and to young people in need. A set of guidelines and regulations have been published aimed at bringing to residential managers and practitioners an understanding of the principles of the Children Act 1989, and to help discussion of the implications for policies, procedures, and practice (HMSO, 1991).

These guidelines have several implications for the management and treatment of difficult and delinquent young people in residential settings (see Table 6.4). They emphasize the importance of safeguarding and promoting the welfare of individual young people. This renewed emphasis of the individual should help to ensure good residential practice and, in turn, help to avoid the implementation of inappropriate management regimes, such as the 'pin-down' regime adopted in some Staffordshire children's homes.

Table 6.4 Implications of the Children Act 1989 for residential settings

- The need to state the purpose and function of the facility, including a description of the adopted 'ethos'.
- The need to specify the number, relevant experience, and qualifications of staff in post.
- The need to promote staff development and ensure that a body of competence and expertise is maintained.
- The need to promote written guidance on important procedures, e.g. methods of care and control, care planning, confidentiality, logbook and diary recording, child protection procedures, and disclosure of sexual abuse procedures.
- The need to provide staff supervision.
- The need for external consultancy for advice on specific issues, e.g. methods of highly specialized intervention.
- The need for good order and discipline.
- The avoidance of the use of prohibited measures, e.g. deprivation of food or drink and corporal punishment.
- The need for individualized case planning and record keeping.

CRIMINAL JUSTICE ACT 1991

Major legislative and policy developments affecting the way in which children and young persons in particular are dealt with after committing an offence have been prolific in Britain over the last decade. The Criminal Justice Act (1982) replaced the indeterminate Borstal Training Order with the determinate Sentence of Youth Custody. It also introduced 'Specified Activity Orders', a form of compulsory intermediate treatment. This was followed by DHSS Circular LAC 1983(3), which initiated alternatives to custody projects. The intention of this alternative to custody initiative was not only to reduce the use of custodial sentences for juvenile offenders, but also to establish inter-agency bodies to manage the projects and improve cooperation in the juvenile justice system.

The Police and Criminal Justice Act (1984) placed several safeguards and regulations around the detention and interviewing of juveniles, and laid down the principle that young people who were unable to return home should not be detained in police custody but should be placed in the care of the local authority. Home Office Circular 14/1985 gave strong official encouragement to the diversion from prosecution of juvenile offenders. This view was supported in Home Office Circular 59/1990, 'The cautioning of offenders', which referred to the need to extend such diversionary tactics to other age groups. The Criminal Justice Act 1988 introduced the power of the courts to certify that a specified Activities Order was made instead of custody. Following this, should there be a breach in proceedings, a custodial sentence would be available to sentencers.

Hard on the heels of the Children Act 1989, came the Criminal Justice Act 1991, the third such Act in the space of five years. If the Act has a central theme, it is the treatment of offenders after conviction (Waskik and Taylor, 1991), but it also addresses issues such as release from custody and service provision to both those convicted and those awaiting trial. Again, it is not our purpose here to review the Act in detail; several helpful guides have been published by the Home Office.

As discussed below, major reforms brought about by the Criminal Justice Act 1991 will have far-reaching effects on those who are involved in the treatment of offenders. One of the most important changes brought about by the Criminal Justice Act 1991 concerns sentencing procedures and practices. In principle, the severity of an individual's sentence should reflect, in the first instance, the severity of the crime that has been committed, or the need to protect the public from the offender. Factors associated with crime prevention and rehabilitation of the offender are not discounted, but should not lead to a heavier sentence in their own right. There is also a sharper distinction made between property offences and offences of a violent or sexual nature committed against the person. The Act recognizes that additional restrictions may need to be placed on the liberty of violent and sexual offenders to protect the public.

Changes have also been made in the procedures for administering sentences. The Act requires that the administration of sentences be both rigorous and fair to ensure that the sentencer's intentions are properly reflected in the way in which a sentence is served. The Act has abolished remission of sentences and replaced it with a system of early release on licence. The details of this system are shown in Table 6.5. Under this system of early release, all prisoners who are released before the end of their sentences remain at risk of having their sentences reactivated if they offend again.

The Act specifies that fines and, in particular, community sentences should not be viewed as an alternative to custody. Rather, such measures should play a part in their own right in the structure of penalties, being seen as methods of restriction of liberty.

Another change within the Criminal Justice Act 1991, of major importance for practitioners, is the way that children and young people are dealt with under

Table 6.5 Early release system under the Criminal Justice Act 1991

Sentence length	Point of release
1 year	Automatic release after serving half of the sentence
1 year to under 4 years	Release on licence at half-way point of sentence
4 years and over	Release between half-way and two-thirds point of sentence at the discretion of Parole Board (if sentence is 7 years or more, of the Home Secretary advised by the Parole Board)

criminal law. The basic standpoint taken by the Act is that the criminal justice system must deal with young offenders in a way that reflects both their age and development. As with the Children Act 1989, the Criminal Justice Act 1991 also seeks to include the principle of parental responsibility for the behaviour of their children. For example, parents are expected to attend court hearings, the court can consider whether parents should be bound over to exercise proper care and control of their children, and if a fine is administered parents will normally be expected to pay it and it is their means, not the child's, that is taken into account when determining the level of the fine or amount of compensation. These provisions, except for binding over, also apply to local authorities that have acquired parental responsibility.

The Act makes changes to the way that young people are dealt with both before and after their cases are heard. First, remand to prison custody for 15- and 16-year-old young men has been abolished (although the abolition has not been implemented at the time of writing). Instead courts have been given new powers to decide whether any young person of this age, male or female, should be held in local authority secure accommodation. To make such a decision the court must be satisfied that there is a need to protect the public from serious harm. The Act provides further new powers to enable the courts to impose conditions when remanding any juvenile to local authority accommodation. Yet further, juveniles should not be kept in police detention before being brought before the court unless it is impractical for the young person to be transferred to local authority accommodation.

Juvenile courts are now renamed Youth Courts. Although 17-year-olds continue to be treated as adults for the purposes of police detention and remand before court appearance, in terms of trial and sentencing 17-year-old offenders are treated as juveniles for the purposes of custodial sentencing.

Under the Act, 16- and 17-year-olds are seen to be nearing adulthood and are dealt with as a distinct group. It is recognized that owing to a range of developmental and social factors some young offenders will need to be dealt with as young adults and sentenced accordingly. However, for other offenders, their treatment may need to be more in line with young offenders. For young offenders under the age of 16 years, the main changes brought about by the Act are in relation to the degree of parental responsibility assumed for their behaviour. The practical impact of this change on parental responsibility has already been noted above.

For those practitioners working with young offenders in an attempt to reduce offence behaviour, the new regulations have had significant effects on the way this work needs to be planned and managed. The Act effectively makes release from custody at the half sentence point the norm for most offenders. Prior to the 1991 Act, those serving sentences of one year or more could normally expect to gain release during the second third of their sentence (in practice at the two-thirds point of the sentence). Thus, in effect there has been a reduction in the amount of time available to carry out any assessment or any treatment programmes. The practical impact of this change is an increase in the need for intervention programmes to be more tightly structured and managed if they are to be effective.

All young offenders who are granted early release on licence will be supervised by either the probation service or social services for at least three months. This period of compulsory supervision may be used to complete follow-up work in the community after release. This may have the benefits of extending the period over which treatment is carried out, and aiding both reintegration and generalization of treatment effects outside the custodial setting. Further, the period in the community may also improve the quality of follow-up data on the effectiveness of specific intervention techniques on recidivism. However, if these beneficial effects are to take place the treatment integrity of the programme needs to be high.

The notion of continuity between custodial and community work to maintain treatment integrity has enormous training implications. The quality of outcome will depend on all workers having the training and skills to carry out the programme. The need for effective liaison and communication networks between different agencies will be of paramount importance. At the same time release on licence recommendations, particularly in the case of violent and sexual offenders, will need to be based on evidence for both the offender's suitability for release and, after release, his or her continued release in the community. For this to be achieved intervention programmes need to be well managed so that it can be readily seen whether or not programme goals have been achieved and are being maintained. As discussed in Chapters 3 and 4, one of the hallmarks of a behavioural approach is the gathering of quantifiable information over the duration of the programme. When gathered reliably, this information can be used to inform decisions regarding release.

The move towards the establishment of new secure units for young offenders, to keep them out of the mainstream penal system, has major implications for the service to be offered. If these new units are not to become just 'holding tanks' for young criminals a rehabilitative ethos needs to be established. If this is to be done along the guidelines developed in this book then the resourcing implications cannot be neglected. However, failure to manage the system and resource it fully is likely to perpetuate juvenile and young adult crime. It is not necessary to be a behaviourist to see that incarcerating a young person with other young offenders with no positive attempt to change criminal behaviour is likely to be counterproductive.

Given that the assessment system is in place, given that treatment programmes are running, given an active staff training programme, given that there is compliance to the legal frameworks, can the manager sit back and watch it all happen? One of the laws of nature is that entropy increases, and any intervention programme left to its own devices will provide a perfect illustration of chaos from order. Perhaps the greatest challenge of all is to maintain programme integrity.

PROGRAMME INTEGRITY

In a book written in 1987, Herbert Quay, Professor of Psychology at the University of Miami, discussed some work he had undertaken a decade earlier.

In this earlier work, Quay had examined in detail an evaluation of a programme of group counselling with adult offenders. This study, originally made by Kassenbaum *et al.* (1971), had reported that the intervention, group counselling, had not had any impact on rates of recidivism. The design of the study, Quay continues, was exemplary, even involving random allocation of participants to treatment and control conditions. At face value we have a well-designed piece of outcome research, which, like so many others, found that a caring, therapeutic programme did not affect recidivism – more fuel, it seems, for the proponents of the 'nothing works' position.

However, when Quay began to look at the minutiae of the intervention it appeared that all was not as might have been wished. The treatment protocol was poorly defined and the delivery of the counselling itself was not well planned. Yet further:

> The majority of those responsible for carrying out the treatment were not convinced that it would affect recidivism (the major dependent variable of the study), and the group leaders (*not* professional counselors) were poorly trained. The treatment was clearly not well implemented.
>
> (Quay, 1987b, p. 246)

Indeed, to quote Quay yet again, 'What was striking was the serious lack of what we termed "program integrity"' (pp. 245–6). Nevertheless, in spite of these operational factors, which clearly would have diluted the impact of the programme, the study itself entered the annals of studies that fail to show any effect of intervention on recidivism.

THREATS TO INTEGRITY

One of the main points to emerge from the meta-analysis studies discussed in Chapter 1 is that the effectiveness of an intervention is dependent upon the rigour with which that intervention is conducted. It is now clear that the most effective programmes, in terms of reducing recidivism, have high treatment integrity: they are carried out by trained practitioners, and the treatment initiators are involved in all the operational phases of the programme (e.g. Lipsey, 1992a). In other words, effective programmes with high treatment integrity are characterized by sound management, tight design, and skilled practitioners.

It is important to note that treatment integrity applies equally to all interventions, regardless of their theoretical base, method of working, or client group. Treatment integrity simply means that the intervention is conducted in practice as intended in theory and design and therefore must be monitored while in progress.

As Moncher and Prins (1991) note, except for individuals such as Quay, concern about treatment integrity has only recently surfaced in the research literature on programme outcome. However, this is now changing rapidly, so that it is not impossible to see a position where in order to be taken seriously programmes will have to show that they have integrity. In order to begin to suggest a way forward, it is useful to identify the potential threats to integrity. There are at least three: (1) programme drift; (2) programme reversal; (3) programme non-compliance.

Programme drift

As described by Johnson (1981), programme drift is characterized by the gradual shift over time of the aim of a programme. Johnson describes how a psychodynamic programme for offenders gradually moved over time from an emphasis on therapeutic issues to a concern with routine administration. Johnson suggests that a lack of management and the attention to the immediacy of routine matters as opposed to longer-term therapeutic goals gradually changed the nature of the programme.

Programme reversal

The phenomenon of treatment reversal is perfectly illustrated by Schlichter and Horan (1981) in their account of a self-control programme to help young offenders work with their anger and aggression. They record how some staff worked to reverse and undermine the self-control approach: 'Some modeled aggressive behavior in response to anger provocations. Others operating from a different theoretical perspective encouraged the subjects to experience and express their "pent up" anger' (p. 34). Clearly these mixed messages from staff are less than satisfactory for all concerned, particularly the unfortunate young people for whom the experience must have been entirely confusing and counterproductive.

Programme non-compliance

Here we have a situation in which those conducting the programme elect, for reasons of their own, to change sections of the programme. At the whim of the practitioner, some sessions are dropped, new methods introduced, fresh targets for change added, the original material chopped about, and so on. The final product of all this, especially if there have been several sessions of in-service training, is rather like the end product of a game of Chinese Whispers. There may be some vestige of the original message, but the meaning is lost forever.

MAXIMIZING INTEGRITY

How then can these threats to integrity be guarded against? What needs to be done to maximize the chances of programme integrity? An applied psychologist might recommend: (1) a correctly formulated treatment protocol; (2) tight programme design; (3) demonstrable methodological rigour; (4) clearly specified independent and dependent variables; and (5) assessment of protocol reliability.

Table 6.6 Translating psychological into managerial jargon

Psychological term	Managerial term
1 Study protocol	Programme aim
2 Study design	Programme objective
3 Methodology and design	Programme target
4 Process and outcome variables	Performance indicators
5 Reliability checks	System audit

Now if this all sounds rather too psychological, what if we change the jargon? As shown in Table 6.6, the message translates reasonably well into management terminology. Programmes should have an *aim*, say to reduce recidivism among offenders placed on probation. There will be an *objective*, perhaps to introduce styles of working with offenders consistent with 'what works'. The *target* may be stated as 'Using trained staff, we will run *x* groups for *y* per cent of offenders in our organization'. There will, of course, be *performance indicators* such as attendance, process measures during the programme, and outcome measures from those completing the programme. Finally, managers will want an *audit system* that encompasses procedures to ensure programme integrity.

Now, clearly, the factors that ensure best practice are not going to happen of their own accord: those responsible for research and management must be aware of several factors.

PROGRAMME INTEGRITY: IN PRACTICE

To achieve high treatment integrity it is necessary to set the scene by paying attention to several areas before a client is seen.

Treatment definition

It is an obvious point, but worth stating, that to be able to follow a treatment programme, it is first necessary to define what is to be done during that programme. In practice this means a statement of quantity and content, for example, the planned number of sessions and length of sessions; knowing which techniques will be used; planning and detailing the content of sessions; and the selection and justification of the measures that will be used to evaluate changes in the client's behaviour. This whole procedure is made much easier when programmes are guided by a *treatment manual*.

A good manual is one that is firmly based on a respectable theory, and is itself meticulously researched and evaluated by proficient researchers and practitioners. A sound manual will contain detailed guidelines for the design, implementation, running, and evaluation of a given treatment programme. For example, suppose you wished to write a social skills training manual. This manual would have to contain a discussion of the theoretical basis of social skills training; details of skills training techniques; information about the equipment needed; suggestions for practice, say how to construct a role-play and some vignettes around which to construct role-plays for different situations; information on the ordering of components of the programme – typically modelling, role-play, practice, feedback; how to handle tricky situations, such as someone not coming 'out of role' after a role-play; and scales for evaluation of outcome.

Having set up the programme, the active part of the process needs to be considered, that is, the methods that can be used to monitor and inform management of treatment integrity. Needless to say, this is enormously time-consuming.

Assessing quantity and quality

There are three sources of information on the quality and quantity of treatment: (1) outside observers of programmes; (2) client report; (3) practitioner report. While there is room for all three, it is generally agreed that outside observers are the most objective and reliable judges, especially of the quality of the intervention.

Observer recording

In order to be effective recorders of treatment integrity, outside observers must be in a position to examine the actual work, not just rely on verbal reports from practitioners and clients. To maximize the utility of outside observers, a number of conditions must be met. The observers, note the plural, must themselves be skilled and trained in the treatment approach, and be familiar with the particular planned programme they are going to observe. The periods of observation, using live or videotaped observation, must be substantial and, ideally, follow a pre-arranged sampling schedule. For example, the decision could be made to sample, say, 50 per cent of sessions; or to observe all the components of the treatment programme. The observers should be trained to follow the same procedures in recording their observations. There are several rating procedures available that can be adapted for most purposes (e.g. Marziali et al., 1981).

The final product of the observational evaluation will be a statement of the match between what was planned at the outset and what was delivered in practice. Such a statement of quality and quantity has a number of uses (for both managers and practitioners): it can be used to answer questions about the client's experience of treatment; it can be helpful in informing the design of future treatment programmes; it can be a useful method of performance feedback to practitioners; and it should be an essential component of outcome studies.

Practitioner and client report

While observer information is important, the need to consider the views of practitioners and clients should not be ignored in measuring treatment integrity. A system should be developed to allow practitioners and clients systematically to record their judgements of the progress and integrity of the programme. A record should be kept of the quantitative aspects – length of sessions, number of sessions, etc. – of the programme. Periodic debriefing interviews should be held with both practitioners and clients, while practitioners should be encouraged to keep a log of contacts, recording both quantitative and qualitative information (Johnson, 1981). Using information on the progress of the programme from observer ratings, practitioner logs, and client feedback, it should be possible to establish the degree of treatment integrity. Basically, this statement of integrity will be across several dimensions, some of which might be put into questions as follows: (1) Was the quantity of treatment as planned? (2) Did the practitioner stay on course or was there a drift away from the planned focus of the programme? (3) Was there significant client change, in the anticipated direction, on the evaluation measures? and (4) Did the client feel that his or her expectations had been met?

There are several examples of schedules designed to assess overall programme integrity. For example, the STOP Probation Programme in mid-Glamorgan in Wales produced a document for practitioners, 'Achieving programme integrity', which not only makes the case for integrity but gives their Programme Integrity Checklist. This checklist, completed by session leaders and programme consultants, gives a number of ratings, such as the extent to which session focus was maintained, and deviations from the planned session. Thus the first report on the STOP Programme was not only able to comment generally on maintenance of integrity, but was able to pinpoint where and how integrity was threatened (Lucas *et al.*, 1992). This procedure has the advantage that the eventual outcome figures of the STOP programme evaluation will be informed by the assessment of integrity. The Correctional Programme Evaluation Inventory by Gendreau and Andrews (1991) is a highly sophisticated psychometric instrument that looks at a range of programme characteristics, including integrity.

What happens when we go to this amount of trouble in thinking about integrity? Once you begin to consider issues of integrity, you are forced to think about quality. Three specific areas – ethics, practice, research – immediately suggest themselves as being of importance.

THE IMPORTANCE OF INTEGRITY

Ethical issues

If as practitioners we enter an agreement with a client to undertake a specific piece of work, then there is a strong argument to say that we are ethically bound to make sure that we can give our clients some basic facts. We should be able to inform clients what that work entails, how long it will last, how it will be carried out, and what might reasonably be expected as an outcome if they participate fully. It is important to note that the definition of 'client' can be extended to include not only the individuals we see on a face-to-face basis, but also the courts with whom we make agreements about what will happen in given cases. As noted, a clear statement of the programme's aims and methods is a prerequisite for treatment integrity, which goes some way towards satisfying the ethical demands. The monitoring of treatment integrity further extends our ability to respond to ethical demands. Not only should we be able to state what we plan to do, we should be able to state whether the planning has turned into practice. Armed with this level of knowledge, we can state to clients, courts, and anyone else who is interested, that the agreement has been kept (and if not, why not).

Practice issues

Leaving aside ethical issues, there are practical benefits to be gained from working towards high levels of treatment integrity through monitoring the effects of one's programme. The first is that many programmes last for lengthy periods of time, and although the intervention is successful the rate of change can be slow. A record of the progress and effects of treatment can both remind practitioner and client of what has been achieved, and reinforce their working relationship. The second practical reason for monitoring progress is that if a programme is failing it can be detected at an early stage and appropriate steps taken. In truth, both these practical reasons are different sides of the same coin: systematically looking to see whether what we are doing is what we set out to do, and whether we are having the desired effect. Armed with this knowledge we should be in a position to improve the quality of practice and therefore the level of the service delivered.

Research issues

It is probably true to say that most practitioners are not researchers in the formal, academic sense of the term. However, there is most certainly research taking place – in Manchester and Glamorgan, for example – that has the potential to have a substantial impact on probation work. Knowledge of treatment integrity, as Quay so graphically described, is essential when it comes to reading the results of studies of the effectiveness of treatment programmes. For research findings to be of impact, it must be shown that all participants followed the same programme, using trained and skilled practitioners, with identical outcome measures.

While structured programmes will go some way towards setting the scene for high treatment integrity, clearly they will not be sufficient on their own. Attention must also be paid to the needs of the practitioners who are going to be using the manuals.

Practitioners

Selection, training, and support

It is true to say that most practitioners have a preferred style of working and like particular client groups. Some people like working with groups, others prefer working with individuals; some practitioners like one style of counselling, some like another; some prefer active methods of working, like role-play and modelling, others prefer more contemplative, less directive methods; some people like working with adolescents, others prefer adults. There is, of course, room for all styles and approaches, but it makes sense at the onset to match practitioners to their preferred style of intervention. This is particularly true when it comes to the type of work being advocated here; for reasons we will return to, it is possible that not all practitioners will be happy for some of their work to be guided by a manual.

For those practitioners who elect to use a structured approach, training is absolutely essential, and likely to increase treatment integrity. Trained practitioners are more likely to be competent practitioners, who understand why they are doing what they are doing and who stay with the programme. In addition, a practitioner whom clients perceive as capable is more likely to be successful. However, it is worth noting that it is unlikely that such training is going to be achieved quickly.

It would be wrong, however, to assume that training will solve all the problems. The availability of supervision is a vital ingredient in maintaining programme integrity. Through supervision by an experienced individual, practitioner performance can be monitored and feedback offered. Needless to say, supervisory arrangements should be negotiated before treatment begins.

PROBLEMS AND PITFALLS

By this stage, it will be evident that the monitoring of programme integrity faces a number of obstacles; there are three potential sources for such obstacles: the organization, the client, and the practitioner.

Organizational resistance

The concept of organizational resistance refers to the obstacles, be they in a community or institutional setting, that hinder and impede the development of programmes with high treatment integrity. In a classic paper Laws (1974) described the problems he faced when attempting to set up a residential treatment programme with offenders. Essentially these difficulties were about who exercised control over the programme to safeguard treatment integrity; who had control over admission of offenders to the programme; who had control over the timing of offenders leaving the programme; who had control over the finances and resources; and who had control over practitioner training to run the programme. Laws, as have others, documented professional clashes with both administrators and fellow practitioners.

Of course it would be foolish to suggest that such organizational issues will be easily resolved. However, if we return to the principles described by Reppucci (1973), as detailed in Chapter 1, some solutions begin to appear. To recap, Reppucci suggested that the chances of treatment integrity will be greatly increased if policies can be formulated according to six principles: (1) a clear guiding philosophy that is understood by *all* those involved in the process of rehabilitation; (2) an organizational structure that facilitates communication and accountability; (3) an involvement of all staff in decision-making; (4) maximizing the use of everyone's skills; (5) maintaining a community orientation; and (6) setting time restraints in developing and 'tuning' programmes, thereby resisting the pressure to try to do too much in too short a space of time.

Clearly the formulation of policies around these points is a highly demanding and involved task. One of the pitfalls that it is easy to fall into is that training will solve all the organization's problems. However, as Ziarnik and Berstein (1982) point out, there are many reasons other than a lack of training that can account for poor organizational performance. There may not be any clear criteria by which staff and management can judge performance; poor performance may be reinforced socially by the organizational culture, or tangibly by the award of incentives such as pay rises and promotion on criteria other than practitioner skills; or practitioner skills are not reinforced in an organization that places greater priority on other matters. In other words, if the organization is not committed to treatment integrity, even the most highly trained, highly skilled practitioners will have little impact. No amount of training is going to change an organizational climate that only gives lip service to the importance of treatment integrity. Training is a strategy to be used within, not instead of, a coherent organizational structure.

Client resistance

In the same way that clients may be reluctant to engage in programmes, so they may similarly be reluctant to engage in evaluation. However, this may be a matter of presentation: if an expectation of contributing towards evaluation is part of the programme, rather than being presented as an optional extra, then client compliance is much more likely. Indeed, with today's consumer-led ethos, clients might well welcome the chance to offer an appraisal of the service they are offered!

Practitioner resistance

We can see two dimensions to practitioner objections to monitoring of treatment integrity: one at a philosophical level, the other at a practice level.

Philosophical objections

To engage in measurement of treatment integrity, one has to accept two related underlying principles. The first is that one adopts a scientist-practitioner approach to one's work; the second is that one accepts that an empirical approach should inform one's practice. In other words, one is committed to the principle that one's practice will be informed by data gathered, as much as possible, according to the rules of scientific enquiry. There are several excellent guides that will help practitioners evaluate their work (e.g. Herbert, 1990).

Related to this empirical approach is the partial surrender of professional autonomy. When practice is based on an established programme, it becomes much more difficult to sustain the position that practitioners each know what is best for their clients and work along those lines, doing what they feel they and their clients will relate to. It is true that when guided by rigorous assessment the practitioner will be uniquely placed to judge his or her client's needs. However, once the decision is made, say, to use a Reasoning and Rehabilitation programme (Ross and Fabiano, 1985), it has to be accepted that one will follow the programme manual. It has to be agreed at the onset that the package has been designed as a package, not something to borrow from and change as one might see fit. This tinkering is a recipe for low treatment integrity, which is known not to be conducive to a good outcome. We know from experience that practitioners will differ in their response to this: some will happily and creatively work within these rules, while others will be unable to accept these principles. This is not to say who is right and who is wrong: we recognize, of course, that there are other equally valid philosophies in this area. However, we maintain that each approach must maintain its own standards of integrity; it is difficult to see any role for a practice based on mix and match eclecticism.

Practical objections

The practical objections are those objections that arise every time evaluation is mentioned: namely, that the evaluation can be intrusive, and that the information could be misused. Both are surely true, but neither is insurmountable. We sit in on our student's work, so why should it be impossible to make acceptable arrangements for others to sit in, or even videotape, our work? It is the case that evaluation data can be used in ways for which it was not intended, say by management, to appraise practitioner performance to inform promotion decisions. To prevent this, stringent conditions must be detailed at the outset about who has access and what purpose the data will serve.

NOTES

1 *Gillick* vs. *West Norfolk and Wisbech Area Health Authority* (1986) AC112, (1985) 3 All ER 402, H.
2 RER, (1993) 4 ALL ER177.

Epilogue

There can be little doubt that at present we are seeing the re-emergence of a treatment ethos in the field of working with offenders (Palmer, 1992). The meta-analyses have pointed us in the direction we should move towards to construct effective programmes. There is a groundswell of optimism among practitioners, a belief that working with offenders can be effective. As managers and supervisors, we should be prepared to listen to and respond to this cultural change.

However, it is not enough to apply knowledge solely to the content of programmes; if we have learnt nothing else from the last twenty years, we must surely have learnt that practice needs support and management. With programme content informed by the outcome studies and with good supervision and management systems in place, programme integrity begins to look possible. It is plain that there are many issues to be grappled with before treatment integrity becomes an accepted part of everyone's practice. It is our genuine hope that this book will make a contribution, no matter how small, towards defining the issues and suggesting the way towards managing the quandary of programme integrity. All of those who work with young people who offend are taking on a crucial task: the penalty for failure is severe, the gains for success are many.

References

Adams, G. L., Tallon, R. J., and Rimell, P. (1980). A comparison of lecture versus role-playing in the training of the use of positive reinforcement. *Journal of Organizational Behavior Management, 2*, 205–12.

Aichhorn, A. (1955). *Wayward Youth* (translation) New York: Meridian Books. (Original work published in 1925).

Aiken, T. W., Stumphauzer, J. S., and Veloz, E. V. (1977). Behavioural analysis of non-delinquent brothers in a high juvenile crime community. *Behavioral Disorders, 2*, 212–22.

Akers, R. L. (1977). *Deviant Behavior: A Social Learning Approach* (2nd edn). Belmont, CA: Wadsworth.

Alberts, G. and Edelstein, B. (1990). Therapist training: a critical review of skill training studies. *Clinical Psychology Review, 10*, 497–511.

Alevizos, P., DeRisi, W., Liberman, R., Eckman, T., and Callahan, E. (1978). The behavior observation instrument: a method of direct observation for program evaluation. *Journal of Applied Behavior Analysis, 11*, 243–57.

Alexander, J. F. and Parsons, B. V. (1973). Short-term behavioural intervention with delinquent families: impact on family processes and recidivism. *Journal of Abnormal Psychology, 81*, 219–25.

Alexander, J. F. and Parsons, B. V. (1992). *Functional Family Therapy*. Monterey, CA: Brooks/Cole.

Anastasi, A. (1982). *Psychological Testing*. New York: Macmillan.

Anderson, J. R. (1980). *Cognitive Psychology and its Implications*. San Francisco, CA: W. H. Freeman.

Andrews, D. A., Zinger, I., Hoge, R. D., Bonta, J., Gendreau, P., and Cullen, F. T. (1990). Does correctional treatment work? A clinically relevant and psychologically informed meta-analysis. *Criminology, 28*, 369–404.

Arco, L. and Birnbrauer, J. S. (1990). Performance feedback and maintenance of staff behavior in residential settings. *Behavioral Residential Treatment, 5*, 207–17.

Argyle, M. (1983). *The Psychology of Interpersonal Behaviour* (4th edn). Harmondsworth: Penguin Books.

Ayllon, T. and Azrin, N. H. (1968). *The Token Economy: A Motivational System for Therapy and Rehabilitation*. New York: Appleton-Century-Crofts.

Balcazar, F., Hopkins, B. L., and Suarez, Y. (1986). A critical, objective review of performance feedback. *Journal of Organizational Behavior Management, 7*, 65–89.

Baldwin, S., Wilson, M., Lancaster, A., and Allsop, D. (1988). *Ending offending: an Alcohol Training Resource Pack for People Working with Young Offenders*. Glasgow: Scottish Council on Alcohol.

Bandura, A. (1977). *Social Learning Theory*. Englewood Cliffs, NJ: Prentice-Hall.

Bandura, A. (1986). *Social Foundations of Thought and Action: a Social Cognitive Theory*. Englewood Cliffs, NJ: Prentice-Hall.

Bank, L., Patterson, G. R., and Reid, J. B. (1987). Delinquency prevention through training parents in family management. *The Behavior Analyst, 10,* 75–82.

Barker, P. (1988). The future of residential treatment for children. In C. E. Schaefer and A. J. Swanson (eds), *Children in Residential Care: Critical Issues in Treatment*. New York: Van Nostrand Reinhold.

Barlow, D. H., Hayes, S. C., and Nelson, R. O. (1984). *The Scientist Practitioner: Research and Accountability in Clinical and Educational Settings*. Elmsford, NY: Pergamon Press.

Barlow, D. H. and Hersen, S. C. (1984). *Single Case Experimental Designs: Strategies for Studying Behavior Change* (2nd edn). Elmsford, NY: Pergamon Press.

Barlow, G. (1979). United Kingdom: The Youth Treatment Centre. In C. J. Payne and K. J. White (eds), *Caring for Deprived Children: International Case Studies of Residential Settings*. London: Croom Helm.

Basta, J. M. and Davidson, W. S. (1988). Treatment of juvenile offenders: study outcomes since 1980. *Behavioral Sciences and the Law, 6,* 355–84.

Bellack, A. S. and Hersen, M. (eds) (1988). *Behavioral Assessment: a Practical Handbook* (3rd edn). Elmsford, NY: Pergamon Press.

Bellack, A. S., Hersen, M., and Kazdin, A. E. (eds) (1986). *International Handbook of Behavior Modification and Therapy* (2nd edn). New York: Plenum Press.

Bernadin, H. J. and Pence, E. C. (1980). Effects of rater training: creating new response sets and decreasing accuracy. *Journal of Applied Psychology, 65,* 60–6.

Bernstein, G. S. (1982). Training behaviour change agents: a conceptual review. *Behavior Therapy, 13,* 1–23.

Berridge, D. and Cleaver, H. (1987). *Foster Home Breakdown*. London: Basil Blackwell.

Blackburn, R. (1993). *The Psychology of Criminal Conduct: Theory, Research and Practice*. Chichester: Wiley.

Blakely, C. H. and Davidson, W. S. (1984). Behavioral approaches to delinquency: a review. In P. Karoly and J. J. Steffen (eds), *Adolescent Behavior Disorders: Foundations and Contemporary Concerns*. Lexington, MA: Lexington Books.

Blasi, A. (1980). Bridging moral cognition and moral action: a critical review of the literature. *Psychological Bulletin, 88,* 1–45.

Blumenthal, G. J. (1985). *Development of Secure Units in Child Care*. Aldershot: Gower.

Blyth, D. A., Simmons, R. G., and Bush, D. (1978). The transition into early adolescence: a longitudinal comparison of youth in two educational contexts. *Sociology of Education, 51,* 149–62.

Bootzin, R. R. and Ruggill, J. S. (1988). Training issues in behavior therapy. *Journal of Consulting and Clinical Psychology, 56,* 703–9.

Bouchard, M. A., Wright, J., Mathieu, M., Lalonde, F., Bergeron, G., and Toupin, J. (1980). Structured learning in teaching therapists social skills training: acquisition, maintenance, and impact on client outcome. *Journal of Consulting and Clinical Psychology, 48,* 491–502.

Boudewyns, P. A., Fry, T. J., and Nightingale, E. J. (1986). Token economy programs in VA medical centers: where are they today? *The Behavior Therapist, 6,* 126–7.

Braukmann, C. J., Bedlington, M. M., Bedlen, B. D., Braukmann, P. D., Husted, J. J., Kirigin, K., and Wolf, M. M. (1985). The effects of community-based group–home treatment programs for male juvenile offenders on the use and abuse of drugs and alcohol. *American Journal of Drug and Alcohol Abuse, 11,* 249–78.

Braukmann, C. J. and Wolf, M. M. (1987) Behaviorally based group homes for juvenile offenders. In E. K. Morris and C. J. Braukmann (eds), *Behavioral Approaches to Crime and Delinquency: a Handbook of Application, Research, and Concepts.* New York: Plenum Press.

Brewin, C. R. (1988). *Cognitive Foundations of Clinical Psychology.* London: Lawrence Erlbaum.

Brophy, J. (1981). Teacher praise: a functional analysis. *Review of Educational Research, 51,* 5–32.

Brown, W. C. (1961). *Freud and the Post-Freudians.* Harmondsworth: Penguin Books.

Brown, B. (1985). An application of social learning methods in a residential programme for young offenders. *Journal of Adolescence, 8,* 321–31.

Brown, B. (1987). Behavioural approaches to working with adolescents in trouble. In J. C. Coleman (ed.), *Working with Troubled Adolescents: a Handbook.* London: Academic Press.

Brown, K. M., Willis, B. S., and Reid, D. H. (1981). Differential effects of supervisor verbal feedback and feedback plus approval on institutional staff performance. *Journal of Organizational Behavior Management, 3,* 57–68.

Bullock, R., Hosie, K., Little, M., and Millham, S. (1990). Secure accommodation for very difficult adolescents: some recent research findings. *Journal of Adolescence, 13,* 205–16.

Burchard, J. D. (1967). Systematic socialization: a programmed environment for the rehabilitation of antisocial retardates. *Psychological Record, 17,* 461–76.

Burchard, J. D. (1987). Social policy and the role of the behavior analyst in the prevention of delinquent behavior. *The Behavior Analyst, 10,* 83–8.

Burchard, J. D. and Burchard, S. N. (eds) (1987). *Prevention of Delinquent Behavior.* Beverly Hills, CA: Sage.

Burchard, J. D. and Harrington, W. A. (1986). Deinstitutionalization: programmed transition from the institution to the community. *Child and Family Behavior Therapy, 7,* 17–32.

Burchard, J. D. and Lane, T. W. (1982). Crime and delinquency. In A. S. Bellack, M. Hersen, and A. E. Kazdin (eds), *International Handbook of Behavior Modification and Therapy.* New York: Plenum Press.

Burchard, J. D. and Tyler, V. (1965). The modification of a delinquent behaviour through operant conditioning. *Behaviour Research and Therapy, 2,* 245–50.

Burdett, C. and Milne, D. (1985). 'Setting Events' as determinants of staff behaviour: an exploratory study. *Behavioural Psychotherapy, 13,* 300–8.

Burg, M. M., Reid, D. H., and Lattimore, J. (1979). Use of a self-recording and supervision program to change institutional staff behavior. *Journal of Applied Behavior Analysis, 12,* 333–75.

Burgess, A. W., Hartman, C. R., and McCormack, A. (1987). Abused to abuser: antecedents of socially deviant behaviours. *American Journal of Psychiatry, 144,* 1431–6.

Burgio, L. D., Whitman, T. L., and Reid, D. H. (1983). A participative management approach for improving direct-care staff performance in an institutional setting. *Journal of Applied Behavior Analysis, 16,* 37–53.

Calabrese, R. L. and Adams, J. (1990). Alienation: a cause of juvenile delinquency. *Adolescence, 25,* 435–40.

Canter, D. and Canter, S. (eds) (1979). *Designing for Therapeutic Environments: a Review of Research.* Chichester: Wiley.

Carney, L. P. (1977). *Probation and Parole: Legal and Social Dimensions.* New York: McGraw-Hill.

Catania, A. C. and Harnad, S. (eds) (1988). *The Selection of Behavior: The Operant Behaviorism of B. F. Skinner: Comments and Consequence.* Cambridge: Cambridge University Press.

CCETSW (1992). *Setting Quality Standards for Residential Child Care.* London: CCETSW.

Chamberlain, P., Patterson, G., Reid, J., Kavanagh, K., and Forgatch, M. (1984). Observation of client resistance. *Behavior Therapy*, *15*, 133–55.

Christensen, A., Johnson, S. M., and Glasgow, R. E. (1980). Cost effectiveness in behavioral family therapy. *Behavior Therapy*, *11*, 208–26.

Ciminero, A. R., Calhoun, K. S., and Adams, H. E. (eds) (1986). *Handbook of Behavioral Assessment* (2nd edn). New York: Wiley.

Clarke, R. V. (1985). Jack Tizard Memorial Lecture: Delinquency, environment and intervention. *Journal of Child Psychology and Psychiatry*, *26*, 505–23.

Clements, J. (1992). I can't explain . . . 'challenging behaviour': towards a shared conceptual framework. *Clinical Psychology Forum*, *39*, 29–37.

Cole, P. G., Chan, L. K. S., and Lytton, L. (1989). Perceived competence of juvenile delinquents and non-delinquents. *Journal of Special Education*, *23*, 294–302.

Coleman, J. C. and Hendry, L. (1990). *The Nature of Adolescence*. London: Routledge.

Corcoran, K. J. (1988). Understanding and coping with burnout. In C. E. Schaefer and A. J. Swanson (eds), *Children in Residential Care*. New York: Von Nostrand Reinhold.

Cornish, D. B. and Clarke, R. V. G. (eds) (1986). *The Reasoning Criminal: Rational Choice Perspectives on Offending*. New York: Springer-Verlag.

Cullen, F. T. and Gendreau, P. (1989). The effectiveness of correctional rehabilitation: reconsidering the 'nothing works' debate. In L. Goodstein and D. MacKenzie (eds), *The American Prison*. New York: Plenum Press.

Cullen, J. E. and Seddon, J. W. (1981). The application of a behavioural regime to disturbed young offenders. *Personality and Individual Differences*, *2*, 285–92.

Davidson, W. S., Redner, R., Andur, R. C., and Mitchell, C. M. (1990). *Alternative Treatments for Troubled Youth: the Case of Diversion from the Justice System*. New York: Plenum Press.

Davidson, W. S., Redner, R., Blakely, C. H., Mitchell, C. M., and Emshoff, J. G. (1987). Diversion of juvenile offenders: an experimental comparison. *Journal of Consulting and Clinical Psychology*, *55*, 68–75.

Davis, H. (1985). Training professionals in behaviour modification. *British Journal of Medical Psychology*, *58*, 241–8.

Davies, W. (1989). The prevention of assault on professional helpers. In K. Howells and C. R. Hollin (eds), *Clinical Approaches to Violence*. Chichester: Wiley.

Dean, C. W. and Reppucci, N. D. (1974). Juvenile correctional institutions. In D. Glaser (ed.), *Handbook of Criminology*. Chicago: Rand McNally.

Department of Health (1989). *An Introduction to the Children Act 1989*. London: HMSO.

Dixon, N. (1984). *Evaluation of the Professional Home Care Project: Working Paper No. 1*. London: Dr Barnardo's.

Doerner, M., Miltenberger, R. G., and Bakken, J. (1989). The effects of staff self-management on positive social interactions in a group home setting. *Behavioral Residential Treatment*, *4*, 313–30.

Donat, D. C. and McKeegan, G. F. (1990). Behavioral knowledge among direct care staff in an inpatient psychiatric setting. *Behavioral Residential Treatment*, *5*, 95–103.

Dunlop, A. B. (1974). *The Approved School Experience*. Home Office Research Study No. 25. London: HMSO.

Edelstein, B. A. and Michelson, L. (eds) (1986). *Handbook of Prevention*. New York: Plenum Press.

Edens, F. M. and Smit, G. N. (1992). Effectiveness of a skills training program for residential child care workers. *Children and Youth Services Review*, *14*, 541–52.

Elliot, D. and Voss, H. (1974). *Delinquency and Dropout*. Lexington, MA: Lexington Books.

Emerson, E. and Emerson, C. (1987). Barriers to the effective implementation of rehabilitative behavioural programs in an institutional setting. *Mental Retardation*, *25*, 101–6.

Emshoff, J. G., Redd, W. H., and Davidson, W. S. (1976). Generalization training and the transfer of prosocial behavior in delinquent adolescents. *Journal of Behavior Therapy and Experimental Psychiatry*, 7, 141–4.

Epps, K. J. (1990). 'Managing violence in institutions for disturbed adolescents'. Paper presented at the 20th European Congress on Behaviour Therapy, University of Paris, Paris. (Available from author.)

Farrington, D. P. (1983). Offending from 10 to 25 years of age. In K. Teilmann Van Dusen and S. A. Mednick (eds), *Prospective Studies of Crime and Delinquency*. The Hague: Kluwer-Nijhoff Publishing.

Farrington, D. P. (1986). Age and crime. In M. Tonry and N. Morris (eds), *Crime and Justice: an Annual Review of Research*, vol. 7. Chicago: University of Chicago Press.

Farrington, D. P. (1987). Epidemiology. In H. C. Quay (ed.), *Handbook of Juvenile Delinquency*. New York: Wiley.

Feindler, E. L. and Ecton, R. B. (1986). *Adolescent Anger Control: Cognitive Behavioral Techniques*. Elmsford, NY: Pergamon Press.

Feindler, E. L., Marriott, S. A., and Iwata, M. (1984). Group anger control training for junior high school delinquents. *Cognitive Therapy and Research*, 8, 299–311.

Fishman, D. B., Rotgers, F., and Franks, C. M. (eds) (1988). *Paradigms in Behavior Therapy: Present and Promise*. New York: Springer.

Fleming, R. K. and Sulzer-Azaroff, B. (1989). Enhancing quality of teaching by direct care staff through performance feedback on the job. *Behavioral Residential Treatment*, 4, 377–95.

Foster, S. L., Bell-Dolan, D. J., and Burge, D. A. (1988). Behavioral observation. In A. S. Bellack and M. Hersen (eds), *Behavioral Assessment: a Practical Handbook* (3rd edn). Elmsford, NY: Pergamon Press.

Fottrell, E. (1980). A study of violent behaviour among patients in psychiatric hospitals. *British Journal of Psychiatry*, 136, 216–21.

Frude, N. (1991). *Understanding Family Problems: a Psychological Approach*. Chichester: Wiley.

Gardner, J. M. (1972). Teaching behavior modification to non-professionals. *Journal of Applied Behavior Analysis*, 5, 517–21.

Gardner, J. M. (1981). *Training Non-Professionals in Behaviour Modification*. Johannesburg: Witwatersrand University Press.

Gardner, W. I. and Cole, C. L. (1987). Behavior treatment, behavior management, and behavior control: needed distinctions. *Behavioral Residential Treatment*, 2, 37–53.

Garrett, C. J. (1985). Effects of residential treatment on adjudicated delinquents: a meta-analysis. *Journal of Research in Crime and Delinquency*, 22, 287–308.

Gelfand, D. M. and Hartmann, D. P. (1975). *Child Behaviour: Analysis and Therapy*. Oxford: Pergamon Press.

Gendreau, P. and Andrews, D. A. (1991). *Correctional Program Evaluation Inventory* (2nd edn). New Brunswick, Canada: University of New Brunswick.

Gentry, M. and Ostapiuk, E. B. (1989). Violence in institutions for young offenders and disturbed adolescents. In K. Howells and C. R. Hollin (eds), *Clinical Approaches to Violence*. Chichester: Wiley.

Goisman, R. M. (1988). Resistances to learning behavior therapy. *American Journal of Psychotherapy*, 42, 67–76.

Green, A. H. (1978). Self-destructive behaviour in battered children. *American Journal of Psychiatry*, 135, 579–82.

Gresswell, D. M. and Hollin, C. R. (1992). Towards a new methodology for making sense of case material: an illustrative case involving attempted multiple murder. *Criminal Behaviour and Mental Health*, 2, 329–41.

Harchik, A. E., Sherman, J. A., Hopkins, B. L., Strouse, B. C., and Sheldon, J. B. (1989).

Use of behavioral techniques by paraprofessional staff: a review and proposal. *Behavioral Residential Treatment, 4*, 331–57.

Harter, S. (1981). A model of mastery motivation in children: individual differences and developmental change. *The Minnesota Symposium of Child Psychology, 14*, 215–25.

Harter, S. (1982). The Perceived Competence Scale for Children. *Child Development, 53*, 87–97.

Hartup, W. W. (1983). Peer relations. In P. Mussen (ed.), *Social and Personality Development: Handbook of Child Psychology*, vol. 4: *Socialization, Personality, and Social Development*. New York: Wiley.

Hawkins, R. P. (1972). It's time we taught the young how to be good parents (and don't you wish we'd started a long time ago?). *Psychology Today*, November, 28–32.

Hawton, K. and Goldacre, M. (1982). Hospital admissions for adverse affects of medicinal agents (mainly self-poisoning) among adolescents in the Oxford region. *British Journal of Psychiatry, 141*, 166–70.

Hawton, K., O'Grady, J., Osborn, M., and Cole, D. (1982). Adolescents who take overdoses: their characteristics, problems, and contacts with helping agencies. *British Journal of Psychiatry, 140*, 118–23.

Hayes, S. C. (ed.). (1989). *Rule-Governed Behavior: Cognition, Contingencies, and Instructional Control*. New York: Plenum Press.

Haynes, S. N. and Wilson, C. C. (1979). *Behavioral Assessment*. San Francisco, CA: Jossey-Bass.

Hazel, J. S., Schumaker, J. B., Sherman, J. A., and Sheldon-Wildgen, J. (1981). The development and evaluation of a group skills program for court-adjudicated youth. In D. Upper and S. M. Ross (eds), *Behavioral Group Therapy, 1981: an Annual Review*. Champaign, IL: Research Press.

Health Services Advisory Committee (1987). *Violence to staff in the Health Services*. London: Health and Safety Commission.

Henderson, M. and Hollin, C. R. (1986). Social skills training and delinquency. In C. R. Hollin and P. Trower (eds), *Handbook of Social Skills Training*, vol. 1: *Applications Across the Life-Span*. Oxford: Pergamon Press.

Henggeler, S. W. (1989). *Delinquency in Adolescence*. Beverley Hills, CA: Sage.

Henggeler, S. W., Melton, G. B., and Smith, L. A. (1992). Family preservation using multisystemic therapy: an effective alternative to incarcerating serious juvenile offenders. *Journal of Consulting and Clinical Psychology, 60*, 953–61.

Herbert, M. (1987a). *Conduct Disorders of Childhood and Adolescence: a Social Learning Perspective* (2nd edn). Chichester: Wiley.

Herbert, M. (1987b). *Behavioural Treatment of Children with Problems: a Practice Manual* (2nd edn). London: Academic Press.

Herbert, M. (1988). *Working with Children and their Families*. Leicester: British Psychological Society/Routledge.

Herbert, M. (1990). *Planning a Research Project: a Guide for Practitioners and Trainees in the Helping Professions*. London: Cassell.

Herbert, M. (1991). *Clinical Child Psychology: Social Learning, Development and Behaviour*. Chichester: Wiley.

Herbert, M. (1993). *Working With Children and the Children Act: a Practical Guide for the Helping Professions*. Leicester: The British Psychological Society.

Hersen, M. and Turner, S. M. (eds) (1985). *Diagnostic Interviewing*. New York: Plenum Press.

HMSO (1991). *The Children Act 1989. Guidance and Regulations*, vol. 4: *Residential Care*. London: HMSO.

Hoghughi, M. S. (1979). The Aycliffe token economy. *British Journal of Criminology, 19*, 384–99.

Hollin, C. R. (1989). *Psychology and Crime: an Introduction to Criminological Psychology*. London: Routledge.

Hollin, C. R. (1990a). *Cognitive-Behavioral Interventions with Young Offenders*. Elmsford, NY: Pergamon Press.

Hollin, C. R. (1990b). Social skills training with delinquents: a look at the evidence and some recommendations for practice. *British Journal of Social Work, 20*, 483–93.

Hollin, C. R. (1992). *Criminal Behaviour: a Psychological Approach to Explanation and Prevention*. London: Falmer Press.

Hollin, C. R. (1993). Contemporary psychological research into violence: an overview. In P. J. Taylor (ed.), *Violence in Society*. London: Royal College of Physicians of London.

Hollin, C. R. and Henderson, M. (1984). Social skills training with young offenders: false expectations and the 'failure of treatment'. *Behavioural Psychotherapy, 12*, 331–41.

Hollin, C. R. and Howells, K. (eds) (1986). *Clinical Approaches to Criminal Behaviour: Issues in Criminological and Legal Psychology No. 9*. Leicester: The British Psychological Society.

Hollin, C., Wilkie, J., and Herbert, M. (1987). Behavioural social work: training and application. *Practice, 1*, 297–304.

Howells, K. (1986). Social skills training and criminal and antisocial behaviour in adults. In C. R. Hollin and P. Trower (eds), *Handbook of Social Skills Training* vol. 1: *Applications across the Life-Span*. Oxford: Pergamon Press.

Howells, K. and Hollin, C. R. (eds) (1989). *Clinical Approaches to Violence*. Chichester: Wiley.

Hudson, B. L. (1986). Community applications of social skills training. In C. R. Hollin and P. Trower (eds), *Handbook of Social Skills Training*, vol. 1: *Applications across the Life-Span*. Oxford: Pergamon Press.

Ivancevich, J. M. (1979). Longitudinal study of the effects of rater training on psychometric error in ratings. *Journal of Applied Psychology, 64*, 502–8.

Iwata, B. A., Bailey, J. S., Brown, K. M., Foshee, T. J., and Alpern, M. (1976). A performance-based lottery to improve residential care and training by institutional staff. *Journal of Applied Behavior Analysis, 9*, 417–31.

Izzo, R. L. and Ross, R. R. (1990). Meta-analysis of rehabilitation programs for juvenile delinquents: a brief report. *Criminal Justice and Behavior, 17*, 134–42.

Jackson, S. (1987). *The Education of Children in Care*. Bristol: School of Applied Social Studies, University of Bristol.

Jeffery, C. R. (1965). Criminal behavior and learning theory. *Journal of Criminal Law, Criminology and Police Science, 56*, 674–82.

Johnson, V. J. (1981). Staff drift: a problem in treatment integrity. *Criminal Justice and Behavior, 8*, 223–32.

Kain, T. J. and Chambers, H. J. (1991). Assessing reoffense risk with juvenile sexual offenders. *Child Welfare, 70*, 333–45.

Kallman, W. M. and Feuerstein, M. J. (1986). Psychophysiological procedures. In A. R. Ciminero, K. S. Calhoun, and H. E. Adams (eds), *Handbook of Behavioral Assessment*. New York: Wiley.

Kanfer, F. H. (1975). Self-management methods. In F. H. Kanfer and A. P. Goldstein (eds), *Helping People Change: a Textbook of Methods* (4th edn). Elmsford, NY: Pergamon Press.

Kanfer, F. H. and Gaelick-Buys, L. (1991). Self-management methods. In F. H. Kanfer and A. P. Goldstein (eds), *Helping People Change: a Textbook of Methods* (4th edn). Elmsford, NY: Pergamon Press.

Kanfer, F. H. and Grimm, L. G. (1977). Behavioral analysis: selecting target behaviors in the interview. *Behavior Modification, 4*, 419–44.

Kassenbaum, G., Ward, D., and Wilner, D. (1971). *Prison Treatment and Parole Survival: an Empirical Assessment*. New York: Wiley.

Kazdin, A. E. (1979). Fictions, factions, and functions of behavior therapy. *Behavior Therapy*, *10*, 629–54.

Kazdin, A. E. (1982). *Single-Case Research Designs: Methods for Clinical and Applied Settings*. New York: Oxford University Press.

Kendrick, D. J. (1984). 'Assessment of social skills: a survey-research experiment'. Unpublished diploma dissertation, University of Leicester, Leicester. (Available from author.)

Kifer, R. E., Lewis, M. A., Green, D. R., and Phillips, E. L. (1974). Training pre-delinquent youths and their families to negotiate conflict situations. *Journal of Applied Behavior Analysis*, *7*, 357–64.

Kinzel, A. F. (1970). Body-buffer zones in violent prisoners. *American Journal of Psychiatry*, *127*, 59–64.

Kirigin, K. A., Braukmann, C. J., Atwater, J., and Wolf, M. M. (1982). An evaluation of Achievement Place (teaching-family) group homes for juvenile offenders. *Journal of Applied Behavior Analysis*, *15*, 1–16.

Kirigin, K. A., Wolf, M. M., Braukmann, C. J., Fixsen, D. L., and Phillips, E. L. (1979). Achievement Place: a preliminary outcome evaluation. In J. S. Stumphauzer (ed.), *Progress in Behavior Therapy with Delinquents*. Springfield, IL: C. C. Thomas.

Klein, M. W. (1984). Offense specialization and versatility among juveniles. *British Journal of Criminology*, *24*, 185–94.

Kline, P. (1984). *Psychology and Freudian Theory*. London: Methuen.

Knowles, M. and Landesman, S. (1986). National survey of state-sponsored training for residential direct care staff. *Mental Retardation*, *24*, 293–300.

Krohn, M. D., Massey, L. L., and Skinner, W. F. (1987). A sociological theory of crime and delinquency: social learning theory. In E. K. Morris and C. J. Braukmann (eds), *Behavioral Approaches to Crime and Delinquency: a Handbook of Application, Research, and Concepts*. New York: Plenum Press.

Kumchy, C. and Sayer, L. A. (1980). Locus of control and delinquent adolescent populations. *Psychological Reports*, *46*, 1307–10.

Lamal, P. A. (ed.) (1991). *Behavioral Analysis of Societies and Cultural Practices*. New York: Hemisphere.

Landy, F. J. and Farr, J. H. (1980). Performance rating. *Psychological Bulletin*, *87*, 72–107.

Lane, T. W. and Murakami, J. (1987). School programs for delinquency prevention and intervention. In E. K. Morris and C. J. Braukmann (eds), *Behavioral Approaches to Crime and Delinquency: a Handbook of Application, Research, and Concepts*. New York: Plenum Press.

Laws, D. R. (1974). The failure of a token economy. *Federal Probation*, *38*, 33–8.

Lee, V. L. (1988). *Beyond Behaviorism*. Hillsdale, NJ: Lawrence Erlbaum.

Levy, A. and Kahan, B. (1991). *The Pindown Experience and the Protection of Children: the Report of the Staffordshire Child Care Inquiry 1990*. Stafford: Staffordshire County Council.

Lipsey, M. W. (1992a). Juvenile delinquency treatment: a meta-analytic inquiry into the variability of effects. In T. D. Cook, H. Cooper, D. S. Cordray, H. Hartmann, L. V. Hedges, R. J. Light, T. A. Louis, and F. Mosteller (eds), *Meta-Analysis for Explanation: a Casebook*. New York: Russell Sage Foundation.

Lipsey, M. W. (1992b). The effect of treatment on juvenile delinquency: results from meta-analysis. In F. Lösel, D. Bender, and T. Bliesener (eds), *Psychology and Law: International Perspectives*. Berlin: Walter de Gruyter.

190   References

Lipton, D., Martinson, R., and Wilks, J. (1975). *The Effectiveness of Correctional Treatment: a Survey of Treatment Evaluation Studies*. New York: Praeger.
Loeber, R. (1990). Development and risk factors of juvenile antisocial behavior and delinquency. *Clinical Psychology Review*, *10*, 1–41.
Loeber, R. and Dishion, T. (1983). Early predictors of male delinquency: a review. *Psychological Bulletin*, *94*, 168–99.
Loss, P. and Ross, J. E. (1988). *Risk Assessment and Interviewing Protocol for Adolescent Sex Offenders*. New London, CT: Peter Loss Inc.
Lowe, C. F. (1983). Radical behaviourism and human psychology. In G. C. L. Davey (ed.), *Animal Models of Human Behaviour*. Chichester: Wiley.
Lucas, J., Rayner, P., and Vanstone, M. (1992). *Straight Thinking on Probation: 1 Year On*. Swansea: University of Swansea.
McCord, J. (1978). A thirty-year follow-up of treatment effects. *American Psychologist*, *33*, 284–9.
McGurk, B. J., Davies, J. D., and Graham, J. (1981). Assaultive behavior, personality and personal space. *Aggressive Behavior*, *7*, 317–24.
McKeegan, G. F. and Donat, D. C. (1988). An inventory to measure knowledge of behavioral methods with inpatient adults. *Journal of Behavior Therapy and Experimental Psychiatry*, *19*, 229–36.
McMurran, M. and Hollin, C. R. (1993). *Young Offenders and Alcohol-related Crime: a Practitioner's Guidebook*. Chichester: Wiley.
Marlatt, G. A. and Gordon, J. (1985). *Relapse Prevention*. New York: Guildford Press.
Marra, A. M., Konzelman, G. E., and Giles, P. G. (1987). A clinical strategy for the assessment of dangerousness. *International Journal of Offender Therapy and Comparative Criminology*, *31*, 291–9.
Martinson, R. (1974). What works? Questions and answers about prison reform. *Public Interest*, *35*, 22–54.
Marziali, E., Marmar, C., and Krupnick, J. (1981). Therapeutic alliance scales: development and relationship to psychotherapy outcome. *American Journal of Psychiatry*, *138*, 361–4.
Masters, J. C., Burish, T. G., Hollon, S. D., and Rimm, D. C. (1987). *Behavior Therapy: Techniques and Empirical Findings* (3rd edn). New York: Harcourt Brace Jovanovich.
Mealiea, L. W. and Duffy, J. F. (1980). Nine pitfalls for the training and development specialist. *Personnel Journal*, *59*, 929–31.
Milan, M. A. (1987). Token economy programs in closed institutions. In E. K. Morris and C. J. Braukmann (eds), *Behavioral Approaches to Crime and Delinquency: a Handbook of Application, Research, and Concepts*. New York: Plenum Press.
Miller, R. J., Chino, A. F., Harney, M. K., Haines, D. A., and Saavedra, R. L. (1986). Assignment of punishment as a function of the severity and consequences of the crime and the status of the defendent. *Journal of Applied Social Psychology*, *9*, 481–90.
Miller, W. R. and Rollnick, S. (1991). *Motivational Interviewing: Preparing People to Change Addictive Behavior*. New York: Guildford Press.
Millham, S., Bullock, R., Hosie, K., and Haak, M. (1986). *Lost in Care: the Problems of Maintaining Links Between Children in Care and Their Families*. Aldershot: Gower.
Millham, S., Bullock, R., Hossie, K., and Little, M. (1989). *The Experiences and Careers of Young People Leaving the Youth Treatment Centres: a Retrospective Study of 102 Leavers from St. Charles and Glenthorne between 1982 and 1985*. Bristol: Dartington Social Research Unit, School of Applied Social Studies, University of Bristol.
Milne, D. L. (1982). A comparison of two methods of teaching behaviour modification to mental handicap nurses. *Behavioural Psychotherapy*, *10*, 54–64.
Milne, D. (1986). *Training Behaviour Therapists: Methods, Evaluation and Implementation with Parents, Nurses and Teachers*. London: Croom Helm.

Modgil, S. and Modgil, C. (eds) (1987). *B. F. Skinner: Consensus and Controversy*. New York: Falmer Press.

Moncher, F. J. and Prins, R. J. (1991). Treatment fidelity in outcome studies. *Clinical Psychology Review, 11*, 247–66.

Morash, M. (1983). Two models of community correction: one for the ideal world, one for the real world. In J. D. Kluegal (ed.), *Evaluating Juvenile Justice*. London: Sage.

Morris, E. K. (1987). Introductory comments: applied behavior analysis in crime and delinquency: focus on prevention. *The Behavior Analyst, 10*, 67–8.

Morris, E. K. and Braukmann, C. J. (eds) (1987). *Behavioral Approaches to Crime and Delinquency: a Handbook of Application, Research, and Concepts*. New York: Plenum Press.

Morton, T. L. and Ewald, L. S. (1987). Family-based interventions for crime and delinquency. In E. K. Morris and C. J. Braukmann (eds), *Behavioral Approaches to Crime and Delinquency: a Handbook of Application, Research and Concepts*. New York: Plenum Press.

Murphy, G. C., Hudson, A. M., King, N. J., and Remenyi, A. (1985). An interview schedule for use in the behavioural assessment of children's problems. *Behaviour Change, 2*, 6–12.

Nahem, J. (1981). *Psychology and Psychiatry Today: a Marxist View*. New York: International Publishers.

Nietzel, M. T. and Himelein, M. J. (1986). Prevention of crime and delinquency. In B. A. Edelstein and L. Michelson (eds), *Handbook of Prevention*. New York: Plenum Press.

Novaco, R. W. (1980). Training of probation counsellors for anger problems. *Journal of Counselling Psychology, 27*, 385–90.

Nye, R. D. (1992). *The Legacy of B. F. Skinner: Concepts and Perspectives, Controversies and Misunderstandings*. Pacific Grove, CA: Brooks/Cole.

O'Dell, S. L., Tarler-Benlolo, L., and Flynn, J. M. (1979). An instrument to measure knowledge of behavioral principles as applied to children. *Journal of Behavior Therapy and Experimental Psychiatry, 10*, 29–34.

Ostapiuk, E. B. and Westwood, S. (1986). Glenthorne Youth Treatment Centre: working with adolescents in gradations of security. In C. R. Hollin and K. Howells (eds), *Clinical Approaches to Criminal Behaviour. Issues in Criminological and Legal Psychology, No. 9*. Leicester: The British Psychological Society.

Palamara, F., Cullen, F. T., and Gersten, J. C. (1986). The effect of police and mental health intervention on juvenile deviance: specifying contingencies in the impact of formal reaction. *Journal of Health and Social Behavior, 27*, 90–105.

Palmer, T. (1992). *The Re-emergence of Correctional Intervention*. Newbury Park, CA: Sage.

Parks, C. W. and Hollon, S. D. (1988). Cognitive assessment. In A. S. Bellack and M. Hersen (eds), *Behavioral Assessment: a Practical Handbook* (3rd edn). Elmsford, NY: Pergamon Press.

Patterson, G. R. (1982). *Coercive Family Process*. Eugene, OR: Castalia.

Patterson, G. R. (1986) Performance models for antisocial boys. *American Psychologist, 41*, 432–44.

Patterson, G. R. and Stouthamer-Loeber, M. (1984). The correlation of family management practices and delinquency. *Child Development, 55*, 1299–307.

Patterson, G. R., Reid, J. B., and Dishion, T. J. (1992). *Antisocial Boys*. Eugene, OR: Castalia.

Paul, G. L. and Lentz, R. J. (1977). *Psychosocial Treatment of Chronic Mental Patients*. Cambridge, MA: Harvard University Press.

Perkins, D. (1987). A psychological treatment programme for sex offenders. In B. J. McGurk, D. M. Thornton, and M. Williams (eds), *Applying Psychology to Imprisonment: Theory & Practice*. London: HMSO.

Peterson, D. R. (1968). *The Clinical Study of Social Behavior*. New York: Appleton-Century-Crofts.

Phillips, E. L., Phillips, E. A., Fixsen, D. L., and Wolf, M. M. (1971). Achievement Place: the modification of the behaviors of pre-delinquent boys with a token economy. *Journal of Applied Behavior Analysis, 4*, 45–59.

Phillips, E. L., Phillips, E. A., Fixsen, D. L., and Wolf, M. M. (1972). *The Teaching Family Handbook*. Kansas, KN: University of Kansas.

Piaget, J. (1932). *The Moral Judgement of the Child*. New York: Harcourt, Brace.

Pithers, W. D. (1990). Relapse prevention with sexual aggressors. In W. L. Marshall, D. R. Laws, and H. E. Barbaree (eds), *Handbook of Sexual Assault*. New York: Plenum Press.

Pithers, W. D., Marques, J. K., Gibat, C. C., and Marlatt, G. A. (1983). Relapse prevention with sexual aggressives: a self-control model of treatment and maintenance of change. In J. G. Greer and I. R. Stuart (eds), *The Sexual Aggressor: Current Perspectives in Treatment*. New York: Nostrand Reinhold.

Polakow, R. L. and Doctor, R. M. (1974). A behaviour modification program for adult drug offenders. *Journal of Research in Crime and Delinquency, 3*, 41–5.

Poser, E. (1967). Training behaviour therapists. *Behaviour Research and Therapy, 5*, 37–41.

Powers, E. and Witmar, H. (1951). *An Experiment in the Prevention of Delinquency: the Cambridge–Somerville Youth Study*. New York: Columbia University Press.

Preston, M. A. (1982). Intermediate treatment: a new approach to community care. In M. P. Feldman (ed.), *Developments in the Study of Criminal Behaviour*, vol. 1: *The Prevention and Control of Offending*. Chichester: Wiley.

Quay, H. C. (ed.). (1987a). *Handbook of Juvenile Delinquency*. New York: Wiley.

Quay, H. C. (1987b). Institutional treatment. In H. C. Quay (ed.), *Handbook of Juvenile Delinquency*. New York: Wiley.

Reid, I. (1982). The development and maintenance of a behavioural regime in a Youth Treatment Centre. In M. P. Feldman (ed.), *Developments in the Study of Criminal Behaviour*, vol. 1: *The Prevention and Control of Offending*. Chichester: Wiley.

Reid, I. D., Feldman, M. P., and Ostapiuk, E. B. (1980). The SHAPE project for young offenders: introduction and overview. *Journal of Offender Counselling, Services and Rehabilitation, 4*, 233–46.

Remington, B. and Remington, M. (1987). Behavior modification in probation work: a review and evaluation. *Criminal Justice and Behaviour, 14*, 156–74.

Reppucci, N. D. (1973). Social psychology of institutional change: general principles for intervention. *American Journal of Community Psychology, 1*, 330–41.

Repucci, N. D. and Saunders, J. T. (1974). Social psychology of behavior modification: problems of implementation in natural settings. *American Psychologist, 29*, 649–60.

Rescorla, R. A. (1988). Pavlovian conditioning: it's not what you think it is. *American Psychologist, 43*, 151–60.

Roberts, A. R. (1987). National survey and assessment of 66 treatment programs for juvenile offenders: model programs and pseudomodels. *Juvenile and Family Court Journal, 38*, 39–45.

Roberts, A. R. and Camasso, M. J. (1991). The effect of juvenile offender treatment programs on recidivism: a meta-analysis of 46 studies. *Notre Dame Journal of Law, Ethics and Public Policy, 5*, 421–41.

Rosen, H. S., Yerushalmi, C. J., and Walker, J. C. (1986). Training community residential staff: evaluation and follow-up. *Behavioral Residential Treatment 1*, 15–38.

Roshier, B. (1989). *Controlling Crime: the Classical Perspective in Criminology*. Milton Keynes: Open University Press.

Ross, R. R. and Fabiano, E. A. (1985). *Time to Think: a Cognitive Model of Delinquency Prevention and Offender Rehabilitation*. Johnson City, TN: Institute of Social Sciences and Arts.

Rutherford, A. (1986). *Growing Out of Crime: Society and Young People in Trouble.* Harmondsworth: Penguin Books.

Rutter, M. and Giller, H. (1983). *Juvenile Delinquency: Trends and Perspectives.* Harmondsworth: Penguin Books.

Rutter, M., Graham, P., Chadwick, O. F. D., and Yule, W. (1976). Adolescent turmoil: fact or fiction? *Journal of Child Psychology and Psychiatry, 17,* 35–56.

Sanson-Fisher, B. and Jenkins, H. J. (1978). Interaction patterns between inmates and staff in a maximum security institution for delinquents. *Behavior Therapy, 9,* 703–16.

Schaefer, C. E. and Swanson, A. J. (eds) (1988). *Children in Residential Care: Critical Issues in Treatment.* New York: Van Nostrand Reinhold.

Schinke, S. P. and Wong, S. E. (1977). Evaluation of staff training in group homes for retarded persons. *American Journal of Mental Deficiency, 82,* 130–6.

Schlichter, K. J. and Horan, J. J. (1981). Effects of stress inoculation on the anger and aggression management skills of institutionalized juvenile delinquents. *Cognitive Therapy and Research, 5,* 359–65.

Serna, L. A., Schumaker, J. B., Hazel, J. S., and Sheldon, J. B. (1986). Teaching reciprocal social skills to delinquents and their parents. *Journal of Clinical Child Psychology, 15,* 64–77.

Seys, D., Kersten, H., and Duker, P. (1990). Evaluating a ward staff program for increasing spontaneous and varied communicative gesturing with individuals who are mentally retarded. *Behavioral Residential Treatment, 5,* 248–54.

Shoemaker, D. J. (1990). *Theories of Delinquency: an Examination of Explanations of Delinquent Behavior* (2nd edn). New York: Oxford University Press.

Short, J. F. (ed.). (1968). *Gang Delinquency and Delinquent Subcultures.* New York: Harper & Row.

Siegal, L. J. (1986). *Criminology* (2nd edn). St. Paul, MN: West Publishing.

Simcha-Fagan, O. and Schwartz, J. E. (1986). Neighbourhood and delinquency: an assessment of contextual effects. *Criminology, 24,* 667–703.

Simmons, R. G., Blyth, D. A., Van Cleave, E., and Bush, D. (1979). Entry into early adolescence: the impact of school structure, puberty and early dating on self-esteem. *American Sociological Review, 44,* 948–67.

Simon, W. T. and Schouten, P. G. W. (1991). Plethysmography in the assessment and treatment of sexual deviance: an overview. *Archives of Sexual Behaviour, 20,* 75–90.

Sinclair, I. A. (1971). *Hostels for Probationers.* Home Office Research Study No. 6. London: HMSO.

Sinclair, I. A. (1975). The influence of wardens and matrons on probation hostels: a study of a quasi-family institution. In J. Tizard, I. A. C. Sinclair, and R. V. G. Clarke (eds), *Varieties of Residential Experience.* London: Routledge & Kegan Paul.

Skinner, B. F. (1974). *About Behaviorism.* London: Cape.

Skinner, B. F. (1986a). Is it behaviorism? *Behavioral and Brain Sciences, 9,* 716.

Skinner, B. F. (1986b). What is wrong with daily life in the Western world? *American Psychologist, 41,* 568–74.

Skynner, A. C. R. (1976). *One Flesh: Separate Persons.* London: Constable.

Snyder, J. and Patterson, G. R. (1987). Family interaction and delinquent behavior. In H. C. Quay (ed.), *Handbook of Juvenile Delinquency.* New York: Wiley.

Stein, A. and Lewis, D. O. (1992). Discovering physical abuse: insights from a follow-up study of delinquents. *Child Abuse and Neglect, 16,* 523–31.

Strong, P. G. (1973). Aggression in the general hospital. *Nursing Times, 6,* 21–4.

Stumphauzer, J. S. (ed.). (1979). *Progress in Behavior Therapy with Delinquents.* Springfield, IL: C. C. Thomas.

Stumphauzer, J. S. (1986). *Helping Delinquents Change: a Treatment Manual of Social Learning Approaches.* London: Haworth Press.

Sutherland, E. H. (1939). *Principles of Criminology*. Philadelphia, PA: Lippincott.

Sutherland, E. H. and Cressey, D. R. (1974). *Criminology* (9th edn). Philadelphia, PA: Lippincott.

Tharp, R. G. and Wetzel, R. J. (1969). *Behavior Modification in the Natural Environment*. New York: Academic Press.

Thornton, D. M. (1987). Treatment effects on recidivism: a reappraisal of the 'nothing works' doctrine. In B. J. McGurk, D. M. Thornton, and M. Williams (eds), *Applying Psychology to Imprisonment: Theory & Practice*. London: HMSO.

Thornton, D. M. and Reid, R. L. (1982). Moral reasoning and type of criminal offence. *British Journal of Social Psychology*, *21*, 231–8.

Tizard, J., Sinclair, I., and Clarke, R. (eds) (1975). *Varieties of Residential Experience*. London: Routledge & Kegan Paul.

Topping, K. J. (1986) *Parents as Educators: Training Parents to Teach their Children*. London: Croom Helm.

Tutt, N. (1982). An overview of intervention with young offenders: the political and legal contexts. In P. Feldman (ed.), *Developments in the Study of Criminal Behaviour*, vol. 1. Chichester: Wiley.

Wahl, G., Johnson, S. M., Johansson, S., and Martin, S. (1974). An operant analysis of child–family interaction. *Behavior Therapy*, *5*, 64–74.

Wahler, R. G. and Fox, J. J. (1981). Setting events in applied behavior analysis: toward a conceptual and methodological expansion. *Journal of Applied Behavior Analysis*, *14*, 327–38.

Waskik, M. and Taylor, R. D. (1991). *Blackstone's Guide to the Criminal Justice Act 1991*. London: Blackstone Press.

Watson, J. B. (1913). Psychology as the behaviorist views it. *Psychological Review*, *20*, 158–77.

Watson, L. S. and Uzzell, R. (1980). A program for teaching behavior modification skills to institutional staff. *Applied Research in Mental Retardation*, *1*, 41–53.

Weiner, R. and Crosby, I. (1987). *Handling Violence and Aggression*. Adolescent Project Training Paper.

Welch, G. J. (1985). Contingency contracting with a delinquent and his family. *Journal of Behavior Therapy and Experimental Psychiatry*, *16*, 253–9.

Welch, S. J. and Holborn, S. W. (1988). Contingency contracting with delinquents: effects of a brief training manual on staff contract negotiation and writing skills. *Journal of Applied Behavior Analysis*, *21*, 357–68.

Wells, K. C., Griest, D. L., and Forehand, R. (1980). The use of a self-control package to enhance temporal generality of a parent training program. *Behaviour Research and Therapy*, *18*, 347–53.

West, D. J. (1967). *The Young Offender*. Harmondsworth: Penguin Books.

West, D. J. (1980). The clinical approach to criminology. *Psychological Medicine*, *10*, 619–31.

West, D. J. (1982). *Delinquency: its Roots, Careers, and Prospects*. London: Heinemann.

White, R., Carr, P., and Lowe, N. (1990). *Clarke Hall and Morrison on Children: Special Bulletin: a Guide to the Children Act 1989*. London: Butterworths.

Whittaker, J. (1979). *Caring for Troubled Children*. San Francisco, CA: Jossey-Bass.

Widom, C. S. (1989). Does violence beget violence? A critical examination of the literature. *Psychological Bulletin*, *109*, 3–28.

Winefield, A. H., Tiggemann, M., Winefield, H. R., and Goldney, R. D. (1993). *Growing Up with Unemployment: a Longitudinal Study of its Psychological Impact*. London: Routledge.

Wing-Sue, D. and Sue, D. (1990). *Counselling the Culturally Different: Theory and Practice* (2nd edn). New York: Wiley.

Wolfgang, M. E., Thornberry, T. P. and Figlio, R. M. (1987). *From Boy to Man, from Delinquency to Crime*. Chicago: University of Chicago Press.

Woodcock, M. (1979). *Team Development Manual*. London: Gower.

Wright, J., Mathieu, M., and McDonough, C. (1981). An evaluation of three approaches to the teaching of a behavioral therapy. *Journal of Clinical Psychology*, *37*, 326–35.

Ziarnik, J. P. and Bernstein, G. S. (1982). A critical examination of the effect of in-service training on staff performance. *Mental Retardation*, *20*, 109–14.

Zlomke, L. C. and Benjamin, V. A. (1983). Staff in-service: measuring effectiveness through client behavior change. *Education and Training of the Mentally Retarded*, *18*, 125–30.

Zuriff, G. E. (1985). *Behaviorism: a Conceptual Reconstruction*. New York: Columbia University Press.

Name index

Adams, G.L. 140
Adams, J. 103, 124
Aichhorn, A. 11
Aiken, T.W. 61
Akers, R.L. 12
Alberts, G. 146
Alevizos, P. 144
Alexander, J.F. 59
Anastasi, A. 95
Anderson, J.R. 7
Andrews, D.A. 20, 21, 103, 176
Arco, L. 142, 143
Argyle, M. 14
Ayllon, T. 113
Azrin, N.H. 113

Balcazar, F. 142, 143
Baldwin, S. 123
Bandura, A. 7, 11
Bank, L. 59, 130
Barker, P. 48, 49, 165
Barlow, D.H. 73, 74
Barlow, G. 33
Basta, J.M. 67
Bellack, A.S. 72, 73
Benjamin, V.A. 146
Bernadin, H.J. 95
Bernstein, G.S. 118, 149, 179
Berridge, D. 108
Birnbrauer, J.S. 142, 143
Blackburn, R. 10
Blakely, C.H. 30
Blasi, A. 13
Blumenthal, G.J. 34
Blyth, D.A. 105
Bootzin, R.R. 138
Bouchard, M.A. 140, 141
Boudewyns, P.A. 137

Braukmann, C.J. 8, 30, 108, 114, 129
Brewin, C.R. 7
Brophy, J. 4
Brown, B. 114
Brown, K.M. 142
Brown, W.C. 1
Bullock, R. 28, 59, 62, 67
Burchard, J.D. 15, 18, 58, 113, 114
Burchard, S.N. 15
Burdett, C. 149
Burg, M.M. 143
Burgess, A.W. 112
Burgio, L.D. 143

Calabrese, R.L. 103, 123
Camasso, M.J. 21, 49, 131
Canter, D. 34
Canter, S. 34
Carney, L.P. 60
Catania, A.C. 3, 6, 148
Chamberlain, P. 85
Chambers, H.J. 134
Christensen, A. 129
Ciminero, A.R. 73
Clarke, R.V.G. 11, 64
Cleaver, H. 108
Clements, J. 106
Cole, C.L. 137
Cole, P.G. 112, 124
Coleman, J.C. 104
Corcoran, K.J. 112, 132
Cornish, D.B. 11
Cressey, D.R. 10
Crosby, I. 64
Cullen, F.T. 18
Cullen, J.E. 22, 25, 114

Davidson, W.S. 16, 28, 30, 67, 110

Davies, W. 38
Davis, H. 138
Dean, C.W. 112
Dishion, T. 53
Dixon, N. 60
Doctor, R.M. 60
Doerner, M. 143, 144
Donat, D.C. 136, 137
Duffy, J.F. 149–51
Dunlop, A.B. 30, 64

Ecton, R.B. 128
Edelstein, B.A. 15, 146
Edens, F.M. 141
Elliot, D. 53
Emerson, C. 118
Emerson, E. 118
Emshoff, J.G. 58
Epps, K.J. 65
Ewald, L.S. 130

Fabiano, E.A. 12, 121, 180
Farr, J.H. 95
Farrington, D.P. 9, 10, 15
Feindler, E.L. 128
Feuerstein, M.J. 86
Fishman, D.B. 7
Fleming, R.K. 142
Foster, S.L. 88
Fottrell, E. 35, 64
Fox, J.J. 149
Freud, Sigmund 1, 3
Frude, N. 59

Gaelick-Buys, L. 86
Galtin, Sir F. 1
Gardner, J.M. 138, 139, 146
Gardner, W.I. 137
Garrett, C.J. 20, 103
Gelfand, D.M. 58
Gendreau, P. 18, 176
Gentry, M. 51, 54, 64
Giller, H. 8, 53
Goisman, R.M. 147, 148
Goldacre, M. 27
Gordon, J. 62
Green, A.H. 27
Gresswell, D.M. 96, 97
Grimm, L.G. 83

Harchik, A.E. 138
Harnad, S. 3, 6, 148

Harrington, W.A. 58
Harter, S. 113, 124
Hartmann, D.P. 58
Hartup, W.W. 128
Hawkins, R.P. 129
Hawton, K. 27
Hayes, S.C. 11
Haynes, S.N. 87
Hazel, J.S. 128
Henderson, M. 14, 21, 30, 54, 67, 103
Hendry, L. 104
Henggeler, S.W. 8, 131
Herbert, M. 80, 94, 97, 126, 130, 162,
    180
Hersen, M. 73, 83
Hersen, S.C. 74
Himelein, M.J. 15
Hippocrates 1
Hoghughi, M.S. 114
Holborn, S.W. 141
Hollin, C.R. 10, 12, 14, 21, 30, 35, 53, 54,
    57, 65, 66, 67, 72, 75, 96, 97, 103, 118,
    121, 125, 128, 156
Hollon, S.D. 86
Horan, J.J. 173
Howells, K. 14, 57, 66
Hudson, B.L. 60

Ivancevich, J.M. 95
Iwata, B.A. 142
Izzo, R.L. 20

Jackson, S. 108
Jeffery, C.R. 11–12
Jenkins, H.J. 105
Johnson, V.J. 121, 173, 176

Kahan, B. 42
Kain, T.J. 134
Kallman, W.M. 86
Kanfer, F.H. 83, 86, 143
Kassenbaum, G. 172
Kazdin, A.E. 3, 74
Kendrick, D.J. 95
Kifer, R.E. 32
Kinzel, A.F. 36
Kirigin, K.A. 108, 109, 114
Klein, M.W. 11
Kline, P. 1
Knowles, M. 137
Krohn, M.D. 12
Kumchy, C. 124

Lamal, P.A. 8
Landesman, S. 137
Landy, F.J. 95
Lane, T.W. 53, 114
Laws, D.R. 22, 25, 42, 178–9
Lee, V.L. 3
Lentz, R.J. 149
Levy, A. 42
Lewis, D.O. 112
Lipsey, M.W. 21, 103, 131, 172
Lipton, D. 19
Loeber, R. 53, 130
Loss, P. 134
Lowe, C.F. 6
Lucas, J. 176

McCord, J. 16
McGurk, B.J. 36
McKeegan, G.F. 136, 137
McMurran, M. 75
Marlatt, G.A. 62
Marra, A.M. 134
Martinson, R. 18–19
Marziali, E. 175
Masters, J.C. 119
Mealiea, L.W. 149–51
Michelson, L. 15
Milan, M.A. 23
Miller, R.J. 28
Miller, W.R. 125
Millham, S. 103, 108
Milne, D. 138, 141, 145, 149
Modgil, C. 3
Modgil, S. 3
Moncher, F.J. 131, 172
Morash, M. 61
Morris, E.K. 8, 14
Morton, T.L. 130
Murakami, J. 53
Murphy, G.C. 84

Nahem, J. 148
Nietzel, M.T. 15
Novaco, R.W. 60

O'Dell, S.L. 144, 145
Ostapiuk, E.B. 51, 54, 58, 64, 115

Palamara, F. 16
Palmer, T. 181
Parks, C.W. 86
Parsons, B.V. 59

Patterson, G.R. 105, 128, 130
Paul, G.L. 149
Pavlov, Ivan 2, 3
Pence, E.C. 95
Perkins, D. 46
Peterson, D.R. 83
Phillips, E.L. 43, 129
Pithers, W.D. 62
Polakow, R.L. 60
Poser, E. 139
Powers, E. 16
Preston, M.A. 29, 110, 114
Prins, R.J. 131, 172

Quay, H.C. 8, 22, 131, 171–2, 177

Reid, I.D. 61, 114, 156
Reid, R.L. 13
Remington, B. 60
Remington, M. 60
Reppucci, N.D. 23, 33, 111, 112, 179
Rescorla, R.A. 3
Roberts, A.R. 21, 49, 65, 131
Rollnick, S. 125
Rosen, H.S. 146
Roshier, B. 15
Ross, J.E. 134
Ross, R.R. 12, 20, 121, 180
Ruggill, J.S. 138
Rutherford, A. 103
Rutter, M. 8, 53, 104, 105

Sanson-Fisher, B. 105
Saunders, J.T. 111
Sayer, L.A. 124
Schaefer, C.E. 63
Schinke, S.P. 146
Schlichter, K.J. 173
Schouten, P.G.W. 107
Schwartz, J.E. 61
Seddon, J.W. 22, 25, 114
Serna, L.A. 128, 130
Seys, D. 146
Shoemaker, D.J. 11
Short, J.F. 26
Siegal, L.J. 10
Simcha-Fagan, O. 61
Simmons, R.G. 105
Simon, W.T. 107
Sinclair, I.A. 64
Skinner, B.F. 3–4, 6, 8, 11, 147–8
Skynner, A.C.R. 50

Smit, G.N. 141
Snyder, J. 130
Stein, A. 112
Stouthamer-Loeber, M. 130
Stumphauzer, J.S. 60, 61
Sue, D. 55
Sulzer-Azaroff, B. 142
Sutherland, E.H. 10–11, 12
Swanson, A.J. 63

Taylor, R.D. 169
Tharp, R.G. 60, 111
Thorndike, Edward 3
Thornton, D.M. 13, 19
Tizard, J. 108
Topping, K.J. 130
Turner, S.M. 83
Tutt, N. 29
Tyler, V. 113

Uzzell, R. 140

Voss, H. 53

Wahl, G. 105
Wahler, R.G. 149

Waskik, M. 169
Watson, John B. 2, 3, 6
Watson, L.S. 140
Weiner, R. 64
Welch, G.J. 130
Welch, S.J. 141
Wells, K.C. 129
West, D.J. 8, 10, 15, 18, 112
Westwood, S. 58, 115
Wetzel, R.J. 60, 111
White, R. 162
Whittaker, J. 48
Widom, C.S. 17
Wilson, C.C. 87
Winefield, A.H. 61
Wing-Sue, D. 55
Witmar, H. 16
Wolf, M.M. 30, 114, 129
Wolfgang, M.E. 9
Wong, S.E. 146
Woodcock, M. 132, 133
Wright, J. 141

Ziarnik, J.P. 149, 179
Zlomke, L.C. 146
Zuriff, G.E. 3

Subject index

absconding 64, 112, 119
Achievement Place projects, Kansas 43, 108–9, 114, 129
admission to programmes 22, 35, 48–51; criteria for 48–9, 68–9, 111; procedures 50–1; process 49–50; *see also* referral problems
admissions unit 51
adolescent developmental processes 104–6
after-care 26, 30, 59, 62
aggression: assaults on staff 56, 64, 69–71, 119; assessment 89; related to environment 35–6; reporting of 64–5, 66, 70; training 155, 158; *see also* self-injury
alcohol abuse, treatment for 123; reversal design of programme evaluation 75–6
analysis 5, 155; *see also* applied behaviour analysis; functional analysis
anger management 109, 128
Annual Social Services Yearbook 46
antisocial behaviour 8
applied behaviour analysis 5–6, 7–8, 23–4, 155; *see also* functional analysis
approved schools 64
architecture *see* building design and structure
assertion training 103
assessment 5, 6, 12, 50, 51, 54, 59, 72–101; behavioural theory and 72–3; conducting 79–90; functional analysis 95–101; key issues 100; planning 18, 73–4, 78; pre-intervention 73–4, 86, 111; 'reactive' effects 73, 86–8, 89; reliability and validity 78–9, 89–90, 93, 94–5, 96; training 154, 155; types of measure 91–5
assessment, programme *see under* evaluation

assessment interviews 72, 82–6, 126
audiotapes *see* videotapes
Aycliffe Children's Centre, Durham 114

'back-up' reinforcers *see* reinforcers
Barnardo's 45, 46, 60
baseline information 73–8
BAY Project 114
behaviour: adolescent 104–5; theories of 1–8
behaviour analysis 3–6
Behaviour Modification Test (BMT) 146
Behaviour Observation Instrument (BOI) 144
behavioural coding systems 94
behavioural contracts 116, 119, 141, 155
behavioural management systems 51, 52–3; designing 110–13; ensuring effectiveness 116–21; evaluation 64–5; types of 113–16; *see also* pin-down regime
behavioural theory 2–8; and assessment 72–3; of delinquency 10–14
behavioural treatment *see* treatment
behaviourism 2–8
bias 33; in assessment 91, 94–5; *see also* objectivity
biological forces in behaviour 1–2
'body-buffer zones' 36
building design and structure 34–9

Cambridge-Somerville Youth Study 16
care orders 163, 165–7
categorization measures 93
change, behavioural 4–5, 17, 155; without intervention 103; *see also* generalization of behaviour change; treatment

checklists 94
child-care provision 51–2, 54–5, 56; legal issues 106, 162–8; monitoring quality 63–4
Children Act (1989) 68, 106, 134, 162–8
Children and Young Person's Act (1933), Section 53 27, 68, 69
Children and Young Person's Act (1969) 165, 167
Children's Society 45
classical conditioning 2–3
client-centred therapies, nondirective 21
client characteristics: implications for service delivery 25–8; monitoring 63
clients: ambivalence about need for change 105; behavioural demands of 28, 110, 111–13; discharge 57–62; management and control of 52–3, 64–5, 110–13; motivation 123–5, 132; performance feedback 112–13, 115, 116, relevance of treatment to 109, 125; resistance to intervention and evaluation 68, 105–6, 110, 125, 179; surveys of views 52, 64
closed-circuit television (CCTV) 36, 37–8
cognitive-behaviour modification 7, 20, 21
cognitive processes in offenders 11–14
cognitive theories of behaviour 7
cognitive therapy 7
communication 33, 39, 41, 125–6, 132, 154
community: care of offenders in 171; relations of service to 28, 31, 32, 108; return of offenders to 18, 30, 57–62, 108
community-based programmes 21, 28–9, 39, 110, 114, 143–4, 164
complaints 52, 64, 106
computer training 154
computerized database systems 63, 159
conduct disorder 8
confidentiality of information 60, 133
consistency 34, 41, 101, 129; promotion in level systems 116; see also treatment integrity
contingency 3–6
contingency management 20
Correctional Programme Evaluation Inventory 176
cost-benefit analysis 46
counselling 21, 44; group 172; services 32, 64

crime, juvenile see delinquency
Criminal Injuries Compensation Board Scheme 71
Criminal Justice Act (1982) 168
Criminal Justice Act (1988) 168
Criminal Justice Act (1991) 168–71
cues 5, 85

data collection 72, 73, 79–95, 101, 171; archival information 80–1, 90, 93; assessment interviews 72, 82–6, 126; casual observation 82, 90, 93; direct observation 87, 88–95; self-report and self-monitoring 86–8
day centres 128
decision-making 23, 41, 134–5
delinquency 8–14, 110, 124; behavioural theories 10–14; definition 8; intervention and 17–22, 102–3; prevalence and incidence of 9–10; related to education 53, 61; responses to 14–17, 29
Department of Social Services, funding by 46
deterrence 15
DHSS Circular LAC 1983(3) 168
differential association theory, and delinquency 10–11, 12
Diploma in Social Learning Theory and Practice 156
discrete categorization 93
diversionary treatment 15, 16–17, 28, 110
duration counts 91, 92

education 26, 30, 53, 61, 108
emergencies: prevention 35–8; responding to 38–9, 41, 119–20
empathy 13, 85
employment see work
environment: and behaviour 6–7; and delinquency ix, 10, 13, 18, 124; influence of physical 35–6, 64; and learning 2–3
errors, rating 95
ethical issues 23, 32, 106–7, 120, 176–7; confidentiality of information 60, 133; direct observation 89
ethics groups, committees 107, 120
evaluation: of behavioural management systems 120–1; of programmes 30, 54, 65, 67–8, 73, 74–8, 94, 103, 175–6; of training 144–6, 150–1, 159; see also

monitoring; outcome studies
experimental behaviour analysis 5

family 30, 59, 108; *see also* parental
    responsibility
family systems approach 59, 130
family work, therapy 21, 49, 59, 127,
    129–31, 164, 165, 166; training 156
Feltham Borstal 114
fire procedures, setting 38, 60, 119
flow diagrams 100–1
follow-up *see* after-care
fostering, professional 59–60
frequency counts 91–2
functional analysis 5, 12, 72, 123, 124,
    155; used in assessment 95–101
functional family therapy (FFT) *see*
    family systems approach
furniture 36–7

gender, and service provision 27
generalization of behaviour change 30,
    32, 58–9, 108–9, 129, 130
genetics, and behaviour 1
Gillick case 164
Glenthorne Youth Treatment Centre 51, 65,
    114, 116, 117, 156; admission criteria
    69–9; organizational structure 40
group activities 45
group counselling 172
group work 127, 128; training in 141

health services 32, 60–1, 64
Home Office, funding 46
Home Office Circular 14/1985 168
Home Office Circular 59/1990 168

incidents, reporting 64–5, 66, 70
income generation 47
individual: emphasis on, in Children Act
    (1989) 167; and functional analysis 96;
    institutional v. individual emphasis in
    programmes 54, 57–8, 118–19
individualized treatment programmes 73,
    118, 121–31
information-gathering *see* data collection
information-processing model 7
injury *see* aggression; self-injury
inspection of services 52, 64; *see also*
    evaluation
intensity measures 93
Intermediate Treatment (IT) 17, 29, 128

interval recording 92
intervention *see* treatment
intervention programmes *see* treatment
    programmes

key worker system 126–8

learning theories: and behaviour 2–7; and
    delinquency 8, 10–14
legal issues 23, 27, 32, 52, 106–7, 110,
    120, 162–71; rights of staff 71
level management systems 115–16, 119
local authorities, child-care
    responsibilities of 68, 69, 163–6, 170
locus of control, and delinquency 13, 124;
    see also environment

management 24, 181; model for
    behavioural management and structure
    25–71; *see also individual aspects*
management systems, behavioural *see*
    behavioural management systems
measures, observational 88, 90; types
    91–5
medical model of behaviour viii, 1, 102
mental disorder 8, 69
Mental Health Act (1983) 106
meta-analysis 20–2, 103, 131, 136, 172,
    181
model for behavioural management and
    structure *see* service provision model
modelling 12, 141, 153
monitoring: of behavioural management
    systems 115, 116, 120–1; of
    programme integrity 67–8, 174,
    175–80; of training 138; of treatment
    programmes 23, 30, 38, 52, 54, 62–5,
    66, 118, 132–4
moral reasoning, delinquency and 13
motivation: cognitive theories 7; of
    clients 123–5, 132; of staff 43, 150
multi-model programmes 80, 82, 133
multiple baseline design of programme
    evaluation 74, 76–8
mystical forces, and behaviour 1

National Children's Home 45
natural contingencies systems 119
negative coercion by clients 105
neobehaviourism 3–8

objectivity 33, 49, 78, 79; of outside

inspection 52; *see also* bias
observation, casual 82, 90, 93
observation, direct 87, 88–90; choice and
    type of measure 90–5
operant behaviour, learning 3, 7, 11–12
organizational barriers to programme
    success 22–3, 33, 111
organizational resistance to behavioural
    treatment 179–80
organizational structures, model of *see*
    service provision model
outcome, evaluating 54, 65, 67, 103
outcome studies 19–22, 67, 103, 172,
    181; residential settings 108; of
    training 145–6
outreach services 47; *see also*
    community-based programmes; family
    work

parent management training (PMT) 59,
    129–30, 131
parental responsibility 163–7, 170
peer relationships 108, 109, 116, 128
penile plethysmography (PPG) 107
performance indicators 132, 174
pin-down regime 42, 51, 167
police: and assaults on staff 70, 71;
    relations with 31–2
Police and Criminal Justice Act (1984)
    168
political influences on programmes 18, 46
positive reinforcement *see* reinforcement;
    reinforcers
pre-intervention assessment, information
    73–4, 78, 86, 111
prevention of crime 14–17, 29
private events 6–7, 86
probation hostels 64
probation orders 27, 106, 110
probation services, work 30, 60, 171, 177
problem checklists 94
problem-solving 44, 94, 130
profiles: organization of information 81;
    programme design 121–5
programmed learning 158–61
proportion recording 92
protection orders 163, 165
psychiatric services 28, 30, 32, 61
psychiatrists, attitude to treatment 23
psychodynamic theories of behaviour 1,
    147
psychodynamic treatments 20, 21, 147

psychological theories of behaviour 1–8
psychological therapy 19
psychology: behavioural 2–8; of
    delinquency 10–14
psychopathology viii, ix, 11, 102
punishment 4–5, 120, 153; programmed
    learning text 159–61; reinforcement
    theory of criminal behaviour 12

race awareness training 55, 158
radical behaviourism 6–7
rating scales 93, 94–5, 116
reactivity, assessment and 73, 86–8, 89
recidivism 19, 20, 21, 64, 67, 103, 107,
    171, 172
record-keeping 133–4; about violence
    64–5, 66, 70
recreational facilities 26, 30, 36
referral problems, and service provision
    28; *see also* admission to programmes
rehabilitation 17, 62, 172
reinforcement 4, 5, 7, 37, 115, 116, 119,
    120, 130; time out from 37, 120;
    training 140, 153–4, 159–61
reinforcement theory of crime 11–12
reinforcers 4, 47, 111, 114–15, 121, 125
relapse-prevention strategies 62
research: and income generation 47;
    practice and treatment integrity 177
residential care, services 37, 39, 57, 63,
    64; admission criteria 48–9, 68–9; costs
    47; legal issues 164, 165, 166–8;
    location of 30; regional 29
residential programmes 109, 128, 129,
    178; effectiveness 21, 108, 146; token
    economics 114
resistance 23; clients 68, 105–6, 110, 125,
    179; 'nothing works' attitude 18–22,
    34, 65; organizational 179–80; to
    training 147–8
resources 28, 46–7, 110, 111, 115, 125–6,
    171
reversal design of programme evaluation
    74–6
role-play 128, 130; training 141, 146

schizophrenia 1–2
seclusion rooms 38–9
Secure Accommodation orders 27, 69, 170
secure units, accommodation 34, 36, 38,
    105, 164, 170, 171
security 37–8, 119

segregation rooms 38–9
self-control 58; lack of, related to
   delinquency 13, 53; training 155,
   173
self-injury 36–7, 38, 39, 119; see also
   aggression
self-report: and assessments 86–8; and
   delinquency 17; and private events 7,
   86
self-report questionnaires 86, 87
separation rooms 38–9
service provision model 25–71;
   administration and funding 45–7;
   admission policy 48–51; aims of
   service 25–8; building design and
   structure 34–9; catchment area 28–9;
   comprehensiveness of provision 51–4;
   discharge and follow-up 57–62;
   location 30–2; monitoring and
   evaluation 62–8; outcome expectations
   29–30; philosophy and operational
   framework 32–4; policy and practice
   54–7, 69–71; staffing 39–45
severity measures 93
sexual harassment 27
sexual offenders 107, 134–5, 169, 171
SHAPE Project 61, 114
skills training 20, 21, 128, 140, 141; see
   also social skills training
Skinner Box 3, 5
Snowdon Unit, Glenthorne Centre 116,
   117
social cognition, and delinquency 12, 13,
   14
social influences on treatment 18; see
   also ethical issues; legal issues
social learning theory 7; and delinquency
   11, 12–14
social problem-solving, and delinquency
   13, 14
social process theory in criminology 11
social services 30, 32, 60, 68, 171
Social Services Inspectorate (SSI) 52
social skills, and delinquency 12, 13–14
social skills training (SST) 32, 76–8, 109,
   128, 140–1, 155, 175
social structure theories in criminology 11
social work 27, 68, 165
Special Interest Group 157–8
staff 26, 39–45; assaults on 56, 64,
   69–71, 119; barriers to success of
   programmes 22–3; behavioural

knowledge 42, 136–7, 144–5 (see also
   staff training and development);
   commitment and motivation 43, 150;
   and delivery of programmes 34, 118,
   131–5; depersonalization of 112;
   interaction with clients 105; legal rights
   71; monitoring 63; organization 39–41,
   115; performance feedback and support
   132, 141–3; resistance 23, 147–8,
   179–80; supervisory duties 36; and
   treatment integrity 178, 179–80; type
   and qualities 42–5; and unit-based
   programmes 128–9; untrained 42; see
   also communication
staff groups, teams 41, 45, 63, 128;
   delivery of programmes 131–5
staff meetings 41, 131–2
staff selection 42–3
staff supervision 83, 101, 115, 178
staff training and development 23, 26, 27,
   28, 42, 63, 101, 104, 106, 115, 116,
   118, 136–61, 171, 178; for assessment
   54, 83, 89, 95; evaluation of 144–6,
   150–1, 159; framework for training
   151–9; induction training 34, 56,
   152–3; levels of 138–9; methods
   140–4, 150, 158–61; pitfalls of 149–51,
   179–80; race awareness 55, 158;
   resistance to 147–8
Staff Welfare Officer 70
START programme 23
STOP Probation Programme 176
subjectivity in assessment 90, 93; see also
   bias; objectivity
supervision orders 163, 165

target behaviours 83, 86–90, 123, 131–2
'teaching family' model 129
terminology 33
three-term contingency 5
time sampling 91–2
token economy programme 112, 113–15,
   119, 120
Training Proficiency Scale (TPS) 146
treatment vii–ix, 54, 181; and
   delinquency 17–22, 102–3; factors
   limiting behaviour change 103–10;
   important principles of 79; 'nothing
   works' attitude to 18–22, 34, 65
treatment integrity: fidelity 21, 22, 23,
   67–8, 101, 118, 131, 136, 151, 171–80,
   181; importance of 176–8; issues of

practice 174–6; maximizing 173–4, 179; problems and pitfalls 178–80; threats to 172–3
treatment meetings 41, 131–2
treatment programmes 12, 17; barriers to success 22–4, 33, 111; delivery 131–5; design and management 18, 102–35; evaluation and assessment *see* evaluation; institutional v. individual emphasis 54, 57–8, 118–19; limiting factors 103–10; manuals 34, 50, 56, 118, 174–5, 178, 180; planning and goal-setting 5, 41, 57, 106, 108, 121–2, 132–3; setting 107–10 (*see also under* service provision model); support from outside agencies and services 32, 33, 45–6, 60, 68, 125–6; *see also* outcome studies
treatment programmes, early 16; individualized 73, 118, 121–31

treatment strategies 72–3

unit-based programmes 127, 128–9
Unit One programme 114

victim support schemes 17
videotapes: in assessment interviews 83, 84; training 155
violence *see* aggression
violent offenders 169, 171
voluntary organizations 45–6, 164

Wardship Court order 68
withdrawal design of programme evaluation 74–6
work 26, 30, 53, 61–2, 64

Youth Treatment Service 40, 114; *see also* Glenthorne Youth Treatment Centre

SOCIAL SCIENCE LIBRARY

Manor Road Building
Manor Road
Oxford OX1 3UQ
Tel: (2)71093 (enquiries and renewals)
http://www.ssl.ox.ac.uk

This is a NORMAL LOAN item.

We will email you a reminder before this item is due.

Please see http://www.ssl.ox.ac.uk/lending.html
for details on:

- loan policies; these are also displayed on the notice boards and in our library guide.

- how to check when your books are due back.

- how to renew your books, including information on the maximum number of renewals. Items may be renewed if not reserved by another reader. Items must be renewed before the library closes on the due date.

- level of fines; fines are charged on overdue books.

Please note that this item may be recalled during Term.